Praise for *The Armchair Birder*

"*The Armchair Birder* will be around for a long time, because it gets to the heart of the matter quickly and stays there. . . . Once you start reading, you won't want to stop until you finish because the writing is so fresh and . . . well, *good*."
—CLYDE EDGERTON, author of *Raney*, *Killer Diller*, and *The Bible Salesman*, among many other books

"Yow is the ultimate gentleman birder, highlighting the omnipresent glory and understated miracle of these feathered friends."
—*BookPage*

"Finally, a bird book for the rest of us! John Yow has empowered . . . us to sit back, to let the birds come to us and to enjoy the sights and sounds. . . . Secrets of birds and birding are out at last!"
—*Anniston Star*

"Fun to read, and anyone, regardless of experience level, will learn something from this book (probably many somethings)."
—birderslibrary.com

"Who says you have to travel to faraway places to watch birds? The delightful essays in John Yow's *The Armchair Birder* take readers on a fascinating voyage of discovery in their own backyards."
—TIM GALLAGHER, author of *Falcon Fever* and *The Grail Bird*

"An excellent literary introduction to . . . the most common North American birds. . . . Colorful and engaging."
—*Englewood Review of Books*

"*The Armchair Birder* offers details of behavior about our most common birds that will enrich your enjoyment long after establishing who's who in the backyard and beyond. This delightful book reveals the reality that even the most familiar birds have lives rich with amazing behavior and mystery."
—STEPHEN W. KRESS, author of *The Audubon Guide to Attracting Birds*

"Ably illustrates facets of bird behavior and instinct, acknowledging their unique adaptations to the natural and human worlds."
—*Library Journal*

"This is a book you will want to sit and read through over and over, not just for the fascinating bird lore, but for the affection and humor that come through in John Yow's fine writing about our familiar birds."
—BAILEY WHITE, author of *Quite a Year for Plums*, among other books

"Yow discusses forty species of birds . . . [and] whets your appetite for knowing what they are up to. . . . [With] stunning black-and-white drawings of each bird by John James Audubon."
—*Booklist*

"I enjoyed the dickens out of this book! Drawing on Audubon, Thoreau, Bent, Forbush, and others in order to characterize the avian species, Yow writes with a light-hearted, cocked-head, tongue-in-cheek approach. These essays are gems."
—JANET LEMBKE, author of *Dangerous Birds: A Naturalist's Aviary*

"Among a list of favorite things in life must be an armchair. If yours is near a window, you can observe the most active creatures this spring— birds—while dipping into John Yow's generous new offering."
—*Asheville Citizen Times*

"Whether you favor random dips into the book or prefer to follow Yow systematically through the seasons, you will be sure to learn something new."
—*Virginia Wildlife Magazine*

The Armchair Birder

goes coastal

The Armchair Birder
goes coastal

The SECRET LIVES *of* BIRDS *of the*
SOUTHEASTERN SHORE

....

JOHN YOW

The University of North Carolina Press
Chapel Hill

This book was published with the assistance of the
BLYTHE FAMILY FUND *of the University of North Carolina Press.*

Library of Congress Cataloging-in-Publication Data
Yow, John.
The armchair birder goes coastal : the secret lives of birds of the Southeastern shore / John Yow.
p. cm.
Includes bibliographical references and index.
ISBN 978-0-8078-3561-6 (cloth : alk. paper)
1. Shore birds—Atlantic Coast (South Atlantic States) 2. Shore birds—Gulf Coast (U.S.) 3. Water birds—Atlantic Coast (South Atlantic States) 4. Water birds—Gulf Coast (U.S.) 5. Bird watching—Atlantic Coast (South Atlantic States) 6. Bird watching—Gulf Coast (U.S.) 7. Yow, John—Travel—Atlantic Coast (South Atlantic States) 8. Yow, John—Travel—Gulf Coast (U.S.) 9. Atlantic Coast (South Atlantic States)—Description and travel. 10. Gulf Coast (U.S.)—Description and travel. I. Title.
QL678.5.Y68 2012
598.3'3—dc23   2011039276

16 15 14 13 12   5 4 3 2 1

for Dede and Ruthie, with love

CONTENTS

Acknowledgments ix

Introduction xi

A Note on the Sources xvii

• • • • • • • • •

spring

Black-Necked Stilt 3

American Oystercatcher 11

White Ibis 18

Black-Bellied Plover 26

Ruddy Turnstone 32

Reddish Egret 40

• • • • • • • • •

summer

Anhinga 51

Wilson's Plover 59

Royal Tern 66

Wood Stork 73

Laughing Gull 81

Brown Pelican 88

• • • • • • • • •

autumn

Forster's Tern 99

Double-Crested Cormorant 106

Clapper Rail 112

Willet 119

Tricolored Heron 127

Snowy Egret 135

. . . .
winter

Sanderling 147

Roseate Spoonbill 155

Short-Billed Dowitcher 163

Greater Yellowlegs and Lesser Yellowlegs 170

Wilson's Snipe 177

American White Pelican 183

Black Skimmer 191

. . . .
(return to) spring

Red Knot 201

Whimbrel 208

American Avocet 215

Bibliography 225

Index 229

ACKNOWLEDGMENTS

First and foremost, I'd like to express my abiding gratitude to my agent, Sally Hill McMillan, whose faith in my work and effort on my behalf have meant more to me than I can say. In what often seems a fruitless endeavor, the words "I would love to represent this book" are like sweet rain on parched earth. Thank you, Sally.

Huge thanks, also, to the gifted folks at the University of North Carolina Press—and most especially to my editor, Mark Simpson-Vos. Both this book and its predecessor, *The Armchair Birder*, owe their existence to Sally and Mark. May the team endure.

While the earlier book celebrated a particular place, this one took me on a journey, and I needed a lot of help along the way—often from people who knew me only slightly or not at all. Along Florida's "forgotten coast," Todd Engstrom and John Murphy, a couple of true gentlemen, not only were willing to take a stranger birding but also seemed genuinely happy to do it. In Florida's Cedar Key, Dale Henderson did not let a little rain stop her from introducing me to the island's renowned Shell Mound site. (I should mention also my dear cousin Elsa Sibley, whose little house on Cedar Key provided a base of operations.) On Alabama's Dauphin Island, the incomparably gracious John ("Sto") Stowers showed me wonders I couldn't have imagined.

Christa Frangiamore and Royce Hayes welcomed me to the little piece of unspoiled paradise known as St. Catherines Island, off the Georgia coast, and on equally beautiful Little St. Simons Island, Stacia Hendricks and her fellow naturalists were ideal guides to the island's spectacular bird life. Brad Winn and Tim Keyes of the Georgia Department of Natural Resources allowed me to tag along on what proved to be a memorable search for Wilson's plover nests.

Many thanks, also, to the great birders and good friends at the Atlanta Audubon Society—especially Lisa and Art Hurt and Theresa Hartz—with whom I was able to explore fabulous birding sites along the Georgia and Florida coasts that would otherwise have remained unknown to me.

Finally, thanks evermore to Dede and Ruthie, who understand that while a little constructive criticism has its place, praise must be constant and fervid.

INTRODUCTION

This book provides something of a sequel to one I wrote a couple of years ago called *The Armchair Birder*. The title was meant to convey my perhaps idiosyncratic idea of birding—that is, to content myself with watching the birds that come to me rather than troubling myself to go to them. Our woodsy little homeplace in the foothills of the Appalachians justified this approach; wonderful surprises continually winged their way into convenient view—tanagers, indigo buntings, yellow-billed cuckoos, rose-breasted grosbeaks. The more I saw, the more I wanted to know about the lives of these beautiful creatures. So, fanny still settled and feet propped up, I began reading.

Not just guidebooks, mind you. I wanted to know what these birds were up to when they weren't cracking open sunflower seeds; I wanted bird *behavior*. What I wanted, I soon found out, was Arthur Cleveland Bent's *Life Histories of North American Birds* and John James Audubon's *Ornithological Biography*. These books and others like them were not just chock-full of incredible information; they were also charming, witty, anecdotal, *readable*. That got me to thinking: Must be a whole lot of folks out there who love to look at the birds in the backyard and who would probably enjoy learning a little more about them. Maybe I ought to share some of this stuff. That got me to writing.

Turns out my approach wasn't so idiosyncratic. I heard from lots of people who were happy to describe themselves as armchair birders and who enjoyed getting their hands on a book that was obviously written with them in mind. Of course, since the information in the book goes well beyond wingbars and eye-stripes, I hoped that it would also appeal to "real" birders, and I heard from some of them, too. Like that evening in Chattanooga, when I gave a talk to the local chapter of the Tennessee Ornithological Society. I was making the point that my book, covering 35 familiar species, might actually be more useful than a guidebook that covered 500 species nobody would ever see, and to clinch the point, I turned to a young woman on the front row.

"For example," I asked, "how many bird species have you seen?"

"Six hundred fifteen," she said.

. . . .

Not long after that, on a family vacation at Fripp Island, South Carolina, brother Richard and I sat with our binoculars on the beachside porch of our rented house and watched the Sandwich terns (bill tips dipped in mayonnaise) turned into the wind, the black-headed laughing gulls wheeling and laughing, the sanderlings scampering along the surf's edge, the black skimmers skimming blackly. Riding bikes over tidal creeks and marshes, we saw snowy egrets with their golden slippers and wood storks with their prehistoric-looking proboscises.

How about a book about these birds? I figured there were plenty of coastal residents and regular beach vacationers who knew these birds—saw them all the time, probably knew their names—just like suburbanites know their cardinals, robins, and chickadees. Wouldn't these people like to learn more about their own "familiar birds"? Couldn't I enhance the "armchair birding" experience of people who lived on or visited the coast?

Sure I could. The only problem was that the shorebirds weren't going to come to my backyard feeders in Acworth. This new book's readers could stay in their armchairs, but yours truly would have to become . . . a birder.

So I did. And, honestly, it's not that bad. You can try to complain about *having* to go to the coast to look at birds, but you won't get a lot of sympathy. I could tell my old friend C. P., for instance, that I hated to miss the Thursday golf game, but I had to travel—you know, business. But he would inevitably inquire as to my destination, and my answer would just about always conclude with the word "island" or "beach."

Like Carrabelle Beach, for example, on old Highway 98 along the Florida panhandle, which was my first destination. Why that particular beach? Well, I knew I couldn't go wrong anywhere on the Gulf coast, since the area's incredible biodiversity has been drawing birders and other naturalists since time immemorial. As a practical matter, though, the place was recommended by a friend who had a friend down there who might be willing to take me out to see the sights.

In fact, I had this kind of friend-of-a-friend experience repeatedly, and it didn't take me too long to figure out that birders by and large are pretty decent people. Not crabby, misanthropic, stay-at-homes like me, but kindly, generous folks who like to watch birds, talk about them, and, particularly, show new species to people who might not have seen 'em yet. John Murphy, for instance, told me he worked during the week in Tallahassee just so he could bird the Gulf coast on the weekends. We had never actually met until I showed up at his house on Alligator Point at 7:30 on a Saturday morning, but by lunchtime he had shown me my first marbled godwit and seven different kinds of plover. Or "Sto" Stowers, to whom I was introduced in Highlands, North Carolina, and who, before the handshake was over, had invited me to spend a weekend at his house on Dauphin Island, Alabama. "We got shorebirds," he told me.

What did Dede and I find when we got to Carrabelle? We found Ochlockonee Bay, Alligator Point, and, right in front of our little rented cottage, a wide expanse of quiet, unpopulated shoreline. We found the peaceful beauty of winter's end on the Gulf of Mexico. This was another thing I figured out: coastal birds tend to seek out lovely places. And unless you're behind the gearbox of a bulldozer, there's not a thing in the world wrong with going to those places to see them. Whether you're on a pristine barrier island, like St. Catherines or Little St. Simons off Georgia's coast, or a spectacular National Wildlife Refuge, like Pea Island on North Carolina's Outer Banks or "Ding" Darling on Florida's Sanibel Island, or even the less developed areas of traditional vacation spots, like the south end of Georgia's Jekyll Island, you're likely to find yourself overwhelmed by the realization of what this poor, overburdened planet of ours once looked like — and still does in more places than you might think.

I discovered that where river systems pour into the ocean, like the Altamaha into the Atlantic in Brunswick, Georgia, or the Lower Suwannee into the Gulf at Cedar Key, Florida, you can find a perfect universe of marshes, islands, bars, creeks, and shoreline, all governed by the power of the moon, not The Man. I also came to realize that a sunset over the marsh is every bit as lovely as a sunset over the ocean.

Then there are the birds. Birds of shore and marsh are not, on the whole, as colorful as many of our neotropical songbirds; nor, for that matter, are they as songful. A good many of them, to my mind, sound like a lawn mower engine that almost catches but then conks out. Others clap, or wheeze, or grunt, or laugh maniacally. But in size, in shape, in anatomical eccentricity, in physical prowess, these birds test the limits of the imagination.

We appreciate the imperatives of evolutionary biology, but so many of these birds—the American oystercatcher, the black-necked stilt, the roseate spoonbill, the reddish egret dancing in shallow water, just to name a few—would seem better explained by the careless conjuring of some droll and whimsical creator.

You'll notice I've named a few of the more distinctive coastal birds—birds as unmistakable in their way as a scarlet tanager or a blue jay. It ain't all that easy. The shore has its clans of sparrows, too—all those sandpipers and smaller plovers, for instance—which, in winter especially, are about as easy to tell apart as Cheerios floating in a bowl of milk.

Sto Stowers and I were leaving Cat Island, the fabulous rookery he had taken me to out in the middle of the Mississippi Sound. I took a last look toward the tip of the island and reported a couple of dunlin down there, a black-bellied plover that hadn't turned yet, and three or four dowitchers.

Sto hoisted his binoculars. "Well, I see a couple of red knots, a ruddy turnstone, and a few willets."

I got better, really, but I'm not saying I became a *great* birder. I won't get to 615 and don't need to. This book, like the first one, selects relatively few species—ones that most readers will already be familiar with—and looks at them in leisurely, appreciative detail. Plus, my own firsthand observations are again supplemented by the work of wonderful writers past and present.

Besides, as even high-octane birders will tell you, it's the journey. Mine, for the purposes of this book, cycled through some fifteen months, from the end of one winter through the spring of the following year. Five seasons of birds and beaches, seafood and salt marshes, ocean breezes and island smiles. Nope, not bad. Not bad at all.

A NOTE ON THE SOURCES

A complete bibliography appears at the end of the book, but, as I did in *The Armchair Birder*, in this book I leaned heavily on a handful of sources that I'd like to say a little about before we get under way.

John James Audubon (1785–1851) remains my favorite bird writer. Yes, he is much more famous as the artist who created *Birds of America*, but he also produced a five-volume prose masterpiece, *Ornithological Biography*, to accompany the artwork. It includes accounts of pretty much every species he ever encountered, and the writing is always vivid, informative, and highly entertaining. Incredibly, the entire opus is now available online from Darlington Library Texts at the University of Pittsburgh (digital.library.pitt.edu). I especially enjoyed reading Audubon alongside his peer (and friendly ornithological adversary, if I'm reading between the lines correctly) Alexander Wilson, whose work is available in an edited volume titled *Wilson's American Ornithology*, published in 1854.

Arthur Cleveland Bent's *Life Histories of North American Birds* again proved an invaluable resource. Bent himself wrote most of the accounts in this twenty-one-volume classic, though some were contributed by other experts; regardless, virtually all of the pieces depend on field notes filed by a wide variety of correspondents. As a result, my citations might refer to Bent, or to "one of Bent's correspondents," or to *Life Histories*. I also again make frequent reference to Bent's contemporary Edward Howe Forbush, the Massachusetts state ornithologist during the early decades of the twentieth century. The work I have, *A Natural History of American Birds of Eastern and Central North America*, is a convenient one-volume abridgement of his three-volume *Birds of Massachusetts and Other New England States*.

Of the several books that I discovered once I turned my attention to coastal birds, two deserve special mention: first, Gardner Stout's *The Shorebirds of North America*, a beautiful coffee-table book whose centerpiece is a superb essay by Peter Matthiessen; and second, Rachel Carson's lovely little book, *Under the Sea-Wind*. In both, the fascinations of natural history are illuminated by great writing.

Finally, I must again bow down before the incredible, and incredibly comprehensive, *Birds of North America Online*. The print version of this critical resource (eighteen volumes covering 716 species), edited by Alan Poole and Frank Gill, appeared in 2002, the culmination of a ten-year effort on the part of the American Ornithologists' Union, the Cornell Lab of Ornithology, and the Academy of Natural Sciences. These days, for a small annual subscription fee, you can get the whole thing online — including audio, video, and recurrent updating based on the latest research.

The Armchair Birder

goes coastal

spring

....

Black-Necked Stilt

Himantopus mexicanus

"So is this a bird a normal person is gonna see?" asked Dede when I showed her some pictures.

Good question, since it touches not only on the habits and habitats of the bird species under consideration, but also on the peculiar psychology of the human subspecies commonly known as the "birder."

Fact is, I had never seen a black-necked stilt, and when John Murphy mentioned that it was one of the relatively few species of shorebird that nested along our southeastern coasts, rather than heading north, I wondered if we might see a pair out on Alligator Point.

"Well, not exactly right here," John said. But not far away, less than an hour back east on Highway 98, was the renowned St. Marks National Wildlife Refuge. I had seen signs, heard the recommendations, and knew I needed to check the place out; I just hadn't decided when. John nudged me: "You're likely to see some stilts in there."

John was a friend of a friend of a friend. I had asked my friend June White if she knew any birders down around Florida's Big Bend, and she had put me in touch with her friend Todd Engstrom, a Tallahassee-based wildlife biologist. Todd kindly advised me to contact his friend John Murphy, who works in Tallahassee but lives on Alligator Point, a birdy spit of sand and scrub sticking out into Ochlockonee Bay between Panacea and Carrabelle Beach on Florida's Gulf coast. John seemed not at all taken aback that a complete stranger, via e-mail, would request a day out of his life. I told him when I was headed down his way, and he said I could pick him up at his house at 7:30 Saturday morning.

Dede and I rented a little cottage on Carrabelle Beach and spent a couple of days coming to appreciate why this area is known as Florida's "forgotten coast." Maybe there would be cars zipping down the old highway and people out walking the shore later in the season, but now, on the first weekend in March, it was marvelously quiet. On

3

our peaceful morning perambulations, cormorants drowsed on ancient pilings, and even the herring gulls sauntered noiselessly along the water's edge. Alligator Point was just a few minutes away, and when Saturday rolled around I had no problem pulling into John's driveway at the appointed hour.

No problem, that is, except for the hour that had been appointed. Seven-thirty might be a routine clock-in time for birders and fishermen, but for slow-starters like me, who require a full two hours before the day's activities begin, it's pretty early. And by noon, to come to the point, I was beat. Not that it hadn't been exhilarating. John showed me my first marbled godwit, which I'm lucky enough to have seen since, and my first golden plover, which I will probably never see again, along with a number of other avian wonders. But this out-of-the-armchair birding is not easy. The walk out to the "point" of Alligator Point was a mile and a half, one way, in soft sand, and we had trekked to a few other sites as well. Maybe the stilts would have to wait.

But when would I be back this way again? I headed east off of Alligator Point and in no more than forty-five minutes saw a big sign that looked like the main entrance to St. Marks. Was this the place? I asked an elderly sun-baked couple selling boiled peanuts at the turn-off. "Straight down the road," said the man. "Six miles in, six miles back out."

After a mile or so I came to the entrance proper, where I was supposed to stick five dollars in an envelope and stuff it in a box. I only had four and wanted help anyway, so I went into the visitors' center and spoke to a lady behind a computer terminal.

"Songbirds?" she asked.

"Waders," I said.

She told me to drive on down to the end of the road and then take one of the trails that wound off behind the restroom building.

There were two. I picked one called Watch Tower Pond Trail and headed out. (The sign indicated the trail was one mile long, and that was about all I felt capable of.) It led through palmetto, saw grass, yaupon holly, pine, and live oak and would occasionally veer out along the "pond." I wasn't seeing much—maybe a couple of scaup. I was wondering if I was wasting my time. Then a portly young couple came along from the direction I was headed. The woman had binoculars hanging around her neck.

"Seen anything?" I asked.

"Like what?" said the man. Clearly not a birder. In fact, I got the impression that they might as well have been looking for Florida panthers as black-necked stilts, so I forged ahead.

Pretty soon I got to a sign that said "Photography Blind" with an arrow pointing off to the right. I found it in a few yards: an elevated wooden box at the edge of the pond, with a couple of chairs and slits to look out of. If nothing else, the chairs looked absolutely wonderful, so I climbed in and plopped down.

Damned if they weren't right there: a pair, two pairs, four pairs, wading and feeding in the shallow water. Fabulous, exotic birds . . . with their absurdly long, bright-red legs, crisp black and white markings, and that long, straight, needle-like bill. As David Allen Sibley says, "Not likely to be confused with any other shorebird."

It's worth noting that I did not see the equally spectacular Ameri-

5

can avocet. The birds are related in the family Recurvirostridae, they often hang together, and John told me I might find both at St. Marks. However, the stilts were by no means alone. At the far end of the pond, off to my right, I saw snowy egrets, great egrets, tricolored herons, and little blue herons. Right in front of me a line of fifteen dowitchers were feeding in formation, advancing slowly, heads bobbing up and down. Across the pond the water had receded to expose a stretch of mud bank, but you couldn't see any mud. It was solid dunlin (one thousand? two thousand?) with some hundreds of willets thrown in.

I hadn't wasted my time.

. . . .

The stilts were interesting to watch: off by themselves, but not together in a group. Two here, two there—paired off for the mating season probably, but not yet in a sexual frenzy. Quietly going about their business, as is their nature. "Unusually gentle and unsuspicious birds," writes Arthur Cleveland Bent, "much more easily approached than most large waders."

They moved slowly, elegantly, through the shallows, or sometimes just stood there, as if they were enjoying the water. I couldn't actually see what they were eating, and there's a reason for that. You'll occasionally see an egret come up with a good-sized fish, so you can say, "OK, there's lunch." But the black-necked stilt eats mostly insects, picking them off the water or sometimes even right out of the air, so there's not a lot of turmoil. The bird might eat a crustacean or tiny fish, but you're unlikely to see a large prey item dangling from that fine, delicate rapier.

Granted, the experts ascribe to the stilt's feeding habits a bit more vigor—even violence—than I have. "Pecking, Plunging, and Snatching" might all be called on, write Julie Robinson and others in BNA *Online*—not to mention the "Scythe-like Sweep," a technique the stilt shares with its avocet cousin (as well as with the spoonbill). In this tactile-feeding method, the bird immerses head and bill and sweeps them back and forth, hoping to bump into something good to eat. No doubt. But I saw pretty much what Bent describes: "The skilful and graceful way in which they wade about in water breast deep. . . . The legs are much bent at each step, the foot is carefully raised and gently but firmly planted again at each long stride."

I would see the stilts again in mid-April, on Little St. Simons Island's Myrtle Pond. The timing was right to witness a little nesting activity, and our formidable guide, Stacia Hendricks, assured us that we were in the right place. But Myrtle Pond is a broad expanse of marshy vegetation, and from our vantage point on the dam road, we did well to pick out the birds; actually locating a nest would have been tough.

But surely the birds had paired off by then, and Robinson tells us just how this happens: "Pair forms when female persistently associates with male and is eventually tolerated." Mating particulars include the standard displays—sexual preening by the male, solicitation posture from the female—with a little water sport thrown in. Like teens flirting in a pool, the male uses his bill to splash water on himself and his mate; the excitement builds until "vigorous splashing" culminates in copulation. In a tender postcoital moment, "birds stand side to side with bills crossed. . . . Male sometimes holds wing over back of female."

As for nest-building, these birds are not all that discriminating when it comes to site selection. Some nests are concealed (as they would certainly be on Myrtle Pond), some are in plain sight; some are scraped out of the dry sand and, says Bent, "profusely lined with small bits of shell and pieces of dry sticks, while those in marshy meadows might be made out of a floating platform of sticks." Out west, Bent correspondent John Tyler has found them in cow pastures, such that "it seems almost a miracle that any of the eggs escape being destroyed [by] cattle tramping everywhere over the fields." They do for the most part escape this fate, for which Tyler has a wonderful explanation: "It is known that few animals will purposely step on any living object of a size large enough to be noticed, and the writer is convinced that a stilt simply remains on her nest and by her vociferousness and possibly even with a few vigorous thrusts of her long bill causes a grazing cow to direct her course away from the nest."

Nests in marshy areas face a surer threat than wandering cattle: rising water. "It is when the water rises that the birds rise to the occasion," Leon Dawson reports to Bent. "Sedges, sticks, water plants with clinging soil, anything movable, is seized and forced under the threatened eggs. Indeed, so apprehensive is the bird of the growing necessity, that as often as she leaves the nest she will seize loose material and fling it over her shoulder for future use. The eggs themselves . . . are mauled about and soiled in the mud, but the day is saved."

By all accounts, black-necked stilts are aggressive guardians of their nests and young. Audubon writes that "while the females are sitting, the males pay them much attention, acting in this respect like those of the American Avoset [*sic*], watching the approach of intruders, giving chase to the Red-winged Starlings, as well as to the Fishing and American Crows, and assailing the truant young gunner or egger." A key defensive stratagem is hollering, at which they persist to such an extent that even the authors at BNA *Online* are driven to write in complete sentences: "Agitated stilts yap incessantly, dive at predators, and feign mortal injuries. After a day of field work near breeding stilts, the yapping echoes in one's head until the next morning when the sound is renewed by the continuing calls of vigilant parents." Edward Howe Forbush adds that the chatter is so unrelenting that the stilt is commonly known as "the lawyer."

As Audubon suggests, aerial enemies might be met by a rising mob of stilts, which are adept at hovering above their nests, their long legs ready for confrontation. Predators on the ground will be led astray, the stilt hopes, by some form of distraction display. The bird has a special knack for two of these tricks, according to Peter Matthiessen: "The stilt may hoist one wing in such a way that the wind twists and rumples it unmercifully, as if it were smashed, and this angular bird has perfected a technique of collapsing one leg which will bring all right-thinking predators on the dead run."

Robinson and her team credit the stilt with a good half-dozen distinct distraction techniques, including the remarkable Popcorn Display, about which more begs to be said. "Popcorn Display," the authors write, "is an amalgamation of birds engaging in Hop-and-Flap behavior," which is occasioned by the arrival on the scene of a "ground predator." The first birds to notice the threat start hopping up and down, and eventually enough birds join in to elevate the Hop-and-Flap into the full Popcorn. Unfortunately, the display is every bit as ineffectual as you might suppose: "Popcorn Display observed to continue for several minutes while ground predator (a gopher snake) ate all the eggs in a nest and then dispersed as the snake departed."

OK. The stilt is just not equipped to deal with a gopher snake. But woe to the chick from another nest that happens to wander too close. Parent stilts, writes Robinson, "are aggressive toward unrelated young and young of other species (particularly American Avocets). Observed pecking avocet chicks repeatedly, such that skin was completely removed from the crown, while parent avocets watched." Wait. The avocet parents did what? At least the stilts do the Popcorn.

Enough. Parents everywhere do what they can. Aspersions need not be cast at the child-rearing skills of Recurvirostridae *in toto*. Instead, let's return to a more appreciative picture of this "graceful and handsome bird," as Forbush calls it, this "pint-sized pied flamingo," in the words of noted zoologist Ralph Palmer. Let's picture it at its ease, wading in the shallows, effortlessly taking a waterbug here, mosquito larvae there. Or, stooping slightly, then springing into the air to take flight, its long red legs trailing out behind, in Peter Cashwell's simile, like Isadora Duncan's scarf.

. . . .

With the image of the bird clearly in mind, let's take another look at Dede's question. Examined from either angle, the answer remains a simple "no." First, the beach vacationer is unlikely to see the black-necked stilt among the peeps, pelicans, gulls, and terns out in front of the oceanside condo. It is a bird to be sought out.

From the other angle the question implicitly addresses those who do see black-necked stilts—that is, birders—and asks, *Are they normal people?* Birders are odd for many reasons. They wear a lot of clothes whatever the season, including, invariably, hats the size of umbrellas. They require specialized and often very expensive gear. They routinely use words ("lores," "axillary," "alula") nobody else knows the meaning of. And they travel enormous distances at the slightest provocation. None of these, though, push the personality of the birder into the categorically "abnormal" range.

At the same time, though, to give up your Saturday to some knucklehead you've never met just because he's had the unmitigated gall to ask you to? No. That ain't normal.

American Oystercatcher

Haematopus palliatus

The lead in the morning paper pretty much said it all: "A fleeing DUI suspect led police on Saturday to his Gwinnett County marijuana grow house." It seems that the suspect, seeing the blue lights flashing in his rearview mirror, pulled over, jumped out of his car, and ran for home. Police followed without difficulty and found not only sixty-nine marijuana plants under cultivation, not only several pounds of processed pot, not only equipment and cash, but also the suspect's partner in crime hiding under a bed.

I'm trying to imagine a male American oystercatcher running back to the nest with, say, a raccoon in pursuit, the mama bird hollering, "Hon', what the heck are you doing?" But, of course, I can't imagine it, because oystercatchers ain't that dumb.

In late April I had the good fortune to be observing these birds on Georgia's Little St. Simons Island, a retreat I could enjoy thanks to the accounting sleight-of-hand known as the tax deduction. This beautiful, unspoiled barrier island, which wraps around larger St. Simons Island's north and east coasts, has had an interesting history. Once part of Major Pierce Butler's coastal empire, the small island was left to the major's grandson, Pierce Butler II, and his wife, the famed British actress (and journalist) Fanny Kemble, in 1836. In 1908, their descendants sold the property to Philip Berolzheimer, who believed that the island's abundance of red cedar trees would make excellent raw material for his Eagle Pencil Company in New York City. Happily, the trees proved too wind-twisted for pencil-making. Just as happily, Berolzheimer decided that the island's beauty and bounty were worth protecting, and he and his family initiated a regimen of stewardship and conservation that continues today.

It's not private. Nobodies like me—a few at a time—can sign up for a stay at the lodge or in one of the cabins, where their every desire will be catered to, as long as those desires fall within the realm of eating, drinking, and enjoying the natural world. (There are no tele-

vision sets, for example, in the otherwise comfortably appointed rooms.) You can go it alone during the day, or you can join an outing (birding, botany, natural history) led by one of the expert naturalists in residence. Yes, it's pricey. But it's *there*.

Now—back to the species in question: On this special spring birding weekend in April, I found myself part of an early-morning expedition to the island's Sancho Panza Beach, where our small group of enthusiasts was marveling at a congregation of about a zillion shorebirds. Among them, but characteristically off to themselves, were a couple of oystercatchers, taking it easy down by the water like a pair of honeymooners. But then a small party of bird researchers appeared back up among the dunes, moving northward, and the oystercatchers immediately bestirred themselves. Steadily (but "sedately," as the progress of these birds is aptly described) they made their way back up into the dunes, moving southward—and no doubt away from the nest that the researchers were approaching.

. . . .

What a striking specimen of nature's profligacy is this American oystercatcher. Oh, it's a handsome bird, with its bold black-over-white coloration, and large enough to set it apart from the peeps and little plovers, but how about that *bill*! What a marvel! What an extravagance! Not just disproportionately long, but brilliant orange-red. In the sunlight, this bill isn't merely bright; it's incandescent. Because of the bill, you know this bird the first time you see it on shore or mudflat. Because you once saw a picture of one in a book, ' and the image of that bill—the impossibility of it—was indelible.

(Oddly, *Haematopus* means "blood-red foot," referring to . . . what exactly? *Palliatus* translates as "wearing a cloak," an understandable reference to this bird's dark-feathered back.)

Of course, the bill is extremely useful, though even the great Alexander Wilson doubted that the bird came by its name honestly. He observed that oystercatchers use their bills merely to probe in the sand in search of small shellfish. "This appears evident on examining the hard sands where they usually resort, which are found thickly perforated with oblong holes, 2 to 3 inches in depth."

Audubon, writing at about the same time, agreed that the oystercatcher will "probe the sand to the full length of its bill," but he also witnessed the oyster-catching spectacle: he watched the birds "seize the bodies of gaping oysters on what are called in the Southern States and the Floridas 'Racoon [*sic*] oyster beds,' and at other times take up a 'razor-handle' or solen, and lash it against the sands until the shell was broken and the contents swallowed." Similar reports continued to be filed, like this one submitted to Bent from C. J. Maynard in 1896: When the outgoing tide left the oyster bars exposed, writes Maynard, the birds "would alight among the oysters and when the bivalves gaped open, as is their habit when the water first leaves them, the birds would thrust in the point of their hard, flat bills, divide the ligament with which the shells are fastened together, then, having the helpless inhabitant at their mercy, would at once devour it." They were proficient, too, says Maynard, "for specimens which I shot after they had been feeding a short time were so crammed that by simply holding a bird by the legs and shaking it gently the oysters would fall from its mouth."

Today no doubt remains that the American oystercatcher is an avid and expert oyster-eater. It can either stab its laterally flattened bill between the two valves or else hammer the shell open, in either case for the purpose of severing the abductor muscle that holds the bivalve clamped shut. Moreover, writes Sibley, "individual oyster-catchers may specialize as 'hammerers' or 'stabbers.' The 'hammerers' break shells open by pounding on them and have blunt-tipped bills. 'Stabbers' have more pointed-tipped bills that they use to pry apart shells." Occasionally, though, even experts make mistakes. According to Erica Nol and Robert C. Humphrey in BNA *Online*, "Accidents have been recorded where an oystercatcher's bill becomes caught by shellfish and held so that bird drowns with rising tide."

John Murphy, who took me birding on the Florida panhandle's Alligator Point, told me that the mating ritual of these birds was a sight to see—the way the two birds run around together with their backs flattened low and their necks stretched out. Nol and Humphrey elaborate: "Birds run side-by-side, with heads bobbing up and down, giving loud Piping Call, which begins slowly, with notes becoming more rapid and changing in pitch. Birds frequently stop and turn 180 degrees, full circle, or at right angles and continue Piping Display." Sounds funny to me, but it's serious business to the oystercatchers, who mate for life and live long.* And while the nest isn't much—just a scrape in the sand with maybe a shell or two for decor—Sibley describes these birds as "very territorial [and] extremely site-faithful; it is routine for a pair to occupy the same territory for many years in succession."

"Shy, vigilant, and ever on the alert," Audubon writes of these birds, and, echoing the sentiment, Bent calls the American oyster-catcher "one of the shyest and wildest of our shore birds, ever on the

---

*Peter Matthiessen, in *The Shorebirds of North America*, adds a curious note: though these birds do pair for life, they "are often promiscuous within the pair-bond and may establish a *ménage à trois*, in which the third bird, usually a cock, assists his colleague by helping to serenade the hen in a three-way 'piping ceremony,' and perhaps in more delicate ways as well; he remains one of the family throughout the incubation."

alert to escape from danger." We might add "determined" and "resourceful" to the list of its attributes, particularly when it comes to producing and protecting its young.

In the first place, that simple scrape of a nest is cunningly inconspicuous, such that it renders the two or three eggs — irregularly spotted on a sand-colored background — equally inconspicuous. About the only thing that might reveal the location of the nest is the presence of the birds, which is why they're quick to leave at the approach of danger. Then begins the highly refined "distraction behavior." The birds circle back over the intruder "giving distress call," write Nol and Humphrey. "May also demonstrate 'cripple-display,' crouch-run, or mock feeding. Birds often adopt mock sleeping attitude or mock brooding in an exposed location. In this posture, will allow predatory birds such as gulls to approach and rarely even touch them."

Pretty ingenious. But how about this, from Bent correspondent Walter J. Hoxie, writing in 1887? Having gotten too close to an oystercatcher nest for the birds' comfort, he watched as the male flew 100 yards off, then called back to his mate. She followed a moment later. "They seemed to be making a lot of fuss out there, kicking up the sand, squatting down, and cackling like mad." Then the mother returned to the nest and "began to act strangely, wiggling round and squatting down again, and I began to think she was going to lay another egg, when off she went and joined her mate who welcomed her coming with the most extravagant cries and gestures."

Hoxie was about to go examine the nest when the mother flew back once more. "Again she went through the same operation, and her second welcome was, if possible, more exuberant that the first." Then all was quiet, with one bird sitting calmly on the sand, the other standing alongside, and neither showing any sign of another return to the nest. "I could only conclude that they had seen me watching them and would not come back until I went away. So I arose from my uncomfortable position and went to pick up the eggs, when to my surprise the little hollow in the sand was empty. While I was watching the curious antics of the female she had lifted the eggs between her legs and carried them off. So without giving time for her to repeat the offense I hurried to her new quarters and secured them successfully."

(Not that I'm doubting, but, for the record, no other source I've come across confirms the oystercatcher's ability to pick up its eggs and fly away with them.)

The precocial chicks, off and running as soon as they hatch, are harder to protect, but the parents do their best, relying again on camouflage. As Audubon puts it, "The old birds run before you, or fly around you, with great swiftness, and emit peculiar notes, which at once induce their little ones to squat among the sand and broken shells, where, on account of their dull greyish colour, it is very difficult to see them unless you pass within a foot or two of them." If you do get that close, he adds, "they run off emitting a plaintive note, which renders the parents doubly angry." Sibley notes that these devoted parents, unlike most shorebirds, feed their chicks for a month or more and continue the child-rearing process for up to six months.

As is the case with most animal species that find themselves cohabitating with the human variety, the oystercatchers need all the diligence they can summon. Historical changes in the bird's breeding range tell a cautionary tale. Bent writes that in spite of the bird's ability to take care of itself, "its range has been greatly restricted and its numbers very much reduced during the past 50 years. It formerly bred abundantly on Cobb Island, Virginia, but when we were there in 1907 we saw very few and found no nests or young." One of his correspondents, H. H. Bailey, offers an explanation for the bird's decline during that era: "This large showy bird fell an easy mark to the spring gunners, breeding as it did during the height of the spring migration of 'beach birds,' from May 10 to 25. Nesting among the sand dunes or flat beaches back from the ocean, over which the spring gunners tramped daily, these birds were right in the line of travel, so to speak, and were either killed or their nests broken up."

With the passage of the Migratory Bird Treaty Act in 1918, which made it "unlawful to pursue, hunt, take, capture, kill or sell" migratory birds, direct human predation on the American oystercatcher for the most part came to an end. BNA *Online* reports that populations started to rebound slowly and a gradual "re-expansion" of the breeding range began. Current populations are stable, we are told, though "significant threats to the future success of this species are human use and development of coastal areas."

. . . .

That party of researchers on Little St. Simons Island, by the way, was participating in an oystercatcher-banding project initiated on nearby St. Catherines Island. The idea is to remove and replace the eggs (with wooden look-alikes, which keep the adults in parenting mode), hatch them in an incubator, band the hatchlings, and return them to the nest. The removal, of course, prevents egg predation and, presumably, enhances the prospects for successful reproduction. For such a site-faithful species especially, the bands will provide important information about the movements, status, and overall well-being of the local population.

Saying is easier than doing. The year before, we were told, some twenty-odd nests were discovered, and every other one was left alone to constitute a control group. But higher-than-usual tides during the breeding season meant less nesting space available above the waterline, which, in turn, made life easier for the raccoons, snakes, and avian predators. As a result, out of those twenty-plus nests (including both the experiment and control groups) not a single bird successfully fledged.

Standing there on the shore, we could still see the breeding pair picking their careful way through the wrack up high on the beach. "But the good news," said Stacia Hendricks, the island's chief naturalist, "is that these birds can live for up to twenty years, so they get lots of chances." That fact, along with these birds' innate resourcefulness, allowed Stacia and her team to hope for better results in nesting seasons to come.

White Ibis

Eudocimus albus

Coming over the causeway and into town, the first thing you see is a sign proclaiming Dauphin Island, Alabama, as "the nation's birdiest coastal community." I wouldn't dispute the claim. The beach at the west end is covered up in shorebirds; along a quiet street in the narrow island's interior is a stand of pine trees where a colony of great blue herons build their nests; and on the north side there's a wooded "shell mound" park where flocks of spectacularly colorful songbirds (prothonotary warblers, indigo buntings, scarlet tanagers, orchard orioles, you name it) habitually pause during their northward migration.

I was the guest of John ("Sto") Stowers and his wife, Jenny, to whom the word "gracious" doesn't quite do justice. By pure coincidence, I had met Sto on a bird hike in the mountains of North Carolina a few months earlier, and before the day was done he had invited me to his springtime house party on Dauphin Island. I accepted.

An outstanding birder, Sto immediately set about showing off the island's amazing avifauna. Among the firsts for me, as we followed the trails through the shell mounds, were an ovenbird and a Louisiana waterthrush. "You never know what you might see this time of year," Sto said as we were leaving the park. "There was a bunch of us out here last spring when word started going around that a Hudsonian godwit had been seen out by the airport. The way people went running for their cars, you'd've thought you were at a NASCAR event."

Sto and Jenny's house is on the north side of the island, sitting right on the channel that leads out into the Mississippi Sound, and when the chop finally settled on the afternoon of my second day there, we hopped in his little motor boat and headed north back toward the mainland. About twenty minutes later we quietly puttered up onto the point of Cat Island, a narrow strip of sand crowned by low-growing wax myrtle and saw grass. Seeing us coming, two hundred white pelicans had already removed themselves from the beach and resettled on the water a hundred yards out. As we picked our way carefully along the shoreline ("'Bout time for the oyster-catchers to start nesting," Sto warned), the air was filled with the low murmur of birds yet unseen in the vegetation rising on our left side. Then, sudden as summer thunder, the white ibises* arose—who knows how many hundreds?—wheeling low overhead in a churning cloud of white and dropped back down out of view.

We walked toward the west end of the island and turned around to set up Sto's scope with the sun at our backs, and from that vantage point we saw a rookery just seething with birds, not only the ibises but every heron and egret imaginable, including the elusive night herons. It was the start of nesting season, and the birds were uneasy at our intrusion. But every now and then, a long, plumed neck would stretch upward as if to check us out, and we would have a perfect look. The lores of the great egret were turning green; those of the snowy were turning red. But the ibises were not to be outdone: in their courtship transmogrification, their faces, bills, and legs all turn from dull pink to bright crimson.

The whole thing was pretty overwhelming—and not just for arm-chair birders. "I got a doctor friend up in Huntsville," said Sto on our way back in. "He and his wife have gone all over the world on birding trips, professional guides and everything. I brought 'em out here and they called it the most amazing place they had ever seen."

---

*"Ibis" is the name given to this bird by the ancient Egyptians and Greeks. Thoth, the Egyptian god of wisdom, had the body of a man and the head of an ibis, and the bird's family name, Threskiornithidae, is Greek for "sacred bird."

As for the genus name *Eudocimus*, that comes from the nineteenth-century Munich ornithologist Johan Wagler and means simply "in good standing." Choate tells us that Wagler "correctly removed these birds from the genus *Scolopax*" and put them into a new genus of his own creation. "It seems he could not resist naming the genus after his own accomplishment in placing the bird in a scientific classification 'in good standing.'" Diana Wells soothes that sting. Wagler, she writes, "loved nomenclature and once described sorting bird names as a way of 'passing the hours in the most pleasant manner imaginable.'"

In any season the white ibis is a beautiful bird, with its long, de-curved bill and pure white plumage, set off by the black-tipped primaries so distinctive in flight. To see them in such numbers was a thrill for me, but for the birds it was business as usual. The gregarious white ibis nests in colonies of hundreds and sometimes thousands of pairs, and island habitats are typical — with the extra advantage of being free from land-based predators.

You might wonder, though, if it took us twenty minutes by boat to get to this little island out in the middle of the sound, where in the world do the ibises go to get something to eat? That little spit of sand and shrubbery wasn't about to support such a population of birds. Not a problem. As Audubon writes, "While breeding, the White Ibises go to a great distance in search of food[,] . . . flying in flocks of several hundreds. . . . They [rise] with common accord from the breeding-ground, forming themselves into long lines, often a mile in extent, and soon disappearing from view." They might head to the nearest mud bank from which the tide has just receded, or to some shallow lake, pond, or marsh, wherever they can find a supply of their favorite foods: fiddler crabs or small fish, frogs, snails, lizards, or even small snakes—not excluding water moccasins.

They have a special fondness for crawfish, according to Bent correspondent Oscar Baynard, who wrote in 1913 that the local ibis colony was doing a great job of controlling the crawfish population in the marshes around Orange Lake in Florida. It was Baynard's observation that crawfish "destroy thousands of the spawn of fish" and that lakes and ponds surrounded by marsh but lacking an ibis colony "are nearly always devoid of any great number of fish." The birds at Orange Lake, though, had kept the crawfish numbers down and the fish numbers up, providing a further boon: "As young fish eat millions of mosquitoes it stands to reason that with ibis and herons we have more fish and less mosquitoes, and any bird that does so much good to a State is of very great value and should be protected for that reason alone."

Audubon, too, noticed the white ibis's fondness for crawfish. And he credits the bird with considerable cunning in foraging for them. In hot weather, he writes, the crawfish burrows deep, deeper than the ibis can reach with its bill, "for before it can be comfortable it must reach the water." So the bird walks "with remarkable care" up to the mound of mud that the crawfish has thrown up in the process of digging its hole, picks a few crumbs off the top, and drops them into the "deep cavity" the crawfish calls home. "Then the Ibis retires a single step, and patiently waits the result. The Cray-fish, incommoded by the load of earth, instantly sets to work anew, and at last reaches the entrance of its burrow; but the moment it comes in sight, the Ibis seizes it with its bill."

Writing for BNA *Online*, James Kushlan and Keith Bildstein add that the ibis's foraging is facilitated by a slight gap in the center of its bill, which effectively turns the bill tips into tweezers. This fine instrument allows the bird not only to grasp its prey but also to remove indigestible appendages, like crawfish claws. Even more interesting, the ibis likes to wash its food before eating—"even if bird must walk to a water source several meters from the capture site."

"I have never seen the courtship of this species," writes Bent, "nor can I find anything about it in print." I haven't seen it either, I'm sorry to say, but thanks to the always dependable BNA *Online*, the whole story is in print—in sometimes unseemly detail. The rites get under way with "bachelor parties," groups of competing males that engage in predictable shenanigans like preening, jousting, and show-offy display flights, in which hundreds of birds might be seen spiraling up and down around the colony site. In one-on-one confrontations, write Kushlan and Bildstein, size matters: "Longer bills are important in determining outcome of fights over mates and nests."

The victorious male's testosterone rush has still not quite subsided when the submissive female approaches. He asserts ownership by grabbing and shaking her head, sometimes with such force that she's bloodied in the process. Once the violence is over, though, you might see the pair with necks crossed, or preening each other, or holding onto the same stick, or just standing there touching. Copulation will follow, with the male on the female's back and her feathers raised to cradle him there. It's a tender scene; unfortunately, the curtain is not ready to fall.

Kushlan and Bildstein describe the marital relationship as "monogamous, with frequent extra-pair copulations," and, in fact, the ongoing compulsion of both birds to "just do it" would seem to be what drives most of their behavior during the rest of the nesting cycle. Nest-building, for example, seems at first to follow a standard pattern. The female selects the site and does most of the construction, with twigs and sticks brought in by the male. But where does he get them? He might very well steal them from nests his neighbors have already built, "often in conjunction with"—you guessed it—"attempted extra-pair copulations."

Of course, the male who is out running around is also running his own risk of being cheated on—which is why these "extremely aggressive males" spend more time at the nest during nest-building and egg-laying than might be expected. As Kushlan and Bildstein put it, "Any departures put nest and its contents at risk and females at risk of extra-pair copulations." Statistics confirm the obvious: "Number of extra-pair copulations correlated with time female spends alone at nest." Clearly, neither male nor female knows when to say no.

Well, when there's no trust, what have you got? The end of civilized life, that's what. Kushlan and Bildstein describe an ugly scene when a male catches a rival with his spouse *in flagrante delicto*: feathers ripped out, facial lesions, eye injuries, crippled legs. And once the male has ousted the intruder, he turns on his unfaithful mate, pecking her about the head and neck. The violence nesting ibises visit on one another goes to the limit: eggs left unattended are likely to be destroyed by rivals from nearby nests. Is it any wonder that, nesting or foraging, ibises can never let their guard down and remain the wariest waders on the pond?

It's a shame, because nesting ibises have more than their share of the usual worries, too. Bent writes of a rookery in Florida that's "infested, during the breeding season, with a horde of Florida crows and fish crows, which are constantly hovering over the nests, looking for a chance to pounce upon and carry off any unguarded eggs." The crows steer clear of "the long, sharp beaks of the herons," he adds, but are unbothered by the soft, blunt bills of the ibises. The result: "Every nest in the vicinity of my blind was cleaned out." BNA *Online* expands the list of threats to include boat-tailed grackles, black-crowned night-herons, and gulls, not to mention land predators like possums, raccoons, and rat snakes. Egg loss at some colonies reaches close to 50 percent.

Thankfully, the picture brightens once the hatchlings come along. Both male and female are dedicated parents, and, remarkably, they get help. Like the socially advanced American crow, the white ibis is among those avian species that put the nonbreeding younger generation to work helping raise the youngest generation. "These second-year helpers," write Kushlan and Bildstein, "often move among nests, interacting with several broods per hour, preening and shading nestlings." Whether they actually feed nestlings is not known, nor is the extent to which their help is critical in the chick-rearing process. The experience they themselves gain may be what's most important. In any case, such a scene of domestic cooperation is a welcome antidote to the mayhem that has preceded it.

· ·

Besides, unless we insist on voyeurism, what we have in the white ibis is a bird that epitomizes the beauty of coastal wetlands all along our southeastern Atlantic and Gulf coasts. After seeing that huge flock on Cat Island, I was gratified to see them up close, in ones and twos, on Sanibel Island, Florida. Walking the Indigo Trail in "Ding" Darling National Wildlife Refuge, I had a great look at a party of ten birds at their leisure in a tidal creek not fifteen feet from where I stood—six in the water and four sunning and preening in the mangroves just above. I was close enough to count four black-tipped primaries on a couple of the roosting birds—meaning, says Audubon, that they were females; the males have five. One of the birds in the water was intent on picking up a stick that looked to be five feet long, though what he planned to do with it was beyond me.

I saw another pair on an early morning walk along Sanibel beach, wading knee-deep into the gently breaking surf and stabbing repeatedly into the rippling water for something to eat. The fine morning light showed how their bright red bills turn a glossy black as they lengthen toward the tip. Headed back, I came upon a single bird higher up on the beach, maybe looking for a fiddler crab hole to probe around in. It wasn't paying me any attention, and I got close enough to realize for the first time that the iris of the white ibis is a startling blue.

We're lucky. These lovely birds can't be as plentiful as they were in early in the nineteenth century, when Alexander Wilson wrote of the Indians in New Orleans offering strings of them for sale. But in spite of steady encroachment by humankind on coastal environments everywhere—to say nothing of the best efforts of rapacious fish crows, the U.S. population of the white ibis appears to be healthy and stable.

A Brief Note on the Glossy Ibis (*Plegadis falcinellus*)

The glossy ibis has much in common with its more conspicuous cousin: same general shape and size (give or take a couple of inches), with the same distinctive decurved bill and same general feeding habits and habitats. The big difference, of course, is color. The glossy ibis is a dark bird. You'd call it black if you saw it feeding in a marsh pond, but good sunlight gives its plumage a metallic sheen with a tinge of green.

Also, although the glossy is the most cosmopolitan of the ibis species, you won't find it nesting in colonies of thousands of birds. According to the *Breeding Bird Atlas of Georgia*, it usually nests in small numbers within mixed-species colonies, often including snowy egrets, tricolored herons, and little blue herons.

On Little St. Simons Island in April, we never failed to see several of these birds feeding in the marshes of Myrtle Pond, always in the company of snowy and great egrets, black-necked stilts, and a variety of other wading birds. In fact, Kushlan and Bildstein speculate that snowy egrets use glossy ibises as "beaters," taking prey scared up by the tactile-feeding ibises. The glossy may even be a "core species," drawing other waders to feed where they see it feeding.

I've come across little information regarding the breeding behavior of the glossy, but I can offer Bent correspondent C. J. Maynard's account of a nesting pair at a Florida rookery. The female has just returned to the nest to relieve the incubating male—apparently with no "extra-pair copulation" in the interim. "Then would ensue about 15 minutes of as neat courting and billing and cooing as one will ever see being done by a pair of doves. This loving disposition toward each other seems to be a characteristic of the glossy ibis, as every pair that I have observed have done it. . . . They will stand erect and seem to rub their bill against the other one, . . . they will preen each other's feathers and act just like a couple of young humans on their honeymoon; these loving scenes continued until the young were able to fly, never seeming to diminish at all."

Exeunt. Curtain.

Black-Bellied Plover
Pluvialis squatarola

All during March and April the bird had to be pointed out to me. At last, in early May, on Sanibel Island, Florida, the black-bellied plover had its black belly—and face, and throat, sharply outlined in white—and it was, even for me, unmistakable. Whether likened to an aristocrat in his tuxedo or to an avian version of the skunk, as some have suggested, it's a striking and unforgettable bird.

Decent birders, of course, have no trouble identifying the black-bellied plover, even on its coastal wintering grounds. Its plumage is generally gray, but its stocky body, thick neck, and, especially, its short, stout, black bill mark it as a plover, and its size—at eleven and a half inches the largest member of the family—identify it as the black-belly. Another clue is revealed when the bird takes flight: the conspicuous black "armpits," or "wingpits," or, formally, axillars, that Bent says "form the most reliable field mark in all plumages."

Those handsome birds I saw on Sanibel, by the way, were not hanging around. Like so many other shorebirds, the black-bellied plover is a far-northern breeder. It is also widely distributed, migrating in the springtime up both U.S. coasts as well as up the Mississippi Valley. Peter Matthiessen gives a fine sense of this bird's cosmopolitan nature: "On the moonlike desert beaches of Peru, shrouded by fogs drifted in off the Humboldt Current, the black-bellied plover runs and watches, runs and watches; already the plumage of its silver breast has taken on a fretting of the bold black that it will carry northward to the Arctic."

I was fascinated to read Alexander Wilson's claim that the black-bellied plover breeds in the mountainous regions of Pennsylvania, particularly in "newly-ploughed fields, where it forms its nest of a few slight materials, as slightly put together." I was even more fascinated to find that Audubon supports this claim, and all the more so given the keen pleasure he takes in correcting Wilson's occasionally misguided notions. He reports that he followed the black-bellies to "the shores of Labrador[,] . . . where some young birds were obtained in the beginning of August." But then he backtracks to the northeastern states: "Individuals of this species spend the summer months in the mountainous parts of Maryland, Pennsylvania, and Connecticut, where they breed. I found their nests near the waters of the Delaware and the Perkioming Creek, when I resided in the first of those states."

It's odd. This opinion is apparently so far off the mark that no contemporary account bothers to dismiss it—or even acknowledge it. I suppose it's possible that those great masters had another species in mind, but I can't imagine what it might have been.

In any case, it is now universally acknowledged that the black-bellied plover's North American breeding grounds stretch from western Alaska through the Canadian Arctic Archipelago—and that it does not dally along the way. As Bent puts it, "I have never seen any signs of courtship during the spring migration, though I have often looked for it. . . . Hence I must infer that it is accomplished after the birds arrive on their breeding grounds." For an eyewitness account of the details, he turns to his Alaska-based correspondent Herbert W. Brandt, whose enthusiasm for this plover is boundless: "During courtship the male spends considerable time on the wing, speeding about like a racer; and amid the constant din of wild-fowl notes his cheery whistle *to lee, to lee,* is one of the pleasant sounds that greet the ear. . . . He carries on his courtship regardless of weather, now mounting high, the next moment skimming low, with beautiful and bewildering grace, his wild whistling call meanwhile rising above the din of the storm."

Dennis Paulson, writing for BNA *Online,* adds that all this time spent in the air is a form of territory defense and that the male black-bellied plover is "fiercely aggressive to other males." Surely some of the "beautiful and bewildering grace" is evident in what Paulson calls the characteristic "butterfly flight," where the male hovers above his territory with shallow, slow wingbeats before gliding to the ground on outstretched wings. The display continues on foot with a quick dash up to the waiting female, at which point the marriage may well be consummated. Or the pair may first decide to indulge in a form of foreplay Paulson calls the Joint Run.

I mention this because Forbush writes of having witnessed it on the mudflats of Cape Cod: "Two beautifully plumaged adult birds apparently run a race for several rods, trotting, and stepping high, with heads in the air. First, one is ahead, then the other; then they turn and run towards us side by side a yard apart. . . . Then one flies away, with the other in full pursuit." Probably a form of courtship, he speculates, meaning that Bent might have missed something after all.

Paulson reports that, prior to copulation, "no special female posture or display noted," which makes me much prefer Matthiessen's account. "The female, tail high in the classic position and scratching earth out toward the rear the while, responds to the addresses of the male by rotating on one spot as, grandly, he circles in. Whether she kicks and excavates in sexual abandon and later makes the most of her own diggings, or whether she scratches out her scrape in some dim instinct that, from the looks of things, it must soon come in handy, are questions as depressing as they are rewarding, concerning as they do the matter of degree to which female ardor is reflexive and unconscious."

Matthiessen is certainly correct that the nest is just a scrape on the open tundra, usually begun by the male, then deepened and haphazardly lined by the female. Brandt adds that the preferred site is on prominent bluffs overlooking the valleys—which makes sense. The sitting birds are visible and vulnerable, and being able to see a long way is a matter of self-protection.

Coloration of the eggs provides another form of defense, says Brandt. Both the eggs and the surrounding vegetation are "mottled with black and white," and the eggs are so well camouflaged that you just about have to touch them to be sure they're there. He cites an instance in which the eggs in a deserted nest were left unprotected for three days, "during which time jaegers, which were continuously hunting overhead and about, were, even with their sharp eyes, not able to distinguish them."

In fact, in many of its habits the black-bellied plover is a wary bird. Its nests are not only hard to discern; they are also widely scattered. The forty that Brandt studied were never any closer to one another than a quarter mile. Both parents incubate the invisible eggs, and, says Paulson, their changeovers are performed quickly, without ceremony. The male calls from on wing as he approaches, and the female immediately exits, flying several hundred yards away to begin feeding. When the eggs are new, the sitting bird will fly at the remotest provocation, leaving the predator little indication where the nest might be. But as hatching time approaches, both birds become vigilant and protective, ready to attack any jaeger or gull that comes too close. "The female often leaves her eggs to join in the attack," writes Brandt, "and even the swift-flying long-tailed jaeger can not avoid their onslaughts but beats a hasty retreat. I have seen a male plover strike a jaeger so hard that it reeled unsteadily in mid-air, but the coward made no effort to retaliate."

When the eggs hatch at last, the parents take one final precaution, removing the shells to a considerable distance and sometimes even hiding them under plant matter. But these chicks are precocial, anxious to get up and go, so there's not much left for the parents to do. The young are beginning to forage at twelve hours old, according to Paulson, and are spending half their time at it before the first full day is done. For those first few days, while the chicks are still relatively close by, the parents will lure predators away from the site by feigning injury, and they'll give an alarm note to warn the young to crouch and freeze, but for these birds parenting is a short-term occupation. Which makes it less unseemly, I suppose, that the mama birds check out early, heading back south a week or two before the males and the young.

From start to finish, it's about a four-month sojourn. The birds that are going to pass the off-season along our southeastern coasts are making their way through the mid-Atlantic states in late August and early September. They'll shortly molt out of that sharp breeding plumage, and for the next seven months or so I'll be once again trying to recognize them as they feed on the wide beaches and mudflats. To aid me in those times — oh, say, 99 percent — when identification is less than certain, I'm collecting useful hints:

- Does it forage (as Paulson says) by the Stop-Run-Peck or Stop-Run-Stop method characteristic of plovers? Check.
- Does it have a special fondness for marine worms and fiddler crabs, and if it happens to nab one of those items, does it rinse it off in the water before gobbling? Check.
- Does it go in for foot-trembling or foot-tapping, as Sibley says, in order to scare tiny critters into moving and giving themselves away? I can't honestly imagine getting a good enough look to confirm such behavior, but . . . check.

Of course, it wouldn't hurt to go ahead and learn to recognize the bird's song, which, by all accounts, is both distinctive and beautiful. I don't mean the courtship song, which I'm unlikely ever to hear, but the "flight call," which, despite that name, the bird makes while standing, flying around, or migrating. Michael O'Brien, in *The Shorebird Guide*, describes it as a "far-carrying whistle, typically a slurred, three-syllable *plEE-uu-ee* with the middle note lower; sometimes shortened to one or two syllables." Matthiessen writes that "the voice of the black-bellied plover carries far, a stirring *toor-a-lee* or *pee-ur-ee* like a sea bluebird, often heard before the bird is seen." Bent is especially rapt: "To my mind the whistle of the black-bellied plover is one of the sweetest and most fascinating of all the Limicoline voices, . . . [having] a mellow and plaintive quality, with a tinge of wildness, which enlivens the solitude of the ocean beaches."

As for *moi*, I've been listening to the recording on BNA *Online*. Wish me luck.

Actually, this dedicated armchair birder noticed something interesting about the behavior of the black-bellied plover on that visit to Sanibel in May. The birds were plentiful on the mud bars ringing the tidal pools along "Ding" Darling's Wildlife Drive; I might see twenty or more together. But on an early-morning beach walk I couldn't help noting that they gave each other considerably more space. I would see a single bird every fifty yards or so, back a few feet from the rippling surf along which the sanderlings ran so tirelessly. The plovers for the most part stood quietly, like lifeguards.

I was gratified to read later that it is in fact this bird's habit to forage singly and that it is often seen alone — and I was even more gratified to read Bent's description: "The black-bellied plover is wont to stand erect, with head held high, in an attitude of dignified yet alert repose . . . a wary sentinel for all of its smaller companions." Later still, reading Paulson, I discovered what was going on: these birds practice "winter territoriality" — that is, they not only insist on their own breeding space; they insist on their own off-season feeding space as well.

So I'm making progress. And the good news is that once I've learned to recognize it, the black-bellied plover will be there. Back in Bent's day, the bird was reported to be on the decline, but he didn't believe it. He noticed that in his neck of the woods (the coast of Massachusetts) "formerly they were much more abundant in the fall than in the spring, but the reverse is now the case." He believed that they had changed their migratory pattern to avoid the autumn hunt in that area, which he saw as "a striking example of the bird's sagacity."

In fact, the population of the species is stable and healthy, and I'm free to imagine myself with Forbush, at low tide on a Cape Cod mudflat, "in a stranded boat with telescope at hand," observing at our leisure the habits of the black-bellied plover. We'll see them run and stop, "apparently without aim or purpose," until one pulls a marine worm out of the sand and proceeds to wash it off in the surf. We'll see another thump a ruddy turnstone on the head and snatch away its morsel of food. Yet another will wade into the water until its breast is partly submerged, and we watch as it "ducks and splashes, throwing water over itself like a timid girl bather." We'll see those two lovers in their carefree race up the beach and back. And when at the end of the day Forbush observes that "the Black-bellied plover is a glorious bird and well worth watching," I'll roger that, one expert to another.

Ruddy Turnstone
Arenaria interpres

At an Atlanta Audubon Society fundraiser not long ago, Dede and I snapped up a beautiful—and pretty funny—photograph by noted nature photographer Don Saunders. It's titled "Ruddy Turnstone vs. Leopard Crab," and it features, in close-up detail, both of those pie-bald creatures, a couple of inches apart, the bird gazing down at the crab with a look of intense interest.

The leopard crab (a species I don't believe I've ever seen live) looks exactly as the name suggests it should: a pattern of irregular, bright reddish-brown spots on a white background. The ruddy turnstone, in full breeding plumage, looks just like Thomas Burleigh says it does: "a chunky, short-necked bird, with short orange legs and, in the spring and summer months, a variegated plumage of reddish-brown, black, and white that has given it the common name of 'calico-bird.'"

The two together create a composition to make an artist happy, but you'll have to include me among the vulgar multitude left asking, "OK, but what happened?" Given the turnstone's omnivoracity and pugnacity at the feeding trough, it's a fair question—and one that would come to mind again when some other birders and I witnessed what looked like a standoff between a ruddy turnstone and a ghost crab—another crustacean almost as large as the bird itself.

We'll come back to the specifics of the turnstone's feeding habits, but a little background will shed light on *why* this bird feeds so hungrily. Audubon calls the turnstone "one of the most beautiful of its family" but quickly adds that it has been wrongly classified: "Were I to place it in a position determined by its affinities, I should remove it at once from the Tringa [sandpiper] family. Its mode of searching for food around pebbles and other objects, the comparative strength of its legs, its retiring disposition, and its loud whistling notes while on wing, will, I think, prove at some period that what I have ventured to advance may be in accordance with the only true system, by which I mean Nature's own system, could one be so fortunate as to understand it."

But there's one thing the ruddy turnstone does have in common with many of its cousins in the extensive family now called Scolopacidae: it's seriously migratory. We're used to seeing this bird during the winter along our southeastern and Gulf coasts, but the folks in Central and South America are used to seeing it on their coasts, too—all the way down to Tierra del Fuego. And when the season turns and the reproductive urge again quickens their pulse, where do these birds return? Northern Greenland, Ellesmere Island, Victoria Island, and other top-of-the-world spots inside the Arctic Circle. From bottom to top, the trip runs to about 8,000 miles, and there's nothing leisurely about it. Peter Matthiessen writes that a banded ruddy turnstone has been known to journey over 450 miles in a single day.

When these birds stop along the way, they're hungry. They need to find places where plenty of food is available, and they need to eat a lot of it before resuming their journey. One food they particularly enjoy is nutrient-rich horseshoe crab eggs, and the horseshoe crabs oblige by crawling up out of the muck and laying their zillions of eggs in the sand during the month of May, just when the turnstones are en route. I got to witness this spectacle on a relatively small scale when our band of Atlanta Audubon birders was treated to a boat trip into St. Catherines Sound off the Georgia coast. We dropped anchor a few feet away from a small grass-and-sand island where the horseshoe crabs had just finished their business, and now the birds were having at it—dunlin, willets, and dowitchers by the hundreds, in addition to the countless turnstones—feeding with such maniacal purpose as to be utterly oblivious of our proximity. Brad Winn, one of our guides from the state Department of Natural Resources, showed us how only the turnstones, with their chisel-like bills, were able to dig into dry sand for the egg deposits, and woe to any other bird—conspecific or otherwise—that tried to horn in on their excavation.

I say our experience with this phenomenon was small scale because, from all reports, it doesn't compare to what happens every
May on Delaware Bay—no doubt the most famous stopover along
the Eastern Seaboard for the turnstones and other long-distance migrants. Here immense flocks of birds, perhaps a million in all, count
on finding the nourishment to sustain them for the 2,400-mile trek
that still remains. "For this remarkable system to work," writes Scott
Weidensaul in *Living on the Wind*, "there must be a profligacy of
crabs, an orgy of Roman proportions, and more eggs than stars in the
sky. It is not enough that there merely be some horseshoe crabs on
the beach, or even a lot—there must be so many that the bay shore
seethes with them like an invading legion, multitudes squandering
their geological capital with utter, reckless bacchanalian abandon."*

*Given Weidensaul's seemingly hyperbolic description of the spawning horseshoe
crabs on Delaware Bay, it's especially interesting to read Alexander Wilson's account
of the same phenomenon, dating from 1828: "Early in the month of May, the horse-
foot crabs approach the shore in multitudes to obey the great law of nature, in de-
positing their eggs within the influence of the sun, and are then very troublesome to

In the company of vast numbers of sanderlings, semipalmated sandpipers, red knots, dunlin, and dowitchers, the ruddy turnstones gather for the feast, each bird consuming as many as 5,000 eggs per day. None is greedier than the turnstone, who, says Theodore Cross, "rudely pushes aside the other shorebirds," particularly the sanderlings that are so quick to jump into the hole that the turnstone has dug and "get a free ride on the turnstone's work." Where it is feeding, adds Bent, the turnstone "will allow no competition . . . from another bird, even of its own species, but with lowered head, drooping wings, and hunched-up back it rushes at the intruder in a threatening attitude and perhaps gives him a few jabs with its sharp bill."

Truculence is one thing, but for sheer audacity the most vivid account I've seen comes from the other side of the continent, where at the same time of year the cosmopolitan ruddy turnstone is coursing northward over the Pacific. On Laysan Island in northwestern Hawaii, writes Bent correspondent Alexander Wetmore, the gray-backed terns had already laid their eggs and were "entirely at the mercy" of the turnstones. "So bold were the shore birds that on one occasion I saw two actually push aside the feathers on the sides of the incubating tern, drag her egg from beneath her breast, and proceed to open and devour it within 6 inches of the nest." The tern kept sitting, as though unable to comprehend what had happened, until at last, writes Wetmore, she "reached out to draw the half-empty

---

the fishermen, who can scarcely draw a seine for them, they are so numerous. Being of slow motion, and easily overset by the surf, their dead bodies cover the shore in heaps, and in such numbers, that for ten miles one might walk on them without touching the ground.

"The hogs from the neighboring country are regularly driven down, every spring, to feed on them, which they do with great avidity; though by this kind of food their flesh acquires a strong, disagreeable, fishy taste. . . . [The eggs] may sometimes be seen lying in hollows and eddies, in bushels, while the Snipes and Sandpipers, particularly the Turnstones, are hovering about, feasting on the delicious fare. The dead bodies of the animals themselves are hauled up in wagons for manure, and when placed at the hills of corn, in planting time, are said to enrich the soil, and add greatly to the increase of the crop."

shell of her treasure again beneath her, while the robbers, temporarily satisfied, pattered away in search of other prey."

So we've established that the turnstone loves eggs — of various sizes — and while we're at it we might as well add a number of other items to the bill of fare. For example, just as it times its arrival on Delaware Bay to exploit the special food source available there, it times its arrival at its northern breeding grounds to coincide with the early-summer hatch of a wide variety of flying insects. If that food proves insufficient, the bird will hunt the bushes for early-season buds and berries, or, pushed further, it is even willing to ransack human garbage or glut itself on sea-creature carrion.

In other words, the bird's diet runs the full spectrum, from prenatal to postmortem, but all that said, we still haven't touched on why it's called the "turnstone" — though that too, of course, pertains to its feeding behavior. Audubon, watching these birds on the coast of Galveston, tells us of his delight "to see the ingenuity with which they turned over the oyster-shells, clods of mud, and other small bodies left exposed by the retiring tide. Whenever the object was not too large, the bird bent its legs to half their length, placed its bill beneath it, and with a sudden quick jerk of the head pushed it off, when it quickly picked up the food which was thus exposed to view." For impediments requiring more force, "they would use not only the bill and head, but also the breast, pushing the object with all their strength, and reminding me of the labour which I have undergone in turning over a large turtle."

Not surprisingly, bird enthusiasts even before Audubon's time were fascinated by this rare ability. From Matthiessen comes this memorable anecdote about Mark Catesby, whose *Natural History of Carolina, Florida and the Bahama Islands* was published in 1731: "Catesby provided a ruddy turnstone with stones to turn, the better to observe the feeding trait that gives the bird its name. In a time when scientific experiments were less complex than they are today, the bird was furnished systematically with stones that had nothing beneath them, whereupon 'not finding under them the usual food, it died.'"

Assuming they have found sufficient food along the way, and despite the distance, the uncertainties, and the hazards of the weeks-long migratory flight, these high-Arctic breeders often touch down on the very same nesting grounds they used the previous year. The males arrive first and, at the first sight of a female, start advertising with aerial displays and loud courtship calls. "The males outnumber the females so the rivalry is keen," reports Elmer Ekblaw in *Life Histories*. "Frequently two males pursue the same female, seeking to win her favor, the while they are combating one another for the advantage. In giddy, reckless flight they sweep back and forth along the shore [and] when alighted the pursuit is just as eager, the female racing about to escape the insistent attentions of the males."

Actually, says David Nettleship in BNA *Online*, the outcome is to some extent predetermined. Very often the female will find herself wooed and won by the same male she wed the year before. In any case, once paired, the male is as jealous of his mate as he is of his meal, giving chase to rivals and watchful for predators. During the days between pairing and egg-laying, writes Nettleship, the turnstones are seldom more than a few paces apart, and if the male loses sight of his betrothed, he gets upset about it: "If separated, male often attacks female when she reappears, aggression that quickly subsides by submissive 'salutation' behavior of female."

Ruddy turnstone sex appears to be a relatively straightforward affair: male mounts, flutters wings for balance, establishes cloacal contact. "Female passive throughout," writes Nettleship. "Once male dismounts, both birds begin to preen or resume previous activities." Matthiessen sees the thing similarly, but expresses it inimitably: "Like the sanderling, the ruddy turnstone has traveled far into the north, and like that other squat and hardy bird, it takes little time for dalliance. Under luminous skies of the aurora borealis, the two get on about the work of love in a silent, implacable manner, looking neither to the left nor the right."

Like many shorebirds, the turnstones don't fuss too much with nest construction. When the female is about to lay her first egg, she turns around a few times to scrape out a little hollow in the tundra, although she might pluck a few willow leaves for lining. As each of the four eggs hatch, the cautious parents immediately remove the tell-tale shell to a considerable distance. Just as immediately, the precocial, down-covered chicks are up and walking, pecking at anything that might turn out to be an insect. The parents, meanwhile, are on high alert. As Bent correspondent A. L. V. Manniche observes, "One of them will keep a lookout from the summit of a large stone or a rock while the other is brooding or guiding the young ones. The bird on guard will discover an approaching enemy at an incredibly long distance and rush toward him uttering furious cries. Especially the skua is a detested enemy of the turnstone. Every day I could observe the hunting skuas pursued by turnstones."

More detested than the skua, perhaps, is its close cousin the jaeger, and against this predator all of the turnstone's ferocity may prove futile. Jaegers patrol the breeding grounds relentlessly, and if the turnstone pursues, so much the better. "Jaegers elicit chasing by flying over turnstone nesting area," writes Nettleship, "which often leaves nest vulnerable to other jaegers, particularly when both members of a pair join pursuit attack." Once their appetite has been whetted, moreover, the predators "may revisit site . . . until all eggs of clutch taken."

Well, the jaegers do what the jaegers have to do. We'll never have to look very far to be reminded that nature, in Tennyson's phrase, is "red in tooth and claw." The hatchlings in other clutches will survive, in sufficient numbers, to see their down transformed to feathers. As that happens, the territorial boundaries that had been so scrupulously established and defended begin to break down, and family groups may be seen foraging in relative tranquility, in search of a promising insect hatch.

As the young fledge, the females begin to depart, leaving the males to oversee the end of the parenting process. Fledging brings independence, though, and soon the young turnstones flock among themselves, perhaps little aware that their male parents have begun to follow the females southward. The children are the last to leave —

rising up one day at the end of July into high, strange skies, to undertake, unguided, an arduous journey to distant, unknown shores.

It's a marvel, isn't it? But it works. The young somehow make it to wintering grounds they've never seen, or at least enough of them do to keep the North American population of the ruddy turnstone relatively stable. Not that the future is certain. Critical staging areas like Delaware Bay face a host of threats to the continued bounty of horseshoe crab eggs—including not only the predictable pressure of more and more people on the shore but also overfishing for the crabs themselves, which are used primarily as bait for more edible species.

For now, though, the little harlequin is looking good, and armchair birders like me, who have been delighted to see one or two of these pretty birds working a shoreline with the peeps and plovers, can actually, if we take the trouble, see flocks of hundreds during the migratory season—always an awesome experience.

Now, as to that standoff between the turnstone and the ghost crab on the beach at Jekyll Island: we kept watching through our scopes, not necessarily hoping for a tussle, but wondering. The crab emerged from its burrow a couple of times, and with the bird standing right there retreated again. We had to conclude that the turnstone finally wasn't interested, and Art Hurt, one of the most knowledgeable of our Atlanta Audubon group, theorized that the bird was digging around for food near the crab hole and the crab was just curious as to the source of the commotion.

Probably accurate, but not all that colorful. How about this? The turnstone figured that if it hung around long enough, the crab would either lay some eggs or die, and in either case the notoriously resourceful glutton would have itself something to eat.

Reddish Egret

Egretta rufescens

How are we to know the heron from the egret
When ornithologists conspire to keep the information segret?
—Anonymous

Earlier I described my visit to Dauphin Island, off the coast of Alabama, as the guest of Sto and Jenny Stowers—a visit that included a boat trip to the incredible rookery on tiny Cat Island out in the middle of the Mississippi Sound.

While I was gaping at the stunning profusion of white pelicans, white and glossy ibises, and herons of every variety, Sto told me to take a look through the spotting scope he had set up. "What do you see?" he asked.

The scope was focused on a gorgeous, pure-white bird with head and neck luxuriantly plumed. "Snowy egret?" I guessed.

"Take a look at the bill," said Sto.

Whoa. The bill was marvelously two-toned, pink at the base and black at the tip. "ok, not a snowy egret," I had to concede, "but . . ."

"Reddish egret," said Sto. "White morph."

Sto was as delighted to have shown me this bird as I was to have seen it. I asked him what percentage of reddish egrets were of this distinctly nonreddish variety. "I don't know exactly," said Sto, "but you ain't gonna see one every time you come out here."

Audubon was certain that all reddish egrets started out white and then matured, after a couple of years, into their true colorful selves. He was amused at the consternation this truth, when fully grasped, would engender among the experts. "The remarkable circumstance of this bird's changing from white to purple," he wrote, "will no doubt have some tendency to disconcert the systematists, who, it seems, pronounce all the birds which they name Egrets to be always white." He goes on to note that these same people, who give the name "heron" only to birds with colored plumage, will also have to

deal with the problem that "the largest of these known to exist in the United States [the great white heron] is pure white."

Morphologically, Audubon was wrong—probably on both counts. Not only does the white reddish egret remain white for the duration, but the great white heron, similarly, is now widely considered to be a white morph of the great blue heron. Nevertheless, where the reddish egret is concerned, Audubon was correct in recognizing that the white bird and the "purple" bird were the same species—an advance on the work of fellow ornithologist Charles Bonaparte,* who believed the white bird to be a separate species, which he named Peale's egret.

Audubon was also right that the whole heron-versus-egret thing was pretty doggone vexing. "It is not my present intention," he writes, "to say what an Egret is, or what a Heron is; but it can no longer be denied that the presence or absence of a loose crest, floating plume, and a white colour, are insufficient for establishing essential characters separating Egrets from Herons, which in fact display the most intimate connection, the one group running into the other in an almost imperceptible gradation."

I agree. We don't need to worry about the distinctions that separate egrets from herons. After all, we're talking about the family Ardeidae here, and in the sense that *ardea* means "heron," all these birds are herons. In fact, the family is so sprawling and diverse (sixty-five species worldwide, ranging in length from eleven to fifty-four inches and in wingspan from seventeen inches to six feet), instead of wondering what separates them, we might wonder just what

---

*Not to get bogged down, but I can't resist passing along that the reference is to Charles Lucien Jules Laurent Bonaparte (1803–57), often referred to by Audubon as his good friend "Prince of Musignano" and one of the eleven children of Napoleon's younger brother Lucien. Charles migrated with wife and family to America and lived for several years in New Jersey and Pennsylvania. During the 1820s, according to Choate, "he re-edited a volume with the longest title in American ornithology even without appending the full names of the author—*American Ornithology, or History of Birds Inhabiting the United States Not Given by Wilson.*" Choate adds that Bonaparte "is considered to be the father of systematic ornithology in the United States."

ties do the binding. Ah! Here, from *The Sibley Guide to Bird Life and Behavior*: "All family members have powder-down breast and rump patches . . . in which the down disintegrates to a powder the birds use for preening their feathers, often with their pectinate middle toes."

Of course, only one heron is under discussion here, and for the present purpose we do need to distinguish it, the reddish egret, from the others. We need to distinguish it from, say, the little blue heron, which also has (1) a basic, more-or-less slate-blue plumage and (2) the sort of confusing morphology Audubon attributed to the reddish egret—that is, the young are pure white and turn "blue" upon adulthood. (In fact, if you saw a reddish egret in white morph, a young little blue heron, and a snowy egret together on a distant spit of sand and were told that they were different species, you'd probably conclude that bird-watching was best left to obsessive-compulsives.)

Enough meandering. Let's go back to where we started—my visit to Dauphin Island—and take a more direct route into our appreciation of the reddish egret. Sto's house sits on the north side of the island, along the little channel leading out into the sound. Just on the other side of this narrow waterway a sand bar emerges from a stand of marsh grass, and among the birds attracted to this bit of microhabitat is a reddish egret that comes in every afternoon to feed. Engaged in this activity, believe me, the bird announces its distinctive self, and our hosts made sure none of the guests missed it. "He's doing his drunken-sailor routine!" one of them would holler from the porch, and we would put aside cocktails and other such indulgences to go out and enjoy the show.

Peter Lowther and Richard Paul, writing for bna *Online*, offer the standard assessment: "The Reddish Egret is remarkable for its extremely active foraging behavior, employing running, hopping, flying, and open-wing techniques to locate and pursue schools of small fish across barren shallow flats." Birders who've witnessed this memorable sight are more likely to come up with a metaphor like Sto and Jenny's. The bird runs erratically through the shallow water, wings akimbo—maybe one raised, maybe the other, maybe both— weaving, jumping, turning, stabbing. It's enough to frighten small children, to say nothing of small fish, and you would swear it was something done for its own sake, some bizarre ballet, but there's no dispute that this is indeed how the reddish egret catches its dinner.

Most of the bird's various feeding techniques, according to Lowther and Paul, fall under the general heading of "Disturb and Chase," and they include Wing-Flicking, Open-Wing Feeding, Canopy Feeding (both wings extended over the head like an umbrella), and Foot-Stirring. I daresay the bird we watched on Dauphin Island displayed the full Disturb-and-Chase gamut, but the reddish egret is credited with yet another technique, which I would dearly love to witness: "Hovering-Stirring," in which the bird launches into flight and, hovering over the water, "gracefully scrapes mud or aquatic vegetation with one foot," then strikes at its prey while still airborne.

If you're looking at this bird in the late spring, as I was, you'll recognize it at once even without the distinctive feeding behavior. At this time of year the head and neck feathers, which at other times blend subtly into the gray-blue of the overall plumage, become a shaggy lion's mane of bright rusty red. As Bent writes, "The reddish egret in its nuptial display, in which it frequently indulges all through the breeding season to express its emotions, fairly bristles with plumes." He compares the head, neck, and breast feathers to "the quills of a porcupine, giving the bird quite a formidable appearance, terrifying to its enemies, perhaps, but probably pleasing to its mate."

Perhaps better to accentuate this distinctive blandishment, the courtship ritual of reddish egrets involves a good deal of "head-tossing." The female might approach the male's territory, for example, and if he's so inclined, he might signal her—"come on over"—with a couple of head tosses. She might well return the gesture. Or one of the birds might ascend, fly around in a circle, and, in Lowther and Paul's words, "return to initiate a vigorous bout of mutual head tossing."

Well, circle flights and head tosses (or any maneuver that draws attention to the seasonal plumes) are typical of the heron family, but the reddish egret has developed its own wrinkle in the routine—what Lowther and Paul call the "Jumping-over Display." Here, one of the birds—either male or female—flies up and over its mate, plumes erect, head tossing emphatically, and lands on the other side. The other bird watches, standing upright, and responds with some "high-intensity head tossing" of its own. The display might be repeated as many as ten times, at which point the other bird takes over, and the whole episode might last fifteen minutes. You'd think all this excitement would lead to the inevitable, but not necessarily. Copulation might well occur "without preamble," write Lowther and Paul, "with individuals standing quietly side by side at nest with plumage relaxed." The male steps up onto the female's back, the two birds position themselves for contact, and there you have it.

Meanwhile, nest-building is in progress, with the male, usually, bringing in sticks and twigs for his mate to use in the construction of their substantial home. The nests might be situated on the top branches of the mangroves, says Audubon, or down in the thick grass "a foot or two above the highest tide-mark." He adds that those that withstand the "winter gales" are repaired and reused season after season. (Nor can he resist mentioning that the three or four eggs typically produced by the female "afford excellent eating.")

Like the other birds in the heron family, the young are helpless and must be fed by regurgitation. Within a few weeks, Audubon reports, they can "sit upright on the nest, with their legs extended forward, or crawl about on the branches, as all other Herons are wont to do." Bent correspondent Alvin Cahn delineates this "sitting-up" phase in more detail: "Before they are able to climb out of the nest, the babies make a valiant defense against an intruder by hissing and jabbing vigorously with their bills. They are so unsteady, however, that they very seldom hit what they are aiming at. They are a comical sight sitting on their heels, their great feet sprawling before them as they vainly endeavor to keep their balance during the violent exercise of defense."

Their very unsteadiness, according to the same writer, sometimes

does them in: "The chief source of mortality among the young egrets
. . . seems to be falling out of the nest, and a young bird is permitted
to die of starvation or to be consumed by the red ants or a stray coy-
ote that may reach the island during low water, right under the nest,
without the old birds showing any sign of comprehending what is
going on."

Assuming it escapes this fate, the young bird that at a few weeks
of age scrambles awkwardly through the branches outside its nest
will soon be fledged, full-grown, and at ease in its surroundings.
Bent describes the "grace and elegance" with which this species
perches on the tree tops, "swaying in the strong breeze, which generally prevails on the Texas coast, maintaining its balance by slight
adjustments of its supple frame and only occasionally bringing its
wings into play."

. . . .

With this lovely image in mind, let's return to the issue of the reddish egret's "mortality." It is odd that Mr. Cahn, reporting to Bent
in 1923, seems unaware that the reddish egret was at that very time
struggling back from the brink of extermination in the United States.
Bent himself was certainly aware of this bird's plight: "Although
once abundant on the coast and islands of southwestern Florida,"
he writes, "this interesting species had practically gone from that
region before the time of my first visit in 1903, for we saw only a
few scattering individuals in the Florida Keys and near Cape Sable."

In the last years of the nineteenth century, the reddish egret suffered the same fate that befell all the other extravagantly plumed
herons: slaughter at the hands of plume hunters who sold the
feathers to makers of ladies' hats. Bent offers this account from
W. E. D. Scott, writing from southwest Florida in 1887: "The trees
were full of nests, some of which still contained eggs, and hundreds
of broken eggs strewed the ground everywhere. Fish crows and both
kinds of buzzards were present in great numbers and were rapidly
destroying the remaining eggs. I found a huge pile of dead, half de-
cayed birds, lying on the ground which had apparently been killed
for a day or two. All of them had the 'plumes' taken off with a patch

of the skin from the back, and some had the wings cut off; otherwise they were uninjured. I counted over 200 birds treated this way."

Looking back on the destruction, Lowther and Paul write that plume hunting between 1880 and 1912 "greatly reduced numbers of all herons and may have extirpated Reddish Egret from Florida, Louisiana, and Texas." At the height of the craze, "back-plumes from a single individual of this species were valued at 40 cents."

Since the middle of the twentieth century, the population has been rebounding—slowly. In Florida, where the bird wasn't seen at all for ten years (1927–37), there are now maybe 400 pairs spread over forty rookeries. That doesn't sound like very many, and the total U.S. population of 2,000 pairs sounds pretty meager, too (maybe 10 percent of pre-1880 levels, according to some estimates). But I suppose a slowly expanding population is preferable to a rapidly declining one, and I suppose, too, that the upward trend explains why the reddish egret is not currently listed as endangered or threatened.

I'm trying to find comfort there, but as the anonymous wag who supplied the epigraph above might put it, "This beautiful bird with its pectinate toe / Came too close to telling a tale of woe."

summer

Anhinga
Anhinga anhinga

Though it's seldom the most riveting aspect of bird study, I think in this case we'd better start with nomenclature. Nobody seems very happy with the name "anhinga," which comes from the Tupi Indians of Brazil and means "devil bird." It's assumed that such an association derives from the anhinga's habit of swimming along with only its head and part of its neck visible on the water's surface, somewhat in the manner of a snake. "Devil bird," to my knowledge, was never adopted by English speakers, but "snake-bird" remains one of the bird's widely used familiar names.

Then there's "darter," a name David Allen Sibley prefers to apply to the entire Anhingidae family: "Darters are large, cormorant-like waterbirds with mostly dark plumage, a long tail, a long, sinuous neck, and a dagger-like bill." "Darter" presumably refers to this last-named appendage, as well as to the bird's technique of spearing fish with same. (It's a small family, by the way, with at most four species worldwide. Our *A. anhinga* is the only one occurring in North America.)

Wilson, for one, had adopted this term, while writing of the bird's curious physiognomy: "Formerly the Darter was considered by voyagers as an anomalous production; a monster, partaking of the nature of the Snake and the Duck." He then quotes his predecessor William Bartram on the same theme: "I doubt not but if this bird had been an inhabitant of the Tiber in Ovid's days, it would have furnished him with a subject for some beautiful and entertaining metamorphoses."

Audubon called the bird "anhinga," which would seem to have set us on the path toward scientific consistency, but a century later both Bent and Forbush listed this bird in their indexes as the "Water-turkey." Why? Diana Wells, in her book on bird names, explains that "anhingas can fan out their tails like turkeys," but apparently not everyone has witnessed this phenomenon. Ernest Choate, the acknowledged bird-name etymology expert, halfheartedly suggests

51

that "the bird looks somewhat like a small, thin turkey." Bent himself was at a loss. The "water" part he could understand, "but I could never see any resemblance to a turkey, and I can not understand how this name happened to be applied to it. The name 'darter' or 'snake bird,' both of which are descriptive, seem much more appropriate."

Today, for whatever reason, we have returned to the unlovely name "anhinga," the objections to which must include the fact that the word is utterly unpronounceable if you've been stung by a bee and are lapsing into anaphylactic shock.

. . . .

Nomenclatural confusion notwithstanding, the anhinga is a striking, fascinating creature. Anhingas are long, elegant birds—three feet from tail tip to bill tip—with generally dark plumage broken by a spattering of white on the tops of their wings. (As Theodore Cross writes, "It is often said that the black-and-white pattern on the wings closely resembles a supermarket bar code.") The female is distinguished by a lighter, almost tawny neck and upper breast (her "shawl") that contrasts sharply against the black plumage of her lower chest and belly. Because of their dark coloration and their habit of sunning themselves, often spread-winged, on a favorite roosting perch, you might confuse them with cormorants, but anhingas have a longer neck and a longer, more lethal-looking bill (without the hooked upper mandible of the cormorant).

Also, cormorants do not swim, like anhingas do, with their bodies submerged and only their heads and necks above the surface—a point which plunges us straight into the subject of this bird's unique abilities, as well as the controversies surrounding them.

Audubon, in fine fettle, insists that he alone is the proper guide to the study of this bird: "Many writers have described what they have been pleased to call the habits of the Anhinga; . . . or even to inform us gravely and oracularly what they ought to be, when the basis of all their fancies was merely a dried skin and feathers appended. Leaving these ornithologists for the present to amuse themselves in their snug closets, I proceed to detail the real habits of this curious bird, as I have observed and studied them in Nature."

Where have the "ornithologists" gone so wrong? Audubon's answer: "The generally received opinion or belief that the Anhinga always swims with its body sunk beneath the surface is quite incorrect; for it does so only when in sight of an enemy, and when under no apprehension of danger it is as buoyant as any other diving bird, such as a Cormorant, a Merganser, a Grebe, or a Diver. This erroneous opinion has, however, been adopted simply because few persons have watched the bird with sufficient care." Audubon adds that the more threatened it feels, the deeper it sinks, "until at last it swims off with the head and neck only above the surface."

I love that picture: a submarine gradually submerging to evade a hostile warship, until only its periscope is visible. I just can't find any corroboration. Peter Frederick and Douglas Siegel-Causey, writing for BNA *Online*, say simply that "while the bird is swimming on the surface, its body is usually submerged, with only the head and snake-like neck visible." It's a more prosaic argument, but it makes sense: the bird sinks because it must; its feathers get saturated. My guess is that to stay on top of the water it would have to make an effort, like a poor swimmer thrashing about to keep from going under.

Of course, the anhinga doesn't need to stay on top of the water, and everyone agrees that its ability to submerge itself is a good thing—"adaptive behavior," as the evolutionary biologists call it. But exactly how it is able to submerge—why it becomes saturated—is in dispute. *The Breeding Bird Atlas of Georgia*, recently issued and authoritative, offers the generally accepted explanation: "Since the Anhinga's feathers lack the waterproofing oils that protect the feathers of ducks and other waterbirds, they become waterlogged, eliminating tiny air bubbles that would cause the bird to float."

Other contemporary experts contradict that theory: "The plumage of darters, like that of cormorants," writes Sibley, "becomes very wet when they dive, but not because their feathers lack waterproofing oils; rather, the microstructure of the feathers lets water into tiny spaces inside them. The resulting loss of buoyancy helps birds submerge and forage." BNA *Online* elaborates on that microstructure: "Breast-feathers lack hooklets that interlock barbules, allowing water to penetrate to the skin."

Now you know.

In any case, the bird gets thoroughly soaked, and that "wettability," along with its "dense bones" (no argument about those), allows it to achieve "neutral buoyancy." In other words, with a wiggle of a webbed foot, it can slip all the way under and go spear itself something to eat, which is what all this submerging business is about. That's right: the anhinga is one of those amazing birds that swim along underwater in search of prey. It's not as dependent as a cormorant on actual pursuit, notes Sibley, because it can "retract its long neck into an S-shape and then thrust it forward like a spear." Once it has speared a fish, the bird returns to the surface, shakes it loose, tosses it into the air and swallows it headfirst. BNA *Online* adds that if the fish is "too heavy to lift out of the water," the bird will drag it to shore and get it off its bill "by repeatedly swiping it against vegetation; it then subdues the fish with vigorous stabbing."

Audubon supplements this account with the observation that "the quantity of fish consumed by this bird is astonishing," citing an instance in which he and his friend John Bachman fed an anhinga, in one meal, "forty or more fishes about three inches and a half long." But he defends the bird against the charge of indiscriminate gluttony: "It did not appear to relish eels, as it eat [*sic*] all the other sorts first, and kept them to the last; and after having swallowed them, it had great difficulty in keeping them down, but, although for a while thwarted, it would renew its efforts, and at length master them."

Once the anhinga has fed, it seeks a comfy spot in the sun—not only to digest, but to dry out. Some writers insist that the bird simply cannot fly while still waterlogged, but that raises the question of how it gets to its sunning perch. I'd go with Frederick and Siegel-Causey, who write that "it is capable of taking off directly from surface of water or even from submerged position, although these methods are rarely used and inefficient, and wings are more often dried on perch before flight." In any case, this is its characteristic posture, at ease in full sun, wings spread. (The BNA *Online* authors add that these birds also enjoy the sun because they lose so much body heat underwater and, furthermore, their "dependence on sun warmth for thermoregulation" limits their distribution to southerly climes.)

What I can add is that it can't get too hot for the anhinga. I was walking (foolishly perhaps, but I didn't want to miss anything) along Wildlife Drive in "Ding" Darling National Wildlife Refuge on Sanibel Island, Florida. It was midday in May, and I needed a little thermoregulation myself. Instead, I saw a male anhinga getting his. A handsome bird with the glossy black throat and chest that sets him apart from the female, he was perched on a limb twenty feet over a tidal creek. He kept opening his bill wide, soundlessly, then closing it again—like he was yawning. Audubon had seen the same thing and noted that it was a response to "the intense heat of the atmosphere."

Once their wings have dried, anhingas put them to good use. Crediting these birds with "splendid powers of flight," Bent writes that one of their "favorite pastimes" is to "indulge in aerial exercise by rising from their roost, mounting high in the air and soaring in circles gradually upwards until almost out of sight." As it glides overhead, wings spread wide, long neck and long tail outstretched, the anhinga is commonly likened to a flying cross. Bent adds that after watching the birds soaring on high, "the observer may be suddenly surprised to see one after another of the birds fold its wings and dart downwards, swift as an arrow."

At the right time of year, those spiraling flights and arrow-swift dives might well be part of a territorial display, and once the male has found his mate, other forms of display will follow. The male's courtship ritual is elaborate, says Sibley: the raised head moving side to side; the wing-waving, "first in unison, then alternately, with great vigor"; and the reverse bow, "with the head, neck, and tail folded onto the back," followed by a forward bow sometimes punctuated by an audible bill-snap.

There is no evidence that the male performs for the same female year after year, but it is likely that both birds have returned to the same breeding grounds. Audubon claims to have seen the same nest in use for three years in a row, the birds "augmenting and repairing it every succeeding spring, as Cormorants and Herons are wont to do." The nest habitat is always characterized by close proximity to water and also, since anhingas are social birds, by the presence of other nesting species—like those herons Audubon mentions. Interestingly, although usually associated with coastal regions, the anhinga generally makes its home beside (or above) fresh water. As Audubon writes, "It gives a decided preference to rivers, lakes, bayous, or lagoons in the interior, always however in the lowest and most level parts of the country."

If a new nest is required, according to BNA *Online*, the male begins the process "by placing large sticks and green material in forks of trees and collects nearly all nesting material; female finishes building nest." By then, of course, the marriage will have been consummated, with all due ceremony: "Copulation may be preceded by female's stepping onto nest, male's performing bows, waving wings, and ruffling feathers on branch just outside the nest, followed by female's performing similar displays, and by mutual twig-offering. During copulation, necks are extended, and male takes a stick or female's bill in his; female's head may be pulled upward and backward by male."

The parents will raise four chicks, on average, and the young will remain at home until they are full-grown and ready to fly. Long before that time they've learned to swim, and even at two weeks old they're quick to jump from the nest into the water below at any sign of danger. When the peril has passed, they'll use bill and feet to clamber back up again. In another week or two, they've begun to hone their feeding skills by throwing sticks into air and catching them.

There are no guarantees; a hungry fish crow might swoop in for dinner. But if the anhinga makes it to adulthood, it can look forward to a life unusually serene by avian standards. At least that's the way Bent sees it: "They seem to be peaceful and harmless neighbors in the large, mixed rookeries where they breed; and, so far as I know, they seem to have no serious enemies. They attend strictly to their own affairs, have their own favorite haunts and usually flock by themselves." They can be provoked, however, especially when a human being is trying to kill them. Audubon describes how a bird he had shot, but not fatally, had stood "erect as it could . . . with its head drawn back, its bill open, and its throat swelled with anger until, when at a sure distance, it would dart its head forward and give a severe wound." In one case, he writes, a wounded bird "struck at my dog's nose, and hung to it until dragged to my feet over a space of thirty paces."

Mercifully, people are no longer permitted to shoot anhingas, and it's reassuring to know that the bird's population appears to be stable. From coastal North Carolina, around the tip of Florida, and westward along the Gulf coast to Texas, we can look forward to seeing this bird swim, soar, and sun.

. . . .

"In truth the very first of fresh-water divers," writes Audubon; "it disappears beneath the surface, and that so as scarcely to leave a ripple on the spot." Bent calls it "a master diver with perfect control of its movements in its favorite element." I can testify.

I mentioned the male anhinga I saw in "Ding" Darling NWR. A little while later, and trudging even more slowly along Wildlife Drive, I came upon a female perched on a bare branch a couple of feet above a roadside tidal pool. Her movements as she preened gave me a great look at her bar-code-patterned back, and her long, pale brown neck looked more furred than feathered. I was still watching when a park guide rolled his vehicle to a stop a few yards away and quietly walked over to join me. "That's her favorite perch," he told me. "She's there pretty much every day about this time."

Just then the bird leaned over, dove headfirst into the water, and disappeared—no sound, no splash, no nothing but effortless grace. I was stunned to see such a thing, which I'm sure was apparent on my face when I turned to the guide.

"It's a ten every time," he said.

Wilson's Plover
Charadrius wilsonia

A late-spring morning somewhere on a Georgia beach. A band of birders. "Hey, got a Wilson's here!"

"Sure it's not a semipalmated?"

"I'm sure. Chunky bill. Pinky legs. Up beyond the tide line. Could be nesting."

Scopes riveting on their tripods like so many M-60s on swivel mounts. . . .

It took me a while to figure out what all the fuss was about. After all, I had seen the Wilson's plover,* and all of his plover cousins, on a single beautiful March morning out on Alligator Point off the Florida panhandle. Truth be told, under the guidance of John Murphy, I had chalked up a "seven-plover day." On a secluded marsh pond we had spotted the three big ones—the black-bellied, the American golden, and the killdeer—and out on the beach we had seen all four of the little guys—semipalmated, Wilson's, piping, and snowy. John, an expert birder as well as a man of quiet dignity, had declined to whoop and holler at this achievement, so for me, taking John's cue, it was pretty much "plovers, schmovers" from that point on.

I began to understand the excitement generated by a Wilson's plover sighting when I happened to read in my Georgia DNR e-news that Georgia's entire population of the species had shrunk to only about 100 nesting pairs—down from estimates of about 350 pairs in the early 1980s and 200–250 pairs in 1986.

With this information, I was more intrigued than I might otherwise have been as I followed a group from the Atlanta Audubon So-

---

*So does *plover* rhyme with *lover* or *rover*? Its roots (Old French *plovier*; Latin *pluvia*) don't answer that question, but they raise a better one. Why *plover*, which means, basically, *rain bird*? Choate, after enumerating some of the reasons that have been offered for associating plovers with rain, concludes, "None of these holds water." He adds, "There seems to be no justification or known valid reason for the name." The scientific family name, Charadrius, makes more sense. It comes from the Greek *charadra*, or "gully," a reference to the bird's nesting site.

ciety out onto to the beach at the south end of Georgia's Jekyll Island in mid-May. Our leader was Lydia Thompson, who for several years has been tracking the local Wilson's population. The year before, she told us, she had counted seven nesting pairs; so far this spring she had seen only three. Maybe this morning she would add to the tally. During a two-hour trek up and down the beach, we saw a lot of shorebirds—royal terns and black skimmers by the hundreds, for example—but nary a Wilson's.

Then came June, and I had the good fortune to be a visitor on St. Catherines Island, another gorgeous pearl on the string of Georgia's barrier islands—and one I had longed to lay eyes on. Christa, the wife of the island's long-time manager, Royce Hayes, happened to be the sister of the wife of an old Atlanta friend of mine, and based on this tenuous acquaintance I summoned the gall to invite myself into this unspoiled paradise of sea, marsh, pre-Columbian history, and current ecological research. Christa permitted the intrusion on the condition that I bring Dede, with whom she was also only slightly acquainted, but whom she correctly divined to be much better company than I.

When we were joined at supper (pink snapper not more than a couple of hours removed from the ocean) by Brad Winn and Tim Keyes of the Georgia DNR, the Wilson's plover again became the subject of conversation. As part of an ongoing Wilson's project, Brad and Tim had gradually been canvassing all the beach habitat on Georgia's barrier islands, and the next day they would be working St. Catherines. They kindly asked if I was interested in an early-morning plover count. How early? "How about we meet here at the main house at six?" said Brad. Whoa, I thought.

The Wilson's, like the American oystercatcher, which they were also counting, nests in the sand, wrack, and sea grass above the tide line, and our plan was to walk the beach and count the "birds on territory." Obviously, I wasn't going to be trusted with my own stretch of beach. Brad was going to walk the middle beach, Tim the south beach, and I was given my choice as to whom I would tag along with. I chose Brad, based on the fact that as a DNR program manager, he was the ranking member of our delegation. We dropped Tim off, motored to the opposite side of the inlet separating south from middle, and anchored our boat in the sand.

We began to make our deliberate way up the beach, keeping close to the high-tide line and leaving the vast expanse of empty beach off to our right. The sun was just up over the water, and it was a pretty nice place to be. Brad explained that we wouldn't need to see the nests; the birds' behavior would be clear enough. "They just can't help themselves. As soon as they see us coming, they'll start giving their alarm call." I'm particularly bad at distinguishing the calls of the various shorebirds, all of which, it seems to me, are variations on a "long e" sound. Brad said this bird's stress call was a "*peet.*" One of Bent's correspondents describes it as "a sharp *wheet*, between a chirp and a whistle." Typical. Still, I looked forward to hearing it for myself.

. . . .

As I say, I had seen the Wilson's early in the year—the season when, writes Bent, the bird "frequented the sand bars and sandy islands on the Gulf shore, together with other small plovers and sandpipers." I had seen it running the beaches and mudflats in pursuit of its favorite food, fiddler crabs, though I never had a close enough look to appreciate the gourmandizing reported by Carol Corbat and Peter Bergstrom, writing for BNA *Online*. They describe how these plovers will pull the legs off a fiddler one by one, then swallow the "legless carapace" whole. Those who want to try it themselves but can't spend a lot of time in the kitchen should be advised that the recipe concludes: "handling time >1 min/crab."

The Jekyll Island trip in May would have been about the right time, but, as I say, the plovers didn't cooperate, so we enjoyed no firsthand observation of courtship behavior. Apparently, the birds waste little time on the preliminaries. Bent describes seeing the male run around the female "in a crouching, hunchbacked attitude," until "finally she accepts his caresses." But Corbat and Bergstrom write that the male courts the female simply by scraping out for her a number of nest sites in his territory. She accepts his advances by entering one of them. Actual copulation is a bit more complicated. It begins with what Corbat and Bergstrom call a "marking-time display"—the male raising his feet to almost touch his breast and flicking his tail from side to side. "Male will then hop on back of a receptive female and continue the marching in reduced form with no tail-flicking. Male grabs back of female's neck with his bill as he makes cloacal contact. Pair may fall over backward at end of copulation."

There's nothing to the nest, just the slight depression the male has scraped out in the sand above the high-tide line, though, as Lydia Thompson told us, the site might be shaded by a clump of sea rocket or morning glory. In fact, the parents, both of whom incubate, carefully monitor the temperature, and in the absence of shade on really hot days, they'll soak their bellies before settling down on the eggs.

Like other shorebirds, Wilson's plovers make up for the fact that their nests are exposed and vulnerable by being extremely protective parents. Their conscientiousness is evident as soon as the chicks hatch; the parents fly off with the shells and drop them far from the nest. The precocial young are immediately out of the nest, and their parents, as Audubon puts it, "employ every artifice common to birds of this family, to entice their enemies to follow them and thus save their offspring."

Bent's correspondent Henry Thurston got the full treatment. "How she coaxed me to follow her," he writes of a female whose nest he had approached. "This I did for a time, trailing behind as she struggled along on one leg, the other crumpled under her. Tediously she kept ahead, calling—sobbing, I should have said—one of the most pathetic yet beautiful notes I have heard. . . . Finally, as though exhausted, she sank to the sand and lay on her side gasping. . . . I was sure now that she was tired by her exertion and hurried to catch her, only to learn that she was 'playing possum.' She allowed me to almost touch her, and fluttered off again." Now the bird added broken wings to her list of apparent enfeeblements, and Thurston continued his pursuit. "As I had about caught up with her she gave a joyous whistle, sprang into the air, and those wounded wings carried her like a bullet around a point of wooded land and out of sight. She had accomplished her purpose, as I had hopelessly lost the place from which she started."

Wait a minute. There I was walking a beach presumably populated by nesting Wilson's plovers, so why am I not supplying my own firsthand account of this remarkable behavior? For the same reason that I am also unable to offer my own rendering of the bird's distress call. Brad and I had been trekking for about a mile when he began saying things like "Mighty quiet this morning." After another mile, when we came to the mouth of the creek that marked the end of the middle beach, that observation had evolved into "I can't believe this. I mean, there should be birds here." On the way back down the beach, we studied the tiger beetles.

Hmmm. Another strike-out. By now I was fully aware of the plight of this bird, listed as threatened or endangered in several southeastern states and, more generally, as a "species of high concern" to the U.S. Shorebird Conservation Plan. But was it too late? Had my formerly blasé attitude somehow brought about the complete disappearance of the Wilson's plover from the Georgia coast?

No. Tim reported having spotted ten pairs on the south beach. It was just I who would never see one again—I and whoever was unlucky enough to be in my company.

On Telling Small Plovers Apart

To birders who want to be able to tell one small plover from another, the armchair birder is tempted to ask, "Why?" But that doesn't mean he's unwilling to help.

John Murphy, during that early March morning on the panhandle, helped me distinguish them according to coloration—from the semipalmated (the darkest) to the snowy (the palest). That's not bad, as long as they are all standing there next to one another. Otherwise, about the best you can do along those lines is be aware that the semipalmated and the Wilson's are darker than the piping and the snowy. In fact, it's now a useful birding aphorism to note that the semipalmated contrasts to the piping as wet sand contrasts to dry. (We're keeping in mind, of course, that during the breeding season, all four species are darker than they are during the winter).

So how do we know it's a semipalmated and not a Wilson's? True, both these birds are likely to have a "complete" neck band, but the semipalmated's may be more conspicuous—which is why it's sometimes called the ring-necked plover. Also, the (possibly hypothetical) birder quoted at the beginning of this essay noted the Wilson's thick black bill, and if you've got a good look, that is a good key. It is noticeably larger than that of any of the other small plovers. And if you've got a *really* good look, you might notice some orange at the base of the semipalmated's bill, compared to the Wilson's utterly black one. Thumbing through your guide books, you might assume there's a striking difference between the "orange" legs of the semipalmated and the "pinkish-gray" of the Wilson's, and there might be, if you've spent a lot of money on your scope.

There's one sure way to tell these two birds apart: look for them during breeding season. If you're on the southeastern coast, the bird you're seeing is by damn a Wilson's. The semipalmated is a thousand or so miles north of you.

As for telling the piping plover from the snowy, Bent would have us believe that geography is once again our best friend. "The charming little snowy plover of the Pacific coast is the counterpart of our familiar piping plover, found in similar haunts, perhaps even tamer and more confiding, but not equal to our eastern bird in melody of voice." It's true that Bent would have been unlikely to see this bird on his New England stomping grounds, but the snowy is actually a year-round resident along the entire Gulf coast, Texas to Florida.

To my undiscriminating eye, these two species are much more alike than different, but the experts will point out a couple of contrasts. The piping plover is slightly larger (seven and a quarter inches to six and a quarter), has a shorter, thicker bill (with some orange at the base during breeding season), and has yellow legs as opposed to the snowy's gray ones. To reiterate, that's what the experts see. The rest of us see a couple of small, nondescript shorebirds with pale backs and even paler undersides. If we manage to discern the incomplete neck bands that mark them as plovers, we're doing pretty well.

I'd be remiss if I didn't point out one final commonality. Like the Wilson's, both species are seriously threatened by continuing degradation of their habitat. They need undeveloped beaches to breed, and the human species apparently has an overriding need to develop those beaches. According to BNA *Online*, the most recent census (2001) counted fewer than 3,000 breeding pairs of piping plovers in the United States and Canada, and the latest estimates put the North American snowy population at 18,000 breeding pairs.

A century ago, when populations of these tasty little plovers were being decimated by gunners, ornithologist Charles Townsend described the melodious song that gives the piping plover its name as "the call of a dying race." The shooting stopped in 1918 with the Migratory Bird Treaty Act. Let's hope the more insidious, still ongoing threat of habitat destruction will not give final validation to Townsend's prophecy.

. . . .

(Happy addendum: The results of Brad Winn and Tim Keyes's survey, published in the fall of 2010, brought good news. The total from Georgia's nineteen barrier islands came to 350 nesting pairs of Wilson's plover, very close to 1980's count and, of course, much higher than the total from ten years ago. "The high numbers this year, coupled with observing many chicks at a number of locations, was an exciting find," Keyes reported.)

....

Royal Tern

Sterna maxima (Americana?)

Audubon called his masterwork *Birds of America*, an apt title to be sure. But it does invite the curious mind to ponder — where are we to find the quintessentially "American bird?" Or, for that matter, where are we to find America?

My own mind began circling around these questions after a recent excursion to Little St. Simons Island, which, at $600 a night, give or take, is a lovely place — quiet, unspoiled, the sanctuary of fine people in their finer moments. But it's not America. To find America, I realized, I had to retrace my steps, back from the little island, back from the larger St. Simons Island, back across the island causeway to Highway 27, and south a few miles to the Super 8 Motel in Brunswick ($60 a night, give or take).

Here, where America lives, I was reminded of a few things.

America doesn't eat eggs Benedict for breakfast. It starts its day with a free cup of coffee from the in-room coffeemaker, a couple of sugar packs, and some powdered creamer stirred in.

America doesn't drink a martini cocktail and then a glass of cabernet with dinner. America drinks beer and bourbon, early to late, sprawled on the outdoor concrete steps leading from the first to the second floor of the Super 8. Right here, on a warm June night, are the throbbing heart and the loud talk and the confused head of America. When America finally crawls into its room, it turns the air conditioner up full-blast and defiles the ratty, cheap bedspread in ways only the ratty, cheap bedspread can bear witness to.

And yes, America smokes. It smokes with that first cup of coffee and that last sip of bourbon. Its streets and gutters and parking lots are littered with cigarette butts and it doesn't give a damn. Because, more than anything, America doesn't like to be told what to do.

....

Sterna maxima winged its way into these musings on a tailwind of psychological transference. I had found America and had failed America. I was hung over, my coffee tasted like crap, and I longed for the kind of pampering America wasn't going to give me. Worst of all, I was doing exactly what I had been told to do—heading out way too early in the morning to join a bunch of other dilettante naturalists. Not a picture America would be proud of.

Suddenly I remembered what I had seen the day before, puttering around the little islands at the mouth of the Altamaha River. A royal tern was fishing for its breakfast, flying back and forth over a stretch of the river, then hovering, diving, and at the last second pulling out if its dive and ascending again. On its third try it hit the water with a splash and rose back up, a sunlight-silvered fish gleaming in its bill.

The bird regained its altitude, but then dropped its prize. Faster than gravity, it darted down and caught it before it hit the water. Aloft once more, the bird dropped the fish again, zoomed down and caught it again. It did the same thing a third time. What was it doing? Practicing maybe, but when the bird dropped and caught the fish a fourth time, I had to conclude that it was just showing off. The fifth time, it missed. The fish plopped back into the water, probably mangled by this point and just floating there to be picked up and eaten, but the tern flew away without looking back.

I was feeling better as I got out of my car and headed toward the beach at the south end of Jekyll Island. I wasn't sure what the bird had shown me—work, achievement, joy, hubris, loss, failure, don't-give-a-damn—but I was thinking that maybe after my own personal debacle I was being given another chance. Maybe here was another glimpse, maybe even an apotheosis.

Of course, the bird's name is a problem: the last thing America wants to be is "royal." But the name turns out to have been a mistake, based on the misperception that the royal tern was the largest of the so-called crested terns. As Choate explains, "If [Pieter] Boddaert, who described this tern in 1783, had looked up the measurements of the Caspian tern described in 1770, he would probably not have used the term *maximus*"—nor, in all likelihood, would we have the familiar term "royal."

No, America is not royal. America is plebian, hard-nosed, and not about to back down from a fight. Audubon's description gets

it right.* He reports that he had to use large shot to bring down these "strong and tough" birds, then continues: "When seized they at once erected their beautiful crest, threw up the contents of their stomach, uttered loud cries, and bit severely. One that was merely touched in the wing, and brought ashore, through a high surf, by my Newfoundland dog, stuck fast to his nose until forced to relinquish its hold by having its throat squeezed, after which it disgorged seven partially digested fishes." See? That's the America I'm talking about.

Audubon also noted, however, that the birds' "shyness" surprised him, such that he "could study their habits only with the aid of a good glass." Bent made a similar observation about the huge colony of royal terns he was studying on Grand Cochere off the coast of Louisiana: "As the birds were shy my attempts at photography resulted in only a few distant snapshots of the colony as a whole." These comments threw me because, friends, America ain't shy. But my own experience quickly reassured me. We hadn't been walking the Jekyll beach but a few minutes before we came upon a mon-

---

*Hard as it is to believe, Audubon failed to distinguish between the royal tern and the very similar Caspian tern, conflating them under the designation cayenne tern. Odds are that the "great flocks" he describes here were the much more abundant royal tern.

strous flock of royal terns, black skimmers, and laughing gulls, and these birds seemed entirely oblivious of our presence. In fact, they acted more like a sold-out crowd at the Daytona 500 — packed tight, noisy, boisterous. Every now and then we would see a couple of the terns stacked on top of one another. Not enough seats to go around? No, this was, in the language of ornithologists, "copulatory behavior." Right out in the open, and on Sunday, too.

I must say I was beginning to like this conceit. Then I found Rachel Carson, describing royal terns alighting on a drifting log: "This was the first time the terns had paused since they had left a beach far to the north the day before. They feared to alight on the water, for although terns take their living from the sea, they are not truly of it. To them the sea was a strange element to which they must often abandon themselves for a brief and frightening instant of contact as they dived for a fish, but not a place on which they would willingly rest their fragile bodies." And didn't I read somewhere that 58 percent of tournament bass fishermen — those quintessential Americans — don't know how to swim? Point is: America doesn't swim. America drinks beer in boats.

Above the water, royal terns are in their element. In the teeth of a gale, writes Audubon, "they beat to windward with remarkable vigour, rising, falling, and tacking to right and left, so as to seize every possible opportunity of making their way." And they love speed. "No published data on flight speeds," write P. A. Buckley and Francine Buckley in BNA Online, "but individuals clocked at up to 90 km/h from car on bridges and causeways." Fast boats, fast cars, fleet wide receivers — how America loves all these things.

Finally, let's look at how well the royal tern represents America in the complex matters of homemaking and child-rearing. First, the fact that the mated pair "alternates in sitting at potential nest sites" (according to Buckley and Buckley), then spends a lot of time kicking sand around to meet one or the other's specifications, indicates that the tern couple has a hard time finding a home that suits both parents. Second, once the site is decided on, the birds immediately subscribe to the "home as castle" mythos, defecating on the nest rim with such purpose as to make the edifice impregnable. At the same time, royal terns pay homage to the ideal of "neighborhood" or "community," nesting in colonies that sometimes include thousands of families. And diversity, too, is prized. Bent describes the species as "a sociable and harmless neighbor on its breeding grounds, where it is intimately associated with Cabot's terns, black skimmers, and laughing gulls, which it apparently never molests."

Most remarkable, royal terns typify America in their ambivalent approach to child-rearing. They want to be there but can't. Result: daycare. As Buckley and Buckley put it, the presence of huge crèches containing young of all ages is "the most typical aspect of posthatching Royal tern colony." These crèches can include as many as ten thousand chicks, continue the authors, and are overseen by perhaps 10 percent of the colony's adults. This is a necessary fact of harried royal tern life, and the adults feel plenty guilty about the arrangement. Not only do they seek out their own single child, among all those thousands, to bring food to, but, then, once the breeding season is over, they overcompensate by welcoming the child back home again: "Parents . . . continue to accompany and feed [chick] during migration and in winter quarters, for at least 5–8 mo after hatching." This kind of parental guilt and remorse syndrome gets a huge thumbs-up from America.

Here's the picture, then: Accomplished but improvident; pugnacious in its own defense; loud, brawling, and pleasure-loving but pious when it comes to "traditional values"; and erratically parental. With apologies to the bald eagle, as well as to Ben Franklin's wild turkey, I believe we've found America's bird.

A Note on Distinguishing among the Crested Terns

Along our eastern and Gulf coasts, we might see any of the three so-called crested terns: the royal, the Caspian, and the Sandwich. The three species have much in common: crowded nesting colonies; clutches of single large eggs; formation of crèches into which the young move shortly after hatching; and, as we noted with the royal tern, parental care that extends well beyond fledging. Now, as for distinguishing one from another . . .

The royal and Caspian are almost impossible to tell apart, particularly during breeding season, when the black cap covers the forehead in both species. At other times of the year, the royal's black cap retreats, leaving its forehead white. Another subtle difference is that the Caspian's bill is heavier and of a deeper red than the orange-red bill of the royal. The Caspian is larger, too, but its length, twenty-one inches, is not going to conspicuously set it apart from the royal's twenty inches. In fact, cut it how you will, these birds look a whole lot alike. From the porch of his house on Dauphin Island, Sto Stowers took evident pleasure in distinguishing for us the royal from the Caspian terns that gathered on the little sandbar out in the channel. And it was possible to tell them apart—as long as the one was standing right beside the other.

The Caspian does have a few behavioral quirks that set it apart from the royal. It's less gregarious and nests in somewhat smaller colonies, and along the same lines, it may be said to have a less sociable disposition. Theodore Cross's observation that the Caspian is an "ill-tempered bird" that "waddles down the beach stealing eggs and systematically swallowing the chicks of other terns" seems a bit of an overstatement, but Bent accurately describes this species as "the dominant ruling spirit in the colonies" and "the largest, strongest, and fiercest of the terns." One other interesting difference: the Caspian, quite unlike the royal, is happy to settle on the water and can ride the swells as buoyantly as a gull.

The Sandwich tern joins the group by virtue of the shaggy black cap, or crest, that conspicuously covers its crown and forehead during breeding season, but which, like that of the royal, recedes from the forehead during the rest of the year. At fifteen inches long, this tern is significantly smaller than the other two, but when a bird is by itself, comparative size is not necessarily helpful. However, if you can make out the Sandwich tern's bill, you won't mistake it for a royal or a Caspian. Instead of orange or red, it's black—with a distinctive pale-yellow tip, as though it had been dipped in a jar of mustard or mayo. (As suggestive as the comparison may seem, Choate tells us that this tern's common name comes from Sandwich, Kent, England, the site of the first specimen.)

Truth is, all three are fine birds—lovely and graceful as they cut through the air on those narrow, swept-back wings. And their smaller cousins—the Forster's, least, and common terns—ain't bad either, but that's a story for another day.

Wood Stork

Mycteria americana

The first day of our summer "shorebird workshop" had started early and ended late—with darkness descending on St. Simons Island's Gould's Inlet and the checklisters checking their lists in the glare of automobile headlights. Early morning of Day Two had been given over to a long and fruitless trek up and down Jekyll Island's beach looking for Wilson's plover nests, and now the dozen of us from Atlanta Audubon were headed to the old amphitheater in the island's interior. I, for one, had no idea there was an amphitheater on Jekyll and couldn't imagine what kind of bird life might inhabit it, but I was tired, and I understood that what the armchair birder does in this kind of situation is keep his mouth shut and his feet moving.

We followed a woodsy trail beyond the amphitheater and came to a small pond bordered by tall pines and the lower, thicker foliage of willow and mangrove. Why this secluded little spot had demanded our attention became quickly apparent. It was a beautiful, intimate rookery, and the trees were full of birds: egrets, herons, roseate spoonbills, and, by no means least, the forty or so wood storks in various stages of the nesting process. Near the top of a single dying pine tree were eight or ten active nests, with the big parent birds still bringing in nesting material, and, in some cases, squabbling over same. We saw two birds in a tug-of-war over a length of willow reed, and you'd've thought the survival of the species depended on the outcome. The big birds' feet, usually a dull flesh color, had turned bright pink for the breeding season.

This spectacular scene would have made a fitting culmination to our weekend field trip, I thought, but one site remained on the itinerary. After lunch, conveniently on the way back north toward home up Highway 27, our small caravan pulled in to Harris Neck National Wildlife Refuge in McIntosh County. It's a big place*—close

---

*Big, and at this point, controversial. Since the end of the Civil War, this piece of property had been the home of some seventy-five African American families, who

to 3,000 acres and fifteen miles of roads and trails, but our leaders from Atlanta, Lisa and Art Hurt, knew to take us straight to Woody Pond—a spreading, shallow marsh pond, covered with duckweed, wide at the near end (where folks can walk out along the levee) and gradually narrowing way off in the distance. The pond was home to an incredible variety of birds (wood ducks with chicks paddling along behind, anhingas sunning spread-winged, red-faced moorhens, and pretty much the whole heron family), but the real attraction was in the trees along the opposite shore. Stretching away into the distance from near end to far, hundreds upon hundreds of wood storks had made their nests. Combined with almost equal numbers of great egrets, also nesting, the effect was a vast curtain of white against the tree-green backdrop—an astonishing sight.

· ·

Maybe because of its big, decurved bill, earlier writers (up to and including Bent) referred to the wood stork as the wood ibis. Forbush continued the tradition, though the opening sentence of his account reads: "The Wood Ibis is really a stork with a down-curved bill, and it is unfortunate that the name 'Ibis' has become attached to it."

Well, "ibis" has become *de*tached, and this imposing bird is indeed a stork; in fact, it's both the only stork and the largest wading bird that breeds in North America. If you're close enough to see the dark-gray, bald, scaly neck and head, the heavy bill hanging down

---

fished it and farmed it in peace and relative prosperity. In 1942 the federal government decided it needed an air base in Georgia, and the area's white politicians suggested the Harris Neck community. The feds condemned the land, razed the dwellings, and paid the owners $26.90 per acre. The government promised to return the land to its owners at the end of World War II, but that didn't happen. In 1962 the Harris Neck NWR was established, under the management of the U.S. Fish and Wildlife Service. It's regarded as "an important link in the chain of refuges along the Atlantic seaboard."

Now the surviving owners and their descendents are petitioning Congress to get the land back. The Harris Neck Land Trust was officially established in 2006 "to reclaim the land wrongfully and illegally taken by the federal government in 1942 and return it to its rightful owners." How this apparent collision between environmentalism and social justice will be sorted out remains to be seen.

on the breast, you can understand the familiar nickname, "old Flint-head," and might even agree with Theodore Cross's description — "one of the world's most lugubrious birds." Cross writes that he has heard the bird likened to "an undernourished, circuit-riding rural preacher."

But as Bent points out, "Distance lends enchantment to this species." When it's sailing high in a blue sky, you see a right hand-some and graceful bird, black flight feathers showing to best advantage against the pure-white body, head and neck outstretched, and long legs trailing behind. "Even more interesting," adds Bent, "are the spectacular aerial evolutions in which these birds so often indulge. Rising in a flock, they soar in wide circles, mounting higher and higher, crossing and recrossing in a maze of spirals, until they are almost beyond vision in the ethereal blue. Then suddenly they dash downward and repeat the operation or else drift away on motionless wings until lost to sight."

Note Bent's use of the plural. Audubon had castigated his predecessors, William Bartram and then Alexander Wilson, for asserting that the "Wood Ibis" was a "solitary bird [that] does not associate in flocks." Never reluctant to set the record straight, Audubon rightly insists that "the Wood Ibis is rarely met with single, even after the breeding season, and it is more easy for a person to see an hundred together at any period of the year, than to meet with one by itself."

Audubon is also at pains to correct the misapprehension that the wood stork is "fearless, easily approached, and easily shot." On the contrary, he is convinced that "we have not in the United States a more shy, wary, and vigilant bird than the Wood Ibis. . . . Move, gently or not, move at all, and you infallibly lose your opportunity of observing the actions of the birds. Some old male has long marked you; whether it has been with eye or with ear, no matter. The first stick your foot cracks, his hoarse voice sounds the alarm." I have to say that the storks we saw nesting by the little pond on Jekyll Island seemed oblivious of our up-close approach, but maybe that's because, like birds generally, they were reluctant to abandon their nests. In any case, all accounts I've seen agree that the wood stork is a wary bird. Bent calls it "exceedingly shy" and notes that at its roost-ing site "a sentinel is always on the lookout."

The wood stork's long, heavy, down-curved bill is certainly its dis-tinctive feature (*Mycteria* derives from the Greek *mykter*, or "nose"), and how the bird uses it is equally impressive. Audubon writes that the storks wade into shallow water, "dance as it were all through it" to turn it muddy and force the fish to rise toward the surface, where the birds kill them with their beaks. How the kill happens is the only thing Audubon leaves unclear: these birds are snappers, not stab-bers. As David Allen Sibley clarifies, wood storks feed by holding their bills open and submerged, "waiting for something to swim be-tween their bill tips." To increase their odds, "they may stir the water with one foot or open their wings, all the while with the bill in the water[,] . . . techniques [that] presumably rouse prey from hiding places." Sibley adds that "when a Wood Stork touches prey with its bill, it can snap the bill shut in 0.025 seconds — one of the fastest re-action times known in vertebrates."

Still, it can't be easy — standing there hoping something good to eat happens to pass between your bill tips. Which is why they like to feed in a thick stew of fish. "To forage effectively with their special-ized technique," writes Sibley, "storks require a high density of prey, which occurs most reliably when ponds dry up and concentrate fish in ever smaller pools. . . . Consequently, adults time nesting so that hatching occurs as ponds are drying up." Obviously, their timing can't always be perfect. Too little rain and ponds dry up before the young have fledged; too much and prey are not sufficiently concen-trated. In either case, the parents may be forced to abandon their nests and even their young. Working in their favor, though, is the storks' ability to cover a lot of territory in the hunt for food. "They can climb to several thousand feet," says Sibley, "scan for miles to locate potential feeding sites (often by spotting egrets and other storks there), and, if necessary, travel 50 miles from the nest."

You won't be surprised to learn that these magnificent bills serve other purposes as well, particularly in courtship and breeding. Ac-cording to M. C. Coulter, and others, writing for BNA *Online*, once the male accepts a female onto his chosen nest site, both birds put their bills to use "autopreening, allopreening, copulating, twig-grasping, and displaying." Wait. Copulating? That's right: there's "Copulation Clattering" by both sexes during the act. "Female spreads wings; male clatters bill, shakes head, and beats female's bill back and forth with his bill; female holds bill down below horizontal or up almost vertically."

The pair together build a big, bulky nest to cradle the eggs that are the likely result of all this happy percussion, and together they incubate those eggs and brood their chicks. By three weeks of age, the young are eating so much that the parents are foraging together as well. Back home, they'll spread their wings to shade the chicks during the hot middle of the day. Or, if that's not enough, they'll use those fine bills to haul water up from the pond and splash it over the heads and backs of the children. (BNA *Online* mentions an even more remarkable strategy to beat the heat: parents and older chicks will release "dilute uric acid solution on legs for evaporative cooling when ambient temperature is above body temperature.")

Young birds still on the nest will set up a clamor to be fed, but once the young have fledged, rookery and roost site return to silence. The truth is that except for the clattering of those bills, the wood stork is a quiet bird. Sibley explains that storks are among the bird species unable to use their syringeal muscles and so are "extremely limited in the range of vocalizations they can make." Bent adds that the only note he has ever heard from one of these birds "is a hoarse croak, usually uttered when disturbed or frightened." At that pond on Jekyll, and then at Harris Neck, the birds clearly were not disturbed by our presence. The great wings flapped as the big birds left and returned to their nests, twigs snapped, leaves rustled, but the storks went about their business voicelessly.

· ·

Back home, I was gratified to read in my DNR e-news that 2010 turned out to be a big year for Georgia's wood stork population. Roughly 2,500 nests were counted, easily surpassing the 2,200 counted in 2008, the previous high since aerial nest surveying began in the 1990s. I was equally pleased to read that Georgia's largest rookery, with 478 nests, was the one I had just returned from, on Harris Neck's Woody Pond.

That's the good news. The bad news is that the wood stork remains an endangered bird in the United States, and that the current population of 15,000 individuals is one-tenth what it was a century ago. One of Bent's correspondents, writing in 1914, describes a single south Florida rookery with 5,000 nests. Another, reporting from a rookery of perhaps 10,000 nests, writes of "a steady stream of birds, perhaps 25 at a time, all flying to some live willows, breaking off twigs and flying back to the rookery with them."

What happened? Well, the decimation wasn't intentional. Unlike the tasty little plovers, wood storks have never been considered a good choice for the table. (The tough, oily meat is "not fit for food," wrote Audubon, and his own attempts to make it palatable "were not crowned with success.") And unlike those of so many herons, the wood stork's feathers were not sought by the millinery trade.

No, it was that other sad story: unintentional avicide through habitat destruction. As Sibley points out, "Colonies usually occur in large trees, often cypresses, in standing water; cypresses were heavily logged early in the 1900s." He goes on to add that "the single most dramatic drop in Wood Stork numbers probably came from the building of outflow channels in the Florida Everglades. This huge area of marsh formerly supported most of the North American stork population, but after much water was drained for agriculture and development, or diverted to the growing cities on Florida's coast, it now supports only a few thousand storks." Most of the remaining wood storks now nest in northern Florida, Georgia, and South Carolina.

So the ones that are left are moving north, but are they happy about it? I wouldn't mistake the wood stork's silence for consent. Not surprisingly, given their formidable size and aspect, storks have figured large in myth and legend over the centuries. In her 1976 poem "Stork," Ellen Bryant Voight pulls together some of these bits of lore, concluding with these lines:

> If a stork is damaged, the weather darkens.
> If you kill a stork, kinsmen surround you, clacking long sticks
>   together like knives.

Laughing Gull

Larus atricilla

Chances are it was a laughing gull that, circling with its cohort twenty feet overhead, pooped into my mother-in-law's Bloody Mary on that ferry ride from Panama City out to Shell Island lo these many years ago. The incident remains a cherished memory, not only because it was hilarious at the time, but also because, in more recent days, it has provided me with a useful illustration of the wonders of bird behavior. After all (as I like to conclude the anecdote), how in the world did the bird know which one was the mother-in-law?

The mother-in-law in question was not charmed to see her fine beverage befouled, but the truth is that, particularly among the Laridae, the laughing gull stands out as a bird with much to recommend it. Wilson calls it "the most beautiful and most sociable of its genus," and even BNA *Online* temporarily sheds its staid objectivity to write of this "lovely gull," whose "laughing call and delicate head tosses . . . are harbingers of spring." In fact, I think I'll go ahead and reclassify the laughing gull as the "good gull" (*Larus benefice*), in contrast to (as we shall see) the herring gull, or *Larus malevolens*.

Consider, first, the laughing gull's diet. Gulls, as a family, are scroungers, or, in Sibley's more delicate phrase, "remarkable opportunists." Which is to say that they eat pretty much anything and are just as willing to dine at the landfill as at the beach. But bird writers seem to agree that the laughing gull is at least somewhat more discriminating than its cousins. "The laughing gull is less of a scavenger than are the other larger gulls," writes Burleigh in *Georgia Birds*, and Bent concurs ("not such scavengers as the larger gulls"), though, in fairness, he adds that laughing gulls "are not above eating quite a variety of garbage."

The real issue, though, is not whether these birds eat refuse, but whether they, like the notorious herring gulls, eat the eggs and young of other birds. Again, their record is not entirely spotless. Audubon, briefly quoting his own journals, reported seeing laughing gulls eating the eggs of sooty terns in the Dry Tortugas (a group of islands at the end of the Florida Keys). Bent was surprised and, I think, saddened to see evidence of this predatory behavior on Grand Cochere, a sandbar island off the coast of Louisiana, where a few laughing gulls were nesting among larger colonies of royal and Cabot's terns. "In marked contrast to our experience elsewhere," he writes, "we found many broken eggs of the terns which had apparently been eaten by the gulls; we therefore thought it wise to discourage their nesting here and broke up all the nests we could find, about 10, and shot several of the birds."

His "experience elsewhere" was principally on Muskeget Island, south of Cape Cod, which was in his day an important breeding site for laughing gulls. There, he writes, the gulls "seem to live in perfect harmony with their neighbors, the common and roseate terns. I have never found any positive evidence of their eating the eggs of these terns." So, while we may not be able to exculpate the birds entirely, this peaceable behavior is clearly more characteristic of the species. BNA *Online* does not include terns' eggs among "foods taken" by laughing gulls, and though it acknowledges the reports from Audubon and Bent, it describes such behavior as "unusual."

Where it can, this kinder, gentler gull seizes the opportunity to eat small fish, which is as it should be. If it sometimes pilfers these morsels from hardworking brown pelicans, it at least offers up an entertaining spectacle. Describing how these birds hovered around a diving pelican and, then, when it resurfaced, "alighted nimbly on its very head" to snatch away the "glittering fry," Audubon adds that "the sight of these manoeuvres rendered me almost frantic with delight. . . . So very dexterous were some of the Gulls at this sport, that I have seen them actually catch a little fish as it leaped from the yet partially open bill of the Pelican." In his account of a similar performance, Bent adds that the birds holler out "*half, half, half,*" as they swoop down on the feeding pelicans — not a bad rendering of their happy cries.

In *Under the Sea-Wind*, Rachel Carson describes yet another kind of opportunity. Always attuned to the interconnecting links of the food chain, here she describes a swarm of launce being pursued by whiting into a cove from which the tide is receding: "As the launce drove deeper into the cove the water began to thin away beneath them, but in their overmastering terror of the whiting they failed to heed the warnings of shoaling water and stranded by hundreds and thousands. The gulls that had followed in expectantly from outside the inlet, sensing what was happening in the seething water below, mewed and squealed and laughed their excitement when they saw the sandy flats beneath them turn to silver. Black-headed laughing gulls and gray-mantled herring gulls came down with flapping wings, plunging shoulder-deep into the water."

Everyone who has been to the beach has seen this gull, but armchair birders like me don't always know it. When Wilson calls it "beautiful" and Joanna Burger, in BNA *Online*, calls it "lovely," they're talking about the bird in its summer plumage. Until then, this so-called hooded gull has no hood, nor is that the extent of its transformation. As Audubon writes, "At the approach of the breeding season, or, as I like best to term it, the love season, this species becomes first hooded, and the white feathers of its breast, and those of the lower surface of its wings, assume a rich blush of roseate tint." Not many writers can match Audubon's rhetorical flair, but here Elliot Coues, quoted in *Life Histories*, outperforms the master. "Decked out for their nuptials in full attire," he writes, the gulls "gain a rich rosy tint over all the white plumage of the under part; then few birds are of more delicate hues than these. Nature blushes, filling the bird's breast with amorous imagery, till the feathers catch a glow and reflect the blush. Burning with inward fire, the whole frame thrills with the enthusiasm of sexual vigor. The dark glittering eye is encircled with a fiery ring; now it flashes defiance at a rival, now tenderly melts at sight of his mate, soon to be sacrificed to masculine zeal."

The mated pair I saw on a tidal flat in "Ding" Darling NWR did not inspire in me quite such a torrent of emotion, but they did make a very pretty picture. Not only were the dark hoods firmly in place, but their normally blackish bills had turned a deep crimson. As I watched, they repeatedly touched their bills together, then threw their heads back, uttering small tender cries instead of the usual raucous laughter. Based on that one scene, I would not have agreed with Audubon that "their loves are conducted with extreme pomposity," but I must have missed some of the preliminary courtship. Burger has much to say about Long Calls, Facing-Away Postures, Head Tosses, Copulation Calls, Wing-Flagging, and the like, along with the arresting detail that just prior to copulation the male regurgitates a little something for the female to eat. Afterward, she writes, "both birds preen, bathe, or sleep on territory." Or, if they've worked up an appetite, they may indulge in cooperative feeding: "male foot-paddles to release horseshoe-crab eggs from soil for female."

On Muskeget, says Bent, the laughing gulls prefer to build their nests near the center of the island, "where the beach grass grows long and thick on the sandy slopes and in the hollows between the dunes." Once the nest is thus situated, you'll find "a well-trodden path over-arched with grass lead[ing] up to it on one side and away from it on the other, so that the bird may enter and leave the nest without turning around at the risk of ruffling its immaculate plumage." Compared to those of a good many other shorebirds, the nests of the laughing gull are carefully constructed and well concealed, and in them the mated pair will try to incubate their three eggs and raise the semiprecocial chicks.

It won't be easy. A host of predators would love to make a meal of those eggs or young birds. Even if the laughing gulls have succeeded in establishing their colony on an island free of mammalian predators, the list of avian enemies is long: crows (especially fish crows), oystercatchers, owls, harriers, and larger gulls, particularly the aforementioned herring gulls. Sometimes the herring gulls simply prevent the laughing gulls from nesting in the first place. As Burger points out, the herring gull is three times larger, has arrived on the breeding ground earlier, and already has eggs and chicks before the laughing gulls begin to set up shop. Sometimes the laughing gulls will return to a traditional colony site to find that it has been usurped by their brawny cousins—in which case they must look elsewhere.

As parents, laughing gulls do all they can. On hot days they'll head for water to soak their belly feathers in order to cool the eggs, and the just-hatched young, writes Bent, are "carefully brooded by their parents, who stand over them to protect them in wet weather or to shield them from the rays of the hot sun." Cleanliness is high on the list of domestic virtues. The birds bathe regularly, according to Burger, and at length—sometimes for as long as twenty minutes. The parent birds leave the nest to defecate, and the young birds do their business over the nest's rim. Moreover, the parents continue to feed and care for their young until after fledging, which, on Muske-get Island, says Bent, is usually at the end of July—"at which time the adults, still in full nuptial plumage, may be seen hovering over the little grassy meadows, where young birds of various sizes may be found hidden in the long thick grass."

At last the season ends, and, if Coues is to be believed, with it goes the glory of the laughing gull. "Its force all spent the change comes; the red mouth pales again; the glowing plumage fades to white; the bird is but the shadow of his former self, dull-colored, ragged, without ambition beyond the satisfaction of a gluttonous appetite. He loiters southward, recruiting an enervated frame with plenteous fare in this season of idleness, till the warm rays of an-other spring restore him."

Not so fast. Audubon offers evidence that the laughing gull's "strong amatory propensities" outlast the fading year. "At St. Augus-tine," he writes, "in the month of December, I have observed four or five males of the present species paying their addresses to one female, who received their courtesies with evident welcome. Yet the females in that country did not deposit eggs until the 20th day of April. The most surprising fact of all was that, although these birds were paired, and copulated regularly, by the 1st of February, not one had acquired the spring or summer plumage, or the dark coloured hood, or the rosy tint of the breast, nor lost the white spots on the tips of their primary quills."

So the bird loses its breeding plumage but not necessarily its desire. According to Audubon's math, this activity does not produce eggs and therefore does nothing to ensure the survival of the species. Hmmmm. Sounds suspiciously like sex for sex's sake. I understand that not everybody is going to agree that such behavior reflects creditably on the character of *Larus benefice*, but I'm going to assume that the female was lonely and that the males were motivated solely by chivalry.

In any case, the species is in good shape. Writing about the gulls on Muskeget Island and elsewhere along the northeastern coast, Bent writes that "constant persecution" almost extirpated this population toward the end of the nineteenth century, but the "passage of suitable laws" reversed the trend. Consequently, during Bent's visits to Muskeget during 1919, the colony had expanded to "several thousand pairs." BNA *Online* adds that the laughing gull is increasing in much of its range these days and was recently documented nesting in New York State for the first time in 100 years.

Many of those northern nesters head south in August to join year-round residents all along the southeastern Atlantic and Gulf coasts, where, if we know how to spot them without their dark hoods, we can enjoy them in great numbers.

. . . .

Now, as for *Larus malevolens*. Sibley divides the gull* family into two groups: the hooded gulls, epitomized for our purposes by the laughing, but also including Franklin's, little, Bonaparte's, and black-headed; and the white-headed gulls, epitomized for our purposes by the herring and encompassing all other North American species. The white-headed gulls tend to be larger than their hooded cousins, and some of them, like the herring gull, are meaner and hungrier, too.

This is your true scavenger gull. Pierotti and Good, in BNA *Online*, note that herring gulls feed on human refuse obtained by following

---

*"Gull" is an interesting word, as it applies to both bird and human species. As Choate wryly observes, from Latin *gula*, via Old French *goule* ("throat"), "we have gotten such words as gulp, gullet, and gullible. This suggests that 'gull' might be related to the bird's indiscriminate scavenging; it appears willing to swallow almost anything."

garbage scows, or roosting at refuse tips, or waiting downstream from sewage outfalls. We've already commented on their fondness for the eggs and young of laughing gulls, but Pierotti and Good add to the indictment: in any given colony there are likely to be a couple of males who "specialize on conspecific chicks."

To be fair (or less unfair), it's not all garbage and godlessness. For example, Audubon admired the herring gull's ingenious method of dropping mussels from on high to break them open on the rocks below. He saw one in particular that, having "met with a very hard mussel, [took] it up and drop[ped] it three times in succession, before it succeeded in breaking it." Audubon was "much pleased to see the bird let it fall each succeeding time from a greater height than before." He also acknowledges that this gull's food "consists principally of herrings," which would seem suitably eponymous. But his account ends with the observation that these birds "suck all the eggs they can find."

In the Rachel Carson passage quoted earlier, laughing and herring gulls shared a feast where there was plenty of food for all. Here's what happens, she writes, when the pickings are slimmer. An early-morning beach is dotted with dead squid, lured up into shallow shoals by the full moon: "The sanderlings did not linger on this part of the beach, for . . . many large birds had gathered and were quarreling over the squids. They were herring gulls, bound from the Gulf coast to Nova Scotia. They had been delayed by stormy weather and were ravenous. A dozen black-headed laughing gulls came and hovered, mewing, over the beach, dangling their feet as though to alight, but the herring gulls drove them away with fierce screaming and jabs of their bills."

To sew up this argument, I was relying on a particularly vivid memory that on the last page of Paul Theroux's *Mosquito Coast*, it was a couple of herring gulls that plucked out Father's tongue as he lay dying on the beach. When I double-checked, it turned out to be vultures. Lesson: Never double-check.

Brown Pelican

Pelecanus occidentalis

"A wonderful bird is the pelican." So begins the memorable limerick generally misattributed to Ogden Nash. You know the rest, but in tribute to the actual author, let's finish it up:

> His bill will hold more than his belican.
> He can take in his beak
> Food enough for a week,
> But I'm damned if I see how the helican.

For the record, the lines were composed by Dixon Lanier Merritt (1879–1972), journalist, humorist, and founding member of the Tennessee Ornithological Society.

Despite the regularity with which the poem is recited, "wonderful" hasn't always been the first word to spring to the lips of people who try to describe this bird. "The Brown Pelican labors under an undeserved burden of opprobrium," writes author and photographer Theodore Cross in *Waterbirds*. "Clumsy, grotesque, graceless, lumbering, and awkward are the standard guidebook adjectives." He goes on to quote a 1908 article in *Scientific American* that referred to the brown pelican as a "disagreeable, wheezing, asthmatic bird of atrocious habit."

I suppose the bird has had its detractors, but my own reading suggests that that kind of sour, fastidious, late-Victorian invective has never constituted a consensus opinion. In fact, the brown pelican has had its champions, ancient and modern. Janet Lembke reminds us of the legend Shakespeare refers to in his mention of "the kind life-rend'ring pelican." The adult bird, according to the fable, uses its bill to pierce its own breast, sacrificing its blood to keep its nestlings alive. "Such piety and devotion," writes Lembke, "such self-sacrifice in the exercise of parental duty, made the bird so admirable, so glorious, that it was installed in the Middle Ages' aviary of heraldic birds."

Coming forward a couple of centuries, Audubon had nothing but admiration for this bird and included among its gifts a remark-

able meteorological intelligence. Not only are they "as well aware of the time of each return of the tide, as the most watchful pilots," he writes, but "in a degree much surpassing that of man . . . they can judge with certainty of the changes of weather. Should you see them fishing all together, in retired bays, be assured, that a storm will burst forth that day; but if they pursue their finny prey far out at sea, the weather will be fine, and you also may launch your bark and go to the fishing."

Bent, watching pelicans pass in characteristic single file low over the waves, applies one of the "standard" pejoratives, but here's the context: "With grotesque and quiet dignity they passed, and with the military precision of well-drilled soldiers they alternately scaled or flapped their wings in perfect unison, as if controlled by a common impulse." Mark Shields, writing for BNA *Online*, uses another: "Webbing between all 4 toes on each foot makes the Brown Pelican a strong swimmer but an awkward walker." I doubt if either observation was meant to convey a crushing indictment.

And then there's Forbush, who, I believe, comes close to capturing what any of us might feel as we watch these pterodactylic creatures pass silently overhead on a summer evening: "In appearance pelicans are strange, weird creatures[,] . . . like relics of a hoary past, alone in a modern world."

Right. Brown pelicans are strange creatures—strange and wonderful.

. . . .

Brown pelicans might also be the most instantly, most universally recognizable of all of our southern coastal birds. Whether drowsing on a weathered piling or flying in those endless files to and from its foraging grounds, this bird is as much a part of our experience of the beach as sand in our bathing suits.

The brown pelican comes into its own, though, and makes its indelible impression on our consciousness, when it goes after its food. Reconnoitering from twenty or thirty feet high, it spots its prey, folds its wings, and crash-dives into the water—headlong, headfirst, huge bill wide open. Air cavities on the surface of its body cushion the blow and keep the pelican from diving too deep, so it quickly bobs back up again and sits on the waves to sift fish from water. "The generally received idea that Pelicans keep fish or water in their pouch, to convey them to their young, is quite erroneous," writes Audubon. "The water which enters the pouch when it is immersed, is immediately forced out between the partially closed mandibles, and the fish, unless larger than those on which they usually feed, is instantly swallowed, to be afterwards disgorged for the benefit of the young."

The pelicans follow the porpoises, Audubon continues, and the gulls and terns follow the pelicans. "The latter having plunged after a shoal of small fishes, of which it has caught a number at a time, in letting off the water from amongst them, sometimes allows a few to escape; but the Gull at that instant alights on the bill of the Pelican or on its head, and seizes the fry at the moment they were perhaps congratulating themselves on their escape." Recording this scene in his journal, Audubon doubts that he "ever felt greater pleasure than I do at this moment . . . ponder[ing] on the faculties which Nature has bestowed on animals which we merely consider as possessed of instinct."

One of Bent's correspondents offered the observation that the brown pelican always dives downwind and then rises from the water facing upwind, so as to be able to take off again with the wind's up-lift. "Thus, by entering the water down wind and emerging from it up wind," Bent explains, "the pelican makes a complete turnover or turnabout under water; many writers have referred to this, and almost every observer has noticed it." I haven't noticed it but certainly plan to watch for it at the earliest opportunity. Meanwhile, Shields confirms only the first half of the proposition: the pelican "usually faces downwind and away from sun when diving."

And here's an even more interesting assertion. In his lovely book *Florida's Forgotten Coast*, John Spohrer writes that "the day-after-day pounding eventually takes a toll on the pelican's eyes and many die of starvation induced by blindness." Really? It does seem likely that the pelican's eyes would take a beating, and it doesn't seem likely that

Spohrer would have simply fabricated such a notion. He doesn't cite a source for the information, however, and no other writer I've come across seconds it. Tellingly, the authoritative BNA *Online*, which includes "causes of mortality" in its accounts of every species, makes no mention of pelican death by blindness-induced starvation. What it does say, on the contrary, is that the brown pelican is an unusually long-lived species and that the oldest individual on record died at forty-three years of age.

But let's back up to a merrier part of the life cycle and picture the goings-on at a crowded pelican rookery. "Some skirmishes have taken place," writes Audubon, "and the stronger males, by dint of loud snappings of their bill, some hard tugs of the neck and head, and some heavy beats with their wings, have driven away the weaker, which content themselves with less prized belles." Well, everybody loves a medieval romance, but pelican courtship actually has a more workaday, domestic flavor — typified, for instance, by the "Nest Material Presentation Display," in which the male woos the female by offering her a bill full of twigs. Spohrer has a fine photograph of this gift-giving ceremony, which, as he notes, is often a prelude to copulation. He showed the picture to his wife, he writes, and explained that "if the female accepted the offering then they would have sex. She asked incredulously, 'For a stick?'"

One of Bent's correspondents documented a more elaborate ritual: "The female squatted close to the bare ground while the male slowly circled her with ponderous, elephantine tread. . . . Neither uttered an audible sound while the male pursued his dignified circuitous meandering. Suddenly she rose from her squatting position with a *gruff-gruff* of wing-strokes and flew to the ocean, but a short distance from the shore, and after stolidly watching her going, he followed, . . . to the consummation of the courtship on the surface of the quiet swelling waters of the gulf."

As always, BNA *Online* stands ready to disabuse us of such quaint fantasies: "Copulation occurs only on nest site," writes Shields. "Male simply grabs female's upper neck with bill prior to mounting and holds it throughout. Male's feet remain stationary on female's back while wings wave slowly. Female never stands during mounting."

It is the male who selects that nest site, by the way, and he sometimes has to hang around and defend it for two or three weeks until the right "belle" happens along. Florida pelicans, for some reason, prefer to site their homes in the mangrove trees; elsewhere along the Atlantic and Gulf coasts they build on the ground. In either case, the male continues to supply materials all during the incubation and nestling periods, and the female continues to weave them into the nest. This is all the more important since the young chicks, impelled from an early age to master the art of stick-handling, tend to dismantle the nests as quickly as they can be repaired.

Brown pelicans incubate their three eggs under their fully webbed feet for about thirty days. The early development of the hatchlings is thoroughly documented by Shields, but Bent does a good job of conveying the general idea: "When first hatched the young are far from attractive, looking more like shapeless masses of half-dried meat than young birds, with swollen protuberances for heads which they are unable to hold up; the livid, dark reddish naked skin gradually turns to dull black; the eyes open during the first few days and by the end of a week the youngster is able to sit up and take notice."

As Audubon correctly observed, the pelican does not use its bill to transport fish back to the nest to feed the young. It swallows and then regurgitates them, more or less digested according to the development of the young. Even when they are big enough to swallow whole fish—by three or four weeks of age—the young still feed by regurgitation, sticking their bills into the parent's throat to trigger the disgorgement.

The young begin to fly and fend for themselves at about three months old, but problems arise along the way. Bent points out that ground-nesting youngsters like to leave the nest as soon as they can walk and band together in "great droves." This behavior complicates the work of the parent who feels obliged to feed its own child, but who "is besieged by a hoard of lusty young, fully her equal in size, and [is] either overwhelmed by the excited mob or forced to retreat."

A more serious problem is the competition for dominance among the siblings, which, says Shields, begins in the first week after hatching and continues regardless of whether food is up for grabs. In most cases the larger, first-hatched chicks peck the younger into submission — or worse. "Fights often lead to siblicide, with subordinate sibling(s) beaten to death or dying from starvation after being driven from nest and/or prevented from feeding." How frequently siblicide occurs varies widely from rookery to rookery, but Shields reports that in one nesting season on Isla Isabel, Mexico, the first-hatched was the sole survivor in 70 percent of the broods.

The young that do manage to make it out of the nest still have a lot to learn. It might take a young bird at least one full year to become fully adept at diving for its dinner. "Hesitant beginners," writes Lembke, "paddle on the surface and imitate the less audacious freshwater pelicans by using their pouches as scoops to catch whatever swims below." On Tarpon Bay in Sanibel, Florida, I witnessed the next stage: a couple of young pelicans rising two or three feet off the water and then splashing down again. They couldn't have been catching much, but certainly must've been working up the kind of appetite that would encourage them to hone their skills.

. . . .

Never expert at defending themselves against the capricious behavior of humankind, brown pelicans have endured a curious demographic history. Audubon wrote that if you were to fire a few shots into a pelican rookery, the parents would flee — "and leave their eggs or young entirely at your disposal." As for the adults, he continued, the Indians "carry them off in considerable numbers . . . and the Negroes kill all they can find, to make gumbo soup of them during winter." Audubon's dire conclusion was that the birds "are, year after year, retiring from the vicinity of man . . . and will yet be hunted beyond the range of civilization."

That prediction had failed to come true by the end of the nineteenth century, but not for lack of trying on our part. Cross reports that "one hundred years ago a favorite pastime of tourists in Florida was a shotgun shoot of Brown Pelicans on the beach. The local newspaper advertisements shouted, 'No skill is required. The birds tumble easily at 40 yards.'" Pelican shoots also failed to extirpate the population, but a few decades later another threat arose. During World War I, according to Diana Wells, Florida fishermen suspected pelicans of depleting their fishing grounds, and since eating more fish was part of the war effort, federal protection of the species was about to be withdrawn. Led by Audubon Society president Gilbert Pearson, a party of ornithologists "made 3,428 pelicans regurgitate their food, and found that only twenty-seven of the fish they had eaten were the kind humans eat. So the pelicans were saved!"

For the time being.

Pelican shoots and winter gumbo amounted to nothing compared to the devastation visited on the brown pelican beginning in the late 1950s, when organochlorine pesticides like endrin and DDT began entering the marine food chain. As Shields reports in BNA *Online*, endrin killed the pelicans directly, while ingestion of DDT resulted in thin-shelled eggs that broke under the weight of incubating parents. Breeding colonies along the Pacific and Gulf coasts were hardest hit, says Shields; the die-off was so massive that "the species disappeared altogether from Louisiana, the 'Pelican State,' by 1963."

The original Endangered Species Protection Act was signed into law in 1966, and the brown pelican joined the list of endangered species in 1970. The huge losses suffered by the pelican (and the bald eagle, among many other species) brought about the U.S. ban on the use of DDT in 1972 and subsequent regulation of the use of endrin. Happily, the pelican population has enjoyed a complete recovery as a result. It was removed from the Endangered Species List in 1985, and its population along the Gulf coast was considered fully restored by the late 1990s.

Its breeding range may even be expanding. Writing in 1958, Thomas Burleigh was puzzled to note that while there were breeding colonies both in South Carolina and Florida, "the Brown Pelican has never been found nesting in Georgia." Today, however, the *Breeding Bird Atlas of Georgia* reports that two pelican rookeries have been active since the early 1990s, one of which, on Little Egg Island

Bar at the mouth of the Altamaha River, has become one of the largest on the southeastern Atlantic coast, averaging close to 3,000 nests a year.

All the good news leads Shields to conclude that though it once was "a symbol of the detrimental effects of pollution in marine eco-systems, the Brown Pelican now symbolizes the success of wildlife-conservation efforts."

The pessimist in me, rejecting good news categorically, longs to point out that we only ban poison when doing so doesn't cause too much inconvenience, and that the folks in the wildlife-conservation business have to work way too hard for the occasional success. But it's late afternoon on a summer beach, the breeze blows, and low over the rippling waves the majestic pelicans glide by—five, fifteen, fifty in their silent single file—and all carping must cease.

autumn

....

Forster's Tern
Sterna forsteri

As a proposition, the house-swap is about as dubious as the spouse-swap, with plenty of downside potential. But our adventurous friends Sallie and Pat Taylor arranged the deal: strangers would take over their charming house in Highlands, North Carolina, for a few days while they took possession of said strangers' house in St. Augustine, Florida. Dede and I were the risk-free beneficiaries of a goodbye-to-summer beach trip.

The house, in a live oak–shaded, not very beachy–looking neighborhood, wasn't perfect—dog-smelly and oddly dark inside. But I wasn't complaining. Walk out the back gate and down a pleasant lane or two and you found yourself in Anastasia State Park, featuring a big, beautiful marsh pond—called the Salt Run by the locals—as well as four miles of wide, undeveloped beach. At the end of a warm afternoon, Pat and I rented a kayak to watch the wading birds come feed in the Salt Run marsh, but we timed it wrong and found ourselves afloat on a rising tide, with no exposed mud bank for the birds to forage on. Still, as we drifted deep into the marsh grass at the pond's south end, a great blue heron suddenly rose above us, flapping monstrously, croaking at the nuisance, but giving us a rush of pleasure.

About that beach, though—it was not only wide, long, and undeveloped; it was also hard-packed—ideal for bicycling. Ever bicycled on the beach? I recommend it. The going is effortless, and if the shorebirds have decided to settle at one far end or another, big deal. You'll get there in no time. So we pedaled along, past the people spilling onto the beach from Joe's Camp Store and Tropical Grille, past the gulls that don't mind the people, and toward the north end of the beach we came upon some sizable flocks at ease on the sand flats—brown pelicans, laughing gulls just slipping out of their black hoods, imposing white-headed herring gulls, a smattering of willets, a solitary whimbrel that I was pleased to point out to my nonenthusiast friends, and a plentiful supply of terns—mostly royal terns of course, but among them the lovely bird that's my subject here.

. . . .

I had been enchanted by the Forster's tern since I first began seeing it along the Gulf coast back in the early spring. What caught my attention was not just the beauty that attaches to all of the smaller terns, but those dashing, pirate-like black eye-patches, set against the pure-white head and face. Then and subsequently, including that afternoon with Pat on the Salt Run, I've had the keen pleasure of watching this bird feed along marsh pond, seacoast, and riverine estuary—watching it fly over, flutter-hover, and dive for the small fry below. The bird wheels and turns so capriciously that it seems no more than a sheet of paper tossed by the wind.

Did other writers share my enthusiasm? It was hard to say, because the common tern had used up all the ink. "One of the most charming creatures of our eastern seacoast," writes Bent of the common tern—"such an elegant and dainty creature, [with] its spotless and delicate plumage and its buoyant, graceful flight." Its "orange legs, bright red beak with a black tip, jet-black cap, and two white tail streamers," says Theodore Cross, mark the common tern as "a jewel among waterbirds." Even bna *Online* gets in on the act: this is the tern known "for its attractive plumage and graceful flight, and for its long history as a symbol of the conservation movement."

When bna *Online*'s writer, Ian Nesbitt, added that the common tern is the most widespread and familiar North American tern, I began to doubt which bird I had been looking at. But then I found reassurance from Thomas Burleigh, who notes that the Forster's is the one we're more likely to see on southeastern coasts during fall and winter, and who has the good taste to add that "no bird is more graceful on the wing, its flight being light and buoyant, and so suggestive of that of a swallow that in many locations it is frequently called a sea swallow."

The problem is that during the breeding season, when the black around the Forster's eyes expands to cover its crown, nape, and forehead, the two species look almost identical. Forbush reports that the

Forster's is "so much like the Common Tern in appearance, habits and behavior that Audubon did not recognize the breeding adult as a different species" and that Wilson never recognized the species at all. For the record, it was George N. Lawrence, in 1858, who was "the first to differentiate the bird in breeding-dress from the Common Tern."

But, of course, it's only during the "off-season," or during its migration to or from its far-flung breeding grounds, that we see the Forster's, and at those times it's likely to be wearing those definitive eye-patches.

Chances are, too, that it will be feeding, with its characteristic combination of grace, agility, and determination. It may make a sudden swoop or turn to pick an insect out of the air or off the surface of the water, but it makes its serious living as a diver. Scott Weidensaul writes that the bird "may dive a dozen times before finally coming up with a fish, and a pair with several young in the nest to feed may make hundreds of strikes in the course of a day, trying to fill hungry mouths." Sometimes, according to Nesbitt's account, catching the fish is just the first hurdle. He writes that while small fish are often swallowed as the tern regains foraging altitude, larger fish (more than three centimeters in length) "may be dropped from 20 m height and recaught at 10 m; this behavior repeated 3–4 times."

You might recall that I reported this strange and wonderful behavior in writing about the royal tern, and I wondered what the heck the bird was up to. Nesbitt hazards the guess that the dropping and recatching "may be necessary part of food processing," but he doesn't discount completely the possibility that the tern is just having fun. When the royal tern I was watching finally failed to recatch the fish and left it lying on the surface of the water (though no doubt well "processed"), my conclusion was that it had been showing off.

The Forster's terns we saw in St. Augustine may have just returned from breeding grounds further north along the eastern seaboard, but these birds breed inland as well—along the marshy borders of lakes and streams in the upper Midwest, north to Canada, and over to Oregon and California. Wherever it makes its summer home, the male of the species will have one more reason to value his fish-catching expertise. In the ritual Nesbitt refers to as "courtship feeding," the glittering morsel in his bill will be the blandishment with which he attempts to seduce the mate of his choosing. Sometimes he presents his gift right away to the "submissive" female; sometimes he parades around her, carrying the fish in his bill, as she turns 'round with him expectantly. In either case, once the gift is accepted, the male stands erect, job well done, then flies away. This romantic gift-giving establishes the pair's bond, provides a preliminary to copulation, and continues throughout the incubation of the eggs.

The nest holding those eggs might be just a scrape in the mud or sand, but these "marsh terns" are more likely to pile up a bunch of reeds or grasses and form themselves a cup on the top. The typical clutch consists of three eggs, incubated virtually nonstop by one parent or the other for twenty-eight days. The semiprecocial young remain in the nest for a few days, says Bent, until they are strong enough to run about or swim, "when they become very lively and pugnacious." They also become quickly adept at hiding in the marsh grass, a critical survival skill.

There's no shortage of predator species eager to dine on the eggs or young of the Forster's tern. From the air come the herring gulls and great horned owls, and wending their way through the long grass come the raccoons, minks, and marsh rice rats. But the parent terns rise up in ferocious defense, screaming and diving repeatedly at potential predators, whether avian or mammalian, until they are driven away. Nesbitt reports that all forty adults of a Minnesota colony mobbed a mink for the eight hours it remained in the area. Intruders of the human variety are equally unwelcome. Calling loudly, the birds will hover, with tail spread, over the interloper's head, writes Nesbitt, "then close tail and wings to dive; usually stopping just above head but sometimes striking human with feet or bill."

Sounds pretty stout, doesn't it? But when it comes to defensive strategies, the common tern goes the Forster's one better: "Adults attacking predator or human intruder," reports Nesbitt, "habitually defecate at lowest point of dive, frequently hitting intruder with feces." So now we know how to tell the Forster's from the common during breeding season. If you hear the plop of bird poop on your big-brimmed hat, you're under attack by common terns.

The common tern exhibits other behavior, too, that would make the species appear somewhat less endearing than the Forster's. They indulge in kleptoparasitism, for example, stealing fish from neighbors who might be flying home to feed it to their young. Similarly, larger chicks are not above stealing fish from smaller chicks in nearby nests. But before we can declare the Forster's to be the morally superior species, we have to deal with Bent correspondent Reverend B. P. Peabody. The Forster's tern "is radically hostile to all other birds," writes Peabody, and while the bird certainly has enough enemies among other species, "the character of this tern himself inclines me to think that he occasionally plays the cannibal." Hmmm. Maybe so. But since the reverend is making an inference based on what he judges to be the bird's "character," rather than on observation, I'll choose to remain unconvinced.

Both of these pretty terns had a rough time before the passage of the Migratory Bird Treaty Act. Toward the end of the nineteenth century, the millinery trade employed feathers, wings, and even entire stuffed terns to adorn the hats of fashionable ladies. Moreover, the terns' habit of flocking and crying over wounded comrades made it easy for shooters to bring them down by the dozens. Once the shooting was outlawed, populations of these terns rebounded, though other threats emerged in the middle of the twentieth century. In the case of the common tern, for example, predatory gulls have displaced them at a number of choice breeding locations.

The Forster's tern, Nesbit assures us, might suffer occasional reproductive failure because of weather or predation, but it generally overcomes these misfortunes thanks to its ability to nest on a variety of surfaces, to breed in colonies of various sizes, and to relay promptly following nest loss. Those advantages, together with efforts at wetland preservation and the creation of artificial breeding sites, provide hope that the population of this tern, overall, is now and can remain stable.

At the same time, the Forster's tern's designation as a species of special concern in Michigan and Minnesota and as endangered in Illinois and Wisconsin will push us, let's hope, to continue our vigilance on behalf of this beautiful bird.

A Note on the Least Tern (*Sterna antillarum*)

Actually, the diminutive least tern is more guilty of stealing the affections of bird writers than either the Forster's or the common tern. "Sylph-like bird of the waters," Audubon calls it. "Nothing can exceed the lightness of the flight of this bird, which seems to me to be among water-fowls, the analogue of the Humming-bird." Wilson writes that "this beautiful little species looks just like [the common tern] in miniature, but surpasses it far in the rich, glossy, satin-like white plumage with which its throat, breast, and whole lower parts are covered." Forbush adds that the least tern is "by far the most delicate and dainty of our sea-birds."

Apparently, though, least terns share with their larger cousins both aggression and ingenuity in defense of their nesting grounds — even if their efforts may not always be successful. John Spohrer, in *Florida's Forgotten Coast*, tells what happened when a phalanx of eight cattle egrets advanced on the small colony of least terns that were nesting along the old causeway from the mainland to St. George Island. Eventually, he writes, the egrets "crossed an invisible but certain boundary and several of the patrolling terns engaged them about twenty yards from the nesting area." The terns dove, struck the backs of the egrets' heads, and slowed their advance, but still the invaders came on. With invasion imminent, the defenders raised their voices to a frantic pitch, summoning the terns who had been fishing or incubating to join the battle.

The terns "attacked in two waves," writes Spohrer, "and it was an amazing battle plan to behold. . . . The first wave tagged the egrets. They all looked up reflexively to defend themselves and the second wave pulled up short and very accurately dropped poop in their faces! Yes, the chemical warfare. You could certainly tell when they scored a direct hit in an egret's eye. A few deserted, the others quickly lowered their heads and shook fiercely trying to be rid of the offensive substance."

The egrets were driven away but were back in an hour and met the same resistance. They retreated again but returned again. Spohrer departed with the issue still in doubt and came back two days later. "I saw only three chicks and they were recently hatched. There were many fewer adults and the egrets came so close each time that I could see their mating plumage and the gulls flew in tight, lazy circles. Three days later there were no chicks and the adults had gone."

Writing for BNA *Online*, Bruce C. Thompson, and others, note that marauding cattle egrets are by no means the gravest of the many ills visited on the least tern. Like the Forster's and common tern, it recovered from the damage inflicted by the millinery trade, but this beach-loving bird has found little sanctuary since. "Diminished by recreational, industrial, and residential development in coastal breeding areas . . . , it is specially classified for protection in much of its North American range. No other wide-ranging North American tern has that unfortunate distinction."

The least tern's coastal breeding range, however, extends down the entire Atlantic seaboard, around the tip of Florida and west along the Gulf all the way to Texas. It is adaptable, determined, and willing to change breeding locations when pushed to do so. Where beach habitat has been overrun by humanity, for example, the bird has responded by nesting on flat gravel rooftops in a number of coastal areas.

That made me feel better about being unable to locate the colony Spohrer documented beside the St. George Island causeway. I could hope the birds found a safe breeding haven on top of some beer joint or bait shack along old Highway 98.

Double-Crested Cormorant

Phalacrocorax auritus

> Thence up he flew, and on the Tree of Life,
> The middle Tree and highest there that grew,
> Sat like a cormorant; yet not true Life
> Thereby regained, but sat devising Death
> To them who lived.
> —John Milton, *Paradise Lost*

I confess that when I see a double-crested cormorant perched on an old piling of some long-since washed-away pier, half dozing, wings spread to catch an afternoon ray, these lines describing Satan's arrival in the Garden of Eden do not spring immediately to mind. In the first place, honestly, *Paradise Lost* is not one of those poems that I reread on a regular basis. But more to the point, the comparison seems a bit harsh. The editors of my old *Complete Milton* try to justify it with the note that the cormorant "was a traditional symbol of greed and greedy men."

Well, OK, if the traditional-symbol people say so. But I wouldn't have thought it. Watch one take off from its perch on that piling. It drops down for that first wingbeat, and then it's *flap-flap-flap-flap-flap-flap-flap-flap-flap-flap-flap-flap-flap-flap-flap-flap*, inches above the water, all the way out to Dog Island. There's no guile here, no wind-cheating, no cruise control. It's just bill to the grindstone.

But that's not the only reason I've come to appreciate the cormorant as the hardest-working bird on the waterfront. I've also watched it feed, or try to. When you see one of these birds disappear again and again into the water and come back up several seconds later empty-billed, you realize the Sisyphean nature of the labor. It's absurd on its face. Double-crested cormorants aren't like the pelicans and terns that get a flying start and plunge a little way beneath the surface to snag their food. No. They *swim underwater* to catch fish.

The experts at BNA *Online*, being scientists, are obliged to treat this behavior matter-of-factly. The bird "dives from surface by simultaneous action of both feet," write Jeremy J. Hatch and D. V. Weseloh, "which may push bird almost out of water before it submerges, or it may slip smoothly underwater." The more vigorous push, or "leap," they continue, "may be associated with deeper dives. During submerged swimming, holds wings against sides and propels itself by simultaneous strokes of both feet." The fact that the bird is underwater in pursuit of fish, the native inhabitants of that element, is too preposterous to dwell on, so we move ahead to the catch: "Grasping of fish is aided by hooklike nail at tip of maxilla (upper half of bill). . . . Small prey may be swallowed underwater; those noticed at the surface are likely to be large or otherwise difficult to handle, such as eels, flounders, or spiny fish."

It helps that cormorants have "effective vision underwater," but these birds also "catch bottom-dwelling fish in turbid water where visibility is very low." The assumption, then, is that to catch such "skulking prey" (mudpuppies, burbot, gunnels, and such), "cormorants probably root around at the bottom."

Wow. I'm not saying it's impossible, but it can't be easy. After all, how many times have you seen a fish jump out of the water and fly after a bird?

So, yes, I was surprised the first time I saw a double-crested cormorant* completely disappear beneath the surface and astonished to note the time that elapsed and the distance that it covered before resurfacing. I wasn't surprised to see that it had nothing to show for its effort; I couldn't imagine any other result. I kept watching. All along the Gulf and Atlantic coasts I've seen the cormorants diligently diving, resurfacing, diving again. The enterprise seemed as likely of success as pulling down the arm of the aptly named one-armed bandit.

Finally, on a tidal pool in North Carolina's Pea Island NWR, I saw one hit the jackpot. This bird came up holding onto a fish that

---

*By the way, don't break your neck trying to locate those "double crests"—nuptial plumes which appear briefly on the side of the head during the nesting season and which Choate describes as "almost invisible" anyway.

seemed almost as big as it was. Hatch and Weseloh write that when the bird catches a big fish, it might have to shake it or hammer it on the water to subdue it, then maybe toss it in the air in order to swallow it headfirst. The bird I watched kept diving with the fish in its bill, apparently wrestling to get it in the right position. Finally, surfacing for the third or fourth time, he managed to gulp it down. I looked for a bulge in the bird's neck, but couldn't see any sign of digestive discomfort. I guess the fish slipped right down the bird's gullet into its stomach. I couldn't imagine it having to eat again for a long time.

I hope that even with that big meal weighing it down the bird was able to flap off to its favorite piling and loaf the rest of the day away. Let it have a little R&R. Because, really, these birds don't do anything the easy way.

Relatively short-winged, they work hard to fly and are forced to be short-range foragers that need lots of trips to bring home sufficient bacon. Plus, if they're on land or water (rather than on a perch), they have a tough time getting airborne. Audubon writes that "to arise from the water . . . they are obliged to run and beat the surface for many yards, before they get fairly on wing." Actually, it's harder than that. Most waterbirds do run along the surface to get airborne, but the cormorant hops, with synchronized wingbeats. If the bird has just had a big meal, the hops and wingbeats can go on and on.

Also, while many of the birds you see along the shore just scrape a little hollow in the sand for their nests, the cormorant builds and keeps building—sometimes in trees or shrubs, sometimes on rock, as in this description from Audubon: "The Double-Crested Cormorant forms its nest of sea-weeds, some sticks, moss, and clods of earth, with grass adhering to them, which it piles up into a solid mass, often as high as three feet from the rock, with a diameter of fifteen or eighteen inches at the top, and of two and a half feet at the base. The whole has an appearance of solidity seldom seen in the nests of water-birds." The seaweed, by the way, is not just lying around waiting to be snatched up. Bent, who documented the process in detail, noted that the birds dove for it "in deep water" and brought it up in their bills.

Both parents work on the nest, the male typically bringing in the material and the female taking charge of construction. They keep adding to it—and cementing it with excrement—until the chicks have fledged, and the diversity of materials they incorporate rivals that of the equally industrious osprey. Forbush tells of a group of nests decorated with "pocket-knives, pipes, hairpins, and ladies' combs" that the birds had retrieved from a schooner sunk off the coast of Labrador. Hatch and Weseloh list "rope, fishnet, plastic buoys, deflated balloons, even a broiler grill" among documented decor and add that the resulting nest "is substantial and, if spared by winter storms, receives additions each year and eventually becomes a tall turretlike structure, especially in areas of low rainfall." Incidentally, the choice of an "arboreal site" proves unwise, long-term, since the tree will eventually die, the nest collapse, and the birds start over again.

The pair bond is strong among these birds, with considerable display of affection during the comings and goings of nest-building and incubation. Bent writes that returning to the nest and "approaching his mate [the male] begins caressing her with his bill. She steps off the nest; then both begin a series of snakelike movements of heads and necks, almost intertwining them. Finally he passes his head over, under, and around his mate, apparently caressing her from head to tail, and he or she settles down on the nest."

They're conscientious parents as well. In the absence of a brood patch, the adults wedge their warm, webbed feet beneath the eggs and lower themselves down. Once the altricial chicks are hatched, the adults are careful to keep them not only fed but watered. On hot days, after a changeover, write Hatch and Weseloh, the relieved parent "fetches water (instead of nest material) and pours it into open mouths of chicks." The young remain in the nest until almost fully grown, and even after they fledge, their parents continue to feed them until they've mastered the art of fishing for themselves.

So what we've got here, it seems to me, is a picture of solid decency—good work ethic, family values—with little about it to suggest the lineaments of the Archfiend. True, the cormorant has been around a long time. As Janet Lembke points out in her fine book, *Dangerous Birds*, 70 million years "is the evolutionary ornithologists' conservative estimate of how long the bird has been in existence as an entity distinct from all others. Its slow, gentle apparition on earth is coeval with the appearances of flowering plants and sequoias, marsupials and the first little mammals." So, OK, the cormorant might have been around to witness the Fall, but that doesn't mean it precipitated the event.

Besides, Lembke also reminds us that "the word *cormorant* condenses the Latin phrase *corvus marinus*, crow of the sea." Call it a stretch, but I'm throwing out the possibility that Milton, needing a couple of syllables to fill out that line of iambic pentameter, wrote "cormorant" when he actually had "crow" in mind. He might not have known too much about cormorants, but, brilliant classicist that he was, he would have known the Latin derivation like the back of his hand. And the crow, a bird Forbush describes as forever "up to some abominable mischief in the back yard," can easily be imagined "devising Death / To them who lived."

I'll close my case with one final argument. The French poet Charles Baudelaire famously observed that "the devil's greatest wile has been to convince us he does not exist." Well, nobody doubts the existence of the double-crested cormorant. Lembke describes them flying in "mile-long . . . ribbon-like bill-to-tail columns" or rafting on the water "almost as thickly as ducks." These gregarious birds pack themselves densely into their night-time roosts, and breeding colonies range from hundreds of pairs to thousands. I myself, returning from North Carolina's Outer Banks on the Ocracoke–Cedar Island ferry, saw at least a zillion cormorants massed on a sand island in the middle of Pamlico Sound.

Overall, in fact, this species' population has been on an upswing since the mid-1970s, a development not to everyone's liking. David Sibley reports that, in 1989, the legislature of Quebec passed a law

authorizing the extermination of 10,000 double-crested cormorants nesting on islands of the St. Lawrence River. "The rationale,"
he writes, "was that the birds' nesting habits were destroying the
vegetation on these islands and making them unsuitable for other
species." The United States followed suit a decade later, with laws
authorizing the killing of cormorants on islands in the Great Lakes
or feeding in aquaculture farms.

True, a crowded colony of nesting cormorants can wreak havoc
on the local vegetation, and even if the birds choose rock rather
than wood, the scene won't be pretty. Audubon writes, "The whole
surface of the rock [on which the colonies build their nests] re-
sembled a mass of putridity: feathers, broken and rotten eggs, and
dead young, lay scattered over it; and I leave you to guess how such a
place must smell on a calm warm day." Bent describes the cormorant
colony as "the filthiest place imaginable": the whole area becomes
"thoroughly whitewashed with excrement, which also accumulates
in slimy pools swarming with flies; the nests are often alive with
fleas, lice, and other vermin; and the odor of decaying fish scattered
about adds to the nauseating stench."

Uh oh. Does this sound like something out of Dante? Has my
argument circled around and bitten me on the butt?

Well, let's see. Overpopulation. Environmental degradation.
Blithe disregard for the well-being of other species. Hmmmm.

....

Clapper Rail

Rallus longirostris

I know I had ten different pieces of paper telling me that the boat trip up "lazy Jekyll Creek" would take off at 9:00 A.M. from Jekyll Island's "Historic Wharf." I'm used to having to travel forty minutes to get anywhere from our outpost in the woods, so I got to the wharf thirty minutes early. Nobody was there. Nobody there at ten till, five till. Nobody there at nine. I found a phone number on a different piece of paper, which also happened to have the correct location—back over the Jekyll causeway and a couple of miles north on Highway 17. Mercifully, Michael, our captain, said they would putter around in the vicinity of the dock till I got there.

What they did was motor out to a little island and look at a tree full of spoonbills and night herons, but I couldn't complain.

This excursion was one of the highlights of the Georgia Coast Birding and Nature Festival, and I jumped on board to join four other festival attendees, along with Michael and our expert guide Clay Taylor. Michael was a laid-back local in a battered, sweat-stained, Indiana Jones–style hat. Clay was something else, standing ramrod straight in his creased khakis and pressed shirt with the official Swarovski Optik logo on the pocket. A native of New England recently transplanted to Texas, he was slim, swarthy, and good-looking, with gray eyes and gray-blond hair. He was a staff ornithologist—and promoter—for the great optics company (headed from Georgia to a similar event in California), and, frankly, I was afraid the guy was a dude.

In fact, Clay was great. He knew all the birds, of course, but he could also imitate their songs and calls like nobody's business. At one point we saw an oystercatcher rise up from a spit of sand, and Clay called out its harsh cry of alarm. Damned if the bird didn't call back to him with exactly the same note. (He also taught us how to pronounce the famous brand name: "You remember Sonny Bono, right? You remember how he died? Well, when I heard the news, that's what I did. I 'swore off skis.'")

We had already seen a good many birds when Michael began to pilot us through an increasingly narrow, increasingly winding water-path deep in the cordgrass. Clay told us to keep our eyes out—we were in perfect clapper rail habitat. Sounded good to me. I'd never seen this secretive bird, though I'd been on plenty of outings where people said things like, "See that clapper? Never mind—he just disappeared back into the grass." As it turns out, we weren't in clapper habitat; we were in clapper heaven. Suddenly they were everywhere, skedaddling on all sides to escape our slow-gliding craft. They don't like to fly, Clay told us. It's a whole lot of work and doesn't get them very far. Sure enough, when we got too close, they would laboriously flap upward, landing gear still deployed, to a likelier hiding place thirty feet away.

We saw at least a dozen of them, after which I confess that I had to wonder: What in the world is the fuss all about? It's not like they're pretty birds (uniformly gray-brown drab), and their cackling vocals are not exactly melodious. Sibley says their bodies are laterally compressed for easy maneuvering through the tight-packed marsh grass, and from that quirk of physiognomy comes our term "thin as a rail." They also have a formidable bill (*longirostris*) and big feet with really long toes. But I'm still wondering. . . .

. . . .

Now, I do understand why nonbirders have long sought the clapper. It is a game bird, and though clapper rail hunting is not as popular today as it has been in times past, the "season" still opens every fall up and down the East Coast and along the Gulf as well. From this activity, I suppose, come the many versions of its more familiar name: "marsh hen," "salt-water marsh hen," and "mud hen." (The family Rallidae, incidentally, includes coots, moorhens, and gallinules, as well as rails.)

Why this particular bird emerged as a favorite among hunters is a question worth asking. In less sophisticated times, the clapper may have been attractive because it presented an easy target. "When put up," Audubon writes, "they fly slowly and generally straight before you, with their legs dangling, so that they are very easily shot by a quick sportsman, as they rarely fly far at a time on such occasions, but prefer pitching down again into the first tuft of rank grass in their way." Consequently, while clappers are threatened by a host of predators both avian and earthbound, Audubon continues, "their worst enemy is man. My friend Bachman has shot so many as sixty in the course of four hours, and others have killed double that number in double the time."

As a nonhunter I'm on thin ice here, but my guess is that over time fewer people agreed that shooting birds should be easy. Bent, for example, was among those who couldn't see the appeal of this bird for true sportsmen. "It seems to possess few of the qualities of a good game bird. Its flight is low, weak and direct and it is so tame that it usually rises at close range." The fact that it is "one of the easiest of birds to shoot" was not, for Bent, an inducement.

Another reason to wonder at the clapper's game-bird allure is that people are far from agreed as to its fitness for the table. Alexander Wilson dismisses it out of hand: "Their flesh is dry, tastes sedgy and will bear no comparison with that of the Common Rail" (by which he probably means the common moorhen). Audubon, writing at about the same time, declares that they were considered good to eat "in the Southern States, especially during winter." He adds that many birds "are destroyed by torch light, which so dazzles their eyes, as to enable persons fond of the sport to knock them down with poles or paddles during high tides." So, if I may presume to decode Audubon, what we're talking about is southern people without guns, or poor southerners, who, Audubon suggests, will eat anything.

Bent treads the middle ground. "The flesh of this rail will not compare in flavor with that of the sora, especially when the latter has been fattened on wild rice; it is said to be insipid and sedgy, but is undoubtedly tender and fairly palatable, as is the flesh of most birds, particularly young birds." To this I can only add the comment of our boat captain, Michael, who confessed to having hunted clappers as a boy. "So how does it taste?" I asked. "Not too bad if you wrap it in a slab of bacon."

There is absolutely no dispute, however, as to the flavor of the clapper rail's eggs. "Exquisite eating," raves Wilson, "far surpassing those of the domestic Hen." Plentiful, too. "So abundant are the nests of this species," Wilson continues, "and so dexterous some persons at finding them, that one hundred dozen of eggs have been collected by one man in a day." Audubon agrees: "As the eggs are in request as a delicious article of food, they are gathered in great numbers, and I myself have collected so many as seventy-two dozens in the course of a day." He reports that in New Jersey he has seen "twenty or more persons gathering them by thousands during the season; . . . when this havock is continued upwards of a month, you may imagine its extent."

The bonanza is abetted by the fact that clappers generally lay somewhere between eight and twelve eggs per clutch, then reluctantly get out of the way. As Audubon describes the scene, "When the birds are sitting, they suffer you to approach within a few feet; but, as if aware of your intention, they glide away in silence to some distance, and remain crouched among the grass until you have retired. When, on returning, the poor bird finds that her treasure has been stolen, she immediately proclaims her grief aloud, and in this is joined by her faithful mate."

Man may indeed be its worst enemy, but the clapper rail is beleaguered on every side. The care with which it sites and constructs its nest—considering both concealment from predators and safety from rising water—suggests the clapper's awareness of its various vulnerabilities. Wilson expresses the dilemma in describing how the birds continue to add to the nest as the number of eggs grows. At last the nest reaches a height of twelve inches or more, "doubtless to secure it from the rising of the tides. Over this the long salt grass is artfully arched, and knit at the top, to conceal it from the view above; but this very circumstance enables the experienced egg-hunter to distinguish the spot at a distance of thirty or forty yards." Bent also notes that these nests, "with pretty little canopies of green grass interlaced above[,] . . . were often conspicuous at a long distance."

So human predators are not fooled. Nor are the laughing gulls, which not only eat the clapper's eggs and chicks, but sometimes even appropriate the clapper's nest (though it must be added that the clapper reciprocates on all counts). Nor are the fish crows, to say nothing of the wide variety of raptors that will take eggs, young, and adult birds as well. Among ground predators, the raccoon is probably the most destructive, but Wilson writes that "the minx and the foxes come in for their share" and that "not content with the eggs, those last often seize and devour the parents also." In a nod to karmic justice, Wilson adds that "the bones, feathers, wings, etc., of the poor Mud Hen lie in heaps near the hole of the minx; by which circumstance, however, he himself is often detected and destroyed."

How about the defense system against the changing water levels of their marshland habitat? Here the clapper brings all its ingenuity to bear. The big nest is securely fastened to the grass stems in the midst of the thickest tufts, writes Audubon, and above high-water mark. "The materials of which it is formed are so well interlaced with the plants around them, as to prevent their being washed away by extraordinarily high tides." But when spring storms flood the marsh, all is for naught. The high waters "sometimes carry off and destroy the eggs, as well as many of the sitting birds, whose attachment to them is so great, that they are now and then drowned while endeavouring to keep them safe."

Wilson describes the devastation of one of these "north-east tempests": "On an occasion of this kind, I have seen, at one view, thousands in a single meadow, walking about exposed and bewildered, while the dead bodies of the females, who perished on or near the nests, were strewed along the shore. This last circumstance proves how strong the ties of maternal affection are in these birds; for of the great numbers which I picked up and opened, not one male was to be found among them; all were females!"

For all the forces that plague them, though, clappers are not helpless. For one thing, they can move quickly and silently through their chosen habitat, and as Audubon puts it, "they have thousands of paths among the rank herbage, crossing each other so often that they can very easily escape pursuit." Sufficiently provoked—by the low strafing of the marsh hawk, for example—the bird will go on the attack. "On such occasions," Audubon continues, "the Rail rises a few yards in the air, strikes at the marauder with bill and claws, screaming aloud all the while, and dives again among the grass, to the astonishment of the bird of prey, which usually moves off at full speed."

If closed in upon on land, clappers take to the water, where they can remain hidden below the surface if need be. Interestingly, Wilson believes that the birds could hold themselves under by grabbing onto aquatic plants, but Audubon dismisses this contention. "It dives well," he writes, "remains a considerable time under water, and in this manner dexterously eludes its pursuers, although it certainly does not possess the power of holding fast to the bottom, as some persons have alleged." Who was right? BNA *Online* goes with Wilson: "Dives only if wounded or in response to immediate threat. Holds onto submersed vegetation in such cases."

Clappers also enhance their prospects for survival by forming strong pair bonds and sharing the work of raising their large families. Males are the chief nest-builders, and their architectural plans often include ramps leading up into the nest to facilitate entrance and exit for themselves and for the young. Both parents incubate, and when hatching time approaches, they build a number of "brood platforms," where the earliest hatchlings can be brooded while the remaining eggs continue to be incubated. As William Eddleman and Courtney Conway point out in BNA *Online*, these platforms "differ from primary nest in lacking a dome and being capable of floating at high tide." Finally, once all the eggs have hatched, the adults again divide the responsibilities, with each parent taking care of half the brood.

In fact, it's probably true that the clapper's best defense is its numbers. The chicks are semiprecocial and out of the nest quickly, increasing their own chances of survival. If one of those nor'easters does wipe out the household, the pair will set about building another nest and producing another dozen eggs. As Sibley puts it, "The abnormally large clutch sizes and semi-precocial chicks, which allow members of this family to produce as many young as they can as quickly as possible, also may have evolved in response to the vulnerability of their habitat." The grand scheme appears to be working. Bent believes that all the hunting and egging had "greatly thinned" the clapper's ranks; "it no longer exists anywhere in anything like the astonishing abundance described by earlier writers." Maybe. But the species today is not threatened, and its population has been stable for some decades.

. . . .

Kek-kek-kek-kek-kek-kek-kek . . . kek . . . kek . . . kek claps the clapper rail from deep in the cordgrass. The hunters have lost interest, but the birders have become obsessed. There's a crowd of us jostling one another, elbows akimbo, eyeballs to eyepieces, atop an observation deck over a marsh somewhere on the Atlantic coast.

The birds are calling because they can't see each other in the thick grass, no more than we can see them. But we're trying. Or some of us are.

"There he is!" somebody shouts. "I've got him. Or . . . no, it's hard to say. Could be a clump of grass. John, what do you think?"

I think I won't mention that I saw clapper rails by the dozen two weeks earlier on a little boat excursion up Jekyll Creek, that the clapper rail is a fine bird, and that I'm waiting for the avocets to make an appearance.

Willet

*Catoptrophorus semipalmatus**

When it comes to two-story beach motels, is age a good thing? More specifically, should the Sea Foam Motel in Nag's Head, North Carolina, offer up as a selling point that it's on the National Register of Historic Places? Maybe not, because if it's been shifting in the sand and mildewing in the salt air for sixty-five years, how good can it be? Or maybe it should, because there's always the chance that some idiot, checking out the website, is gonna say to himself, "Hey, National Register of Historic Places. How bad can it be?"

Actually, it was quaint. When I checked in, the proprietor handed me a real key, from which dangled one of those plastic doodads with the room number stamped on it, and told me to make myself at home. The room had the usual amenities, including a small refrigerator, and my second-floor accommodation came with a fine little patio perched right over the beach. I liked that to get out there you didn't open a sliding-glass door, but rather a real door and then a screen door with an old-timey latch. I also liked that, as soon as I went through that door, I was assaulted by a dozen or so laughing gulls, who, when they realized I hadn't just fallen off the turnip truck, desisted and never bothered me again.

Now, "quaint" does come with a downside. The bathroom fixtures certainly showed their age, and Dede, whose olfactory system is keener than any bloodhound's, would no doubt have sensed a few objectionable accents in the room's atmosphere. More noticeable to me was the fact that from all four walls the floor sloped toward the middle, as though, at one time in its long history, this upper-story room had somehow flooded and been equipped with a shower-stall-

---

*Hold the presses! This just in from the editors of *BNA Online*: "Analysis of mitochondrial and nuclear DNA sequences in members of the shorebird tribe Tringini suggests that the genus *Catoptrophorus* is embedded within *Tringa* and should be merged into it. Thus the 47th Supplement to the American Ornithologists' Union's *Checklist of North American Birds* now recognizes Willet as *Tringa semipalmata*."

type drainage system. Honestly, I couldn't figure out why the TV didn't just slide off the chest of drawers and crash onto the floor.

But it didn't. And my laptop didn't slide off the little worktable. And I didn't slide off the bed. And, anyway, it would have taken a long list of shortcomings to overcome the exceedingly pleasurable experience of going to sleep every night with that back door open, listening to the sound of the surf rolling onto the shore. And so your armchair birder found himself quite happily doing his armchair thing: sitting with beverage and binoculars on his plastic patio chair, watching the laughing gulls, the herring gulls, the sanderlings, and one lone willet.

. . . .

You might see a bunch of willets together, especially during migration. Our Atlanta Audubon group saw big flocks on the Georgia coast in early May, possibly headed as far north as Nova Scotia. But my experience on Nag's Head in October (and elsewhere at other times) is in line with Sibley's observation that these birds are "usually solitary." If you're walking along a beach populated by the usual company of gulls, terns, and peeps, and you notice an individual bird that doesn't seem to fit in, there's a good chance it's a willet. If it seems to have little else to recommend it—except for those long legs on which it stands out—there's an even better chance it's a willet.

"Plain old Will," as the birders sometimes call it, is not going to be confused with majestic waders like the snowy egret or the tricolored heron, and most descriptions focus on the bird's "always drab" plumage and lack of distinctive markings. No question—this is a gray bird: gray on top, paler gray underneath, and gray legs. It dresses up slightly for the wedding, but not so as to knock anybody's eyes out.

And yet as we walked the beach together on Nag's Head, I came to appreciate the willet.* I couldn't help but admire the way those all-gray head and neck feathers lie down tight and neat, giving this bird a clean-cut look like a just-shorn GI. I might've even been tempted to imagine our nation under the protection of soldiers such as this one—serious-minded, hard-working, resolute—when all of a sudden, for some reason, the bird would flick open a wing and close it again. What was that? Personality? Beauty? Art? A satchel of contraband smuggled back from Bangkok? The fantasy of national security has collapsed, but the bird has been transformed.

It really is hard to believe that the willet with wings open, or in flight, is the same gray bird you see working the beach. As Bent observes, when the willet "lifts its black and white wings or when flying, no bird is more easily recognized, for its color pattern is unique and conspicuous; the black wings, with their broad white band extending across the base of the tail, advertise the willet as far as they can be seen." It works the other way, too. You watch a willet come in for a landing on a sandbar, wonderful wings outspread, then suddenly it disappears into a lump of amorphous grayness.

Not that my bird was interested in flying anywhere. It was hun-

---

*You've noticed by now that I'm not distinguishing between the eastern and western willet. Some birders can, and do, but I'm not among them.

gry, and my proximity wasn't about to put it off its feed. It watched the surf, which was fairly heavy; when it withdrew, the bird ran out on long gray legs to where the shells were turning over in the suck and jabbed away with that long dark bill. Sometimes, when it was after a real prize, it went deep, almost up to its eyeballs. At last it came up with something worth the trouble, something big and plump, some kind of crab, I assumed. It dropped the thing a couple of times, or the thing wrestled free, and it looked to me like the bird was clearly worried about losing it in the rush of water. On the third or fourth try, it finally gulped the meal down and started looking for the next one.

I was interested to read later in BNA *Online* (in the account by Peter Lowther, Hector Douglas, and Cheri Gratto-Trevor), that my interpretation of my willet's behavior may not have been entirely accurate. The menu item probably was a crab, since willets are known to probe for crabs "along the wave outwash," but this bird may not have been dropping its prey accidentally. According to the authors, the willet "grasps crab by leg and shakes until body flies off, then eats leg and process repeated until legless carapace is swallowed whole." While I'm at it, I might as well mention what else I learned: that these birds forage by night as well as by day, and their nighttime techniques apparently depend on what the moon is up to. On moonlit nights, the birds visually forage for fiddler crabs on the mudflats; on dark nights they move to flooded pools and switch to tactile probing with their bills.

I was in Nag's Head in October, well after the breeding season, so my bird wasn't flying off in that direction either. But back in the spring, from the observation tower behind the visitors center on the Jekyll Island causeway, I had a glimpse of courtship behavior. One bird arose out of the marsh, another joined it, and together they circled and dove, ascended and circled—clearly smitten with one another. After a few minutes they landed on a little path beside the marsh and followed each other around. When I read in *The Shorebird Guide* that "the courtship display is a duet, with male rising first, hovering over territory on quivering wings, then joined by female, which hovers and descends to the ground with male," I had to agree, that, yeah, that's just about right.

The pair I was watching, still on the ground, disappeared from view. If the moment of truth was about to unfold, I missed it, but Matthiessen's account is hard to beat: "The willet, should his mate tilt forward in response to all his wing-waving, mounts and copulates without further ado, emitting a kind of jaunty clicking, as if snapping unseen fingers; the female, in these moments, has been heard to give small grunted exclamations. However, she tires of their intimacy before he does. Sometimes she brings matters to a sudden end by throwing her partner forward over her shoulder." I have to add that BNA *Online* includes a terrific sequence of four photographs depicting a pair of willets *in flagrante*. In the final shot, the female does in fact appear to be about to pitch the male forward over her downward-tilting head, but at the same time the male, with his bill firmly pinched around his mate's neck, is clearly not quite ready to disembark.

Probably because the pair I saw had not yet proceeded to actual nesting, I also missed out on all the noise. "This is one of the most noisy and noted birds that inhabit our salt marshes in summer," writes Wilson. "It arrives from the south on the shores of the Middle States about the 20th of April, or beginning of May; and from that time to the last of July, its loud and shrill reiterations of *pill-will-willet, pill-will-willet*, resound, almost incessantly along the marshes, and may be distinctly heard at the distance of more than half a mile." Bent adds that the clamor increases if you approach anywhere near their nests: "No sooner does one land on an island where they are breeding than an outcry is started and one after another the birds arise and fly out to meet the intruder, until the whole colony is in a state of great excitement. Regardless of their own safety they circle about at short range, pouring out a steady stream of angry invectives in a great variety of loud, ringing notes. And this performance is kept up as long as the intruder is anywhere near their nests."

Might my willets build their nest right there in the marsh I was looking out over? Yes, says Audubon. "The Willets retire to the interior of the larger salt-marshes for the purpose of forming their nests and raising their broods in security. There, in the vicinity of the shallow pools, which frequently occur in such places, the bird prepares a nest on the ground, among the rank grass, of which the tenement is composed." Bent isn't so sure: "Its favorite nesting places are on sandy islands overgrown with grass," he writes, and then adds this amplification: "Roger Tory Peterson writes to me that, among 11 nests found by him on the South Carolina coast, 'five sets of eggs on one particular strip of beach were located on the open sand with no preparation at all made for a nest.' Another set was 'in a very heavy, well-made nest of weeds and grass, out on the open sand, far from any grass or bushes.'" (I pass this along mostly because I think it's pretty cool that Peterson, who was born in 1908, apparently was filing field reports to Bent while still in his teens.)

In fact, as BNA *Online* clarifies, willets will nest most anywhere — in the marsh grass, on the sand dunes, in upland meadows, on coral cobble, and even in sphagnum bog. Wherever the nest happens to be, these birds protect it fiercely. "The sight of a Crow, a Turkey Buzzard, a quadruped of any kind, and more especially of a gunner," writes Audubon, "at once excites the greatest alarm. . . . Should they have young broods, they not unfrequently alight within sight, emit clicking and querulous notes, raise their wings upright, and run over the ground as if wounded, moving in so pitiable a manner as frequently to excite a good feeling towards them in the gunner, who, should he be a parent himself, is almost sure to leave them unmolested."

Matthiessen includes the willet among those few species which "astonishingly" have been known to pick up their young between their legs and carry them from danger. "These reports are so numerous," he adds, "that one must repress an impulse to dismiss them out of hand." I've seen one such account, submitted to Bent by one of his regular correspondents, Arthur T. Wayne, in May 1899: "I found a nest in an oat field, which contained one young bird just hatched and three eggs on the point of hatching. I remained near the place until the eggs were hatched, and the willets were greatly alarmed all the time. Presently I saw one of the old birds remove a young one and [holding it between its thighs] fly with it across three creeks and marsh land to an island a quarter of a mile away. This was repeated until all the young were removed." BNA *Online* also cites this report, but not without a raised eyebrow: "This single instance often re-ported, with impression that such behavior might well be common. Never observed in 6 yr in s. Alberta, with considerable observations of parents with broods, nor in 3 yr in N. Dakota."

Still, there's no question that willets are aggressive in the defense of their own. High on the list of enemies are the fish crows, who will sometimes team up to force a willet off its nest. More often, the wil-lets will meet the fish crows halfway, rising up to mob them, and as Wilson puts it, "in united numbers, attack and pursue them with loud clamors." Matthiessen observes that the willet is something of a specialist at the mobbing defense, "with a temperament so well suited to this practice that it will often mob just for the sake of mob-bing, whether or not it has been stimulated by intruders."

Assuming all such dangers are survived, the young willets are fledged and on their own in four weeks' time. Interestingly, only their fathers see them off. If the female finds copulation tiresome before her partner does, she likewise tires of parenting. She sees the job halfway through and leaves the final two weeks to her mate. More interesting, he forgives her for it. Willets pair for life.

. . . .

"Man has been the chief enemy of the willet," writes Bent, "and the main cause of the restriction of its breeding areas. . . . Being a large, fat bird, it helped to fill the game bag rapidly and so was a favor-ite with sportsmen or market hunters." The birds as well as their eggs—considered "a legitimate article of food"—were harvested relentlessly during the breeding season, with the ultimate conse-quence that by the end of the nineteenth century willets had ceased breeding between Nova Scotia and South Carolina.

Happily, that trend was reversed in the latter part of the twen-tieth century, and our eastern willet now once again breeds along the entire Atlantic seaboard from Newfoundland to Florida and also along most of the Gulf coast. So that flock I saw on the Georgia coast in the spring may indeed have been on its way to Nova Scotia, but not necessarily.

As for my friend on Nag's Head, had it settled in for the winter? Audubon writes that "all the individuals betake themselves in winter to the shores of Carolina, Georgia, Florida, and the countries bordering the Mexican Gulf." Bent agrees but notes that "it is rather rare as far north as South Carolina." It had been an unusually mild autumn on the Outer Banks and was still warm while I was there. Maybe this bird had decided to linger but was nevertheless prepared to move on when the weather turned. Maybe I'll see it again in Florida's Merritt Island NWR when I'm there in January. And if I say I do, who's to contradict me?

....

Tricolored Heron
Egretta tricolor

Don't talk to me about armchair birding. I have fought the mosquitoes in Pea Island NWR. That's Pea Island, North Carolina. Outer Banks, North Carolina. Thirteen hours from Acworth, Georgia. I went to find the avocets. I found the mosquitoes.

The only time I've seen mosquitoes like that was in hot, humid Picayune, Mississippi, at my mother-in-law's funeral. In Mississippi, unreconstructed and unregenerate, people still smoke. And they mean it. After the service, we were eating the postfuneral meal at a relative's house, and I noticed a knot of people standing out in the yard — in a thin cloud of smoke made thick by a billion mosquitoes. They were out there because having that cigarette was the most important thing in the world. Sweltering in their funereal garb didn't matter. Antisociability didn't matter. Even the especially hellish torment of swarming, blood-sucking *Culex pipiens* failed to matter. Only smoking mattered.

If somebody had seen me that October morning, walking north along the west bank of North Pond, trying to get to an alleged gathering of wading birds a quarter mile in front of me, beating like a maniac at the blanket of mosquitoes that no amount of repellent could repel, stopping every fifty yards to spray down one more time, that person would have said, "Only birding matters to that poor son of a bitch."

I gave up, eventually, and scurried back to the observation platform at the west end of the dike that bisects the pond. I had discovered the day before — and on other platforms at other coastal locations — that mosquitoes won't always follow you up into that rarefied atmosphere, and I was ready for that refuge. In clambering up those twenty steps I was also returning to what John Fussell, in *A Birder's Guide to Coastal North Carolina*, calls "arguably the single best birding spot in the state," where "on a good day in autumn a sharp birder could undoubtedly tally a hundred species." Well, it is a beautiful spot. From the vantage point of the platform, the vast marsh

pond spreads out north and south; back across the dike, to the east, are the great dunes that somehow hold the Atlantic off this impossibly skinny strip of land, and to the west, just over the marsh line, spreads Pamlico Sound. As for the hundred species: maybe so, if the thousands upon thousands of waterfowl that covered the pond represented, say, ninety-five different species. About that your discriminating narrator wouldn't know. He doesn't do ducks.

As it had the day before, the pond offered up the standard collection of waders: several great egrets, a great blue heron, a few white ibises. Of avocets there were none. Then I turned around and looked west of the big pond, where a few smaller ponds arose amid the marsh. In one of these, alone, a tricolored heron was foraging for breakfast. This wasn't a new bird for me, but it was a particularly good look. The morning sun was at my back, and the bird's raiment — blue-gray, white, and russet — shone in the perfect light. It was a birding moment.

. . . .

Based on my own earlier observations, I was not surprised to see this lovely bird feeding by itself, and experts confirm that it is a solitary forager. They also agree that it is a bird of rare elegance and beauty. "Delicate in form, beautiful in plumage, and graceful in its movements," writes Audubon, "I never see this interesting Heron, without calling it the Lady of the Waters." (By the way, Audubon refers to this bird as the Louisiana heron, and so did everybody else until the American Ornithological Union formally changed its name in 1983.) For Bent these slender herons were "beautiful, dainty creatures[,] . . . agile and graceful. . . . For harmony in colors and for grace in motion this little heron has few rivals."

I was able to appreciate some of that graceful agility, because the bird I was watching was by no means standing still and waiting for the little fishes to swim up and say hello. Sibley says that tricolored herons, like reddish egrets, are "active" feeders, "often prancing and pirouetting with one wing extended while they forage," which corresponds pretty closely to my notes: "dancing around, wings spread, trying to scare something up." Peter Frederick, writing for BNA *Online*, breaks the "active pursuit" into two forms: "loping chases, with flapping wings and lunging strikes, or tight pirouetting while turning in direction of open wing." In any case, like Bent says, "it is a pleasure to watch them."

It must be a pleasure to watch their highly ritualized courtship, too — about which much has been written. It's the male's duty to select the nest territory, and he may even begin constructing the nest's foundation before choosing his mate. Then, writes Frederick, after the female is allowed to enter the established domain, "male and female may engage in Bill-Nibbling—male and female open and close mandibles in close proximity to each other's head and body, creating a gentle rattling sound—neck-entwining, mutual preening, and joint twig manipulation."

Bent describes their lovemaking with an uncharacteristic lack of restraint: As the male "dances along from branch to branch toward his mate, . . . the plumes on his back are raised and lowered, like a filmy veil of ecru drab, and the pure white head plumes are raised and spread like a fan, in striking contrast to the blue and drab. It is a picture of irresistible beauty; his mate finally yields and the conjugal pact is sealed right there on the tree tops, without loss of poise." For a detailed look at the pair's ceremonial nesting behavior he turns to the account he received from Julian Huxley. Because it's fascinating, and because you, like me, may have had little opportunity to appreciate the work of the famous biologist (and brother of the even more famous novelist), I'll pass it along.

After deciding on a nest site, but before the real building gets under way, Huxley writes, the two birds "spend several days in a regular honeymoon. During most of this time they sit side by side, with one resting its head against the other's flanks. Now and again a special ceremony, which I have not seen at other times[,] is indulged in; with loud cries the birds face each other and lean their necks forward, partly or wholly intertwining them, each feverishly nibbling at the other's aigrettes."

During this honeymoon period, one of the birds remains at the nest site while the other goes to feed. On the absent bird's return, we see the more common "greeting ceremony." Huxley writes that in both birds "the crest, neck feathers, and aigrettes are raised, the head is somewhat thrown up, revealing the patch of buff on the chin, the wings are spread and a special cry is uttered as the returning bird alights and walks through the branches to its mate." This ceremony persists throughout the actual nest construction. "It is my experience that the male usually, perhaps always, finds the sticks for the nest, and brings and gives them to the female, who then does the actual building. The giving of each stick is accompanied by a greeting ceremony."

Once the eggs are laid and incubation begins, nest relief offers an opportunity for the greeting ceremony to play out while the birds are changing places. "This, however, does not close the performance," writes Huxley. "Almost invariably the bird which has been relieved goes and fetches one or (almost always) several sticks, which it presents to the sitting bird. The presentation is made in the greeting attitude. The sitting bird then builds the stick into the nest. I have seen as many as 11 sticks presented after one nest relief." Not that we have any reason to doubt Huxley, but Frederick confirms that the greeting ceremony—"arriving bird passes a twig to mate, with all feathers fully erect, wings held out to sides, bill pointed repeatedly upwards, then down towards nest"—is used throughout the nesting period "to aid in recognition and to reduce aggression during nest exchanges."

Tricolored herons may be solitary feeders, but their rookeries are often densely populated. Audubon writes of a breeding colony on an island in the Keys, where "among the branches some hundred pairs of these lovely birds had placed their nests, which were so low and so close to each other, that without moving a step one could put his hand into several." These herons might build their nests in the branches of willow or mangrove trees a few feet off the ground, or they might build on the ground in the thick marsh grasses. In either case, as the nest is being completed and the female begins to lay, the male steps up. He guards the nest, the territory, and his mate with intense dedication, sometimes going several days without food.

Under the care of both parents, the young make their impatient way toward fledglinghood. At two weeks old they begin to climb out of the nest and onto the surrounding branches, pulling themselves up with their bills, returning to the nest only to be fed. After another two weeks they're done with the nest, climbing into the treetops with feet and wings and looking for other kids to hang out with. The neighborhood hums with the noisy business of life. "Quite a variety of croaking notes and squawks, some in soft conversational tones and some loud and vehement, are heard in the rookeries," writes Bent. His observation is that the tricolor "seems to get along well with its neighbors," with some exceptions. He once saw one of these birds, unprovoked, land on a little blue heron's nest "and deliberately poke the eggs out of it onto the ground." Then there's "the pilfering of sticks from the nests of others . . . which often leads to a quarrel."

Of course, into the rookery come the marauders—the fish crows, the vultures, and, as Audubon recounts, the gunners, who find the tricolor to be particularly easy prey. Flying home, they do the hunter the favor of alighting "at once among the lowest branches." Worse, even when being shot at, "they seldom fly to a great distance," and at the cry of a wounded bird, others come flying to the rescue "and may be shot in great numbers by any person fond of such sport." All in all, he writes, "their apparent insensibility to danger has given rise to the appellation of *Egrette folle*, which is given to them in Lower Louisiana."

Bent also laments the havoc wrought by another "human enemy"—"the bird photographer, who sets up his blind in a rookery and keeps the herons off their nests, often for long periods." Confessing his own guilt, he recalls the scene after he and his team had spent parts of three days in one particular rookery: "The crows and vultures had cleaned out practically all the nests anywhere near our blinds; the roseate spoonbills and American egrets had been completely broken up and driven away; hundreds of nests of the smaller herons had been robbed; and the ground was strewn with broken egg shells all over the rookery." He recommends that the safest—and most rewarding—time to practice bird photography "is when the young are partially grown, when there are no eggs for the crows to steal and when the young are too large for the vultures to swallow."

Tricolored herons breed all along our Atlantic and Gulf coasts, and those that nest along the more southerly coasts never have to leave home. Historically, their populations have been robust; in the 1920s Bent declared them to be "by far the most abundant of the southern herons." Those healthy numbers, and the herons' dependable fondness for coastal estuaries, have always been a boon to birders, who knew where to look and could count on success.

For the beautiful birds themselves, however, fortune's wheel seems to have turned. According to the *Breeding Bird Atlas of Georgia*, the tricolor's numbers have declined considerably since the early twentieth century. "The main conservation threat" write the authors, "is continued loss and degradation of wetland habitats. Because this species is so dependent on estuarine resources, it is highly susceptible to loss of habitat due to coastal development."

You probably don't need me to tell you that, while some birds deal with it better than others, the development of coastal habitat for human use is a trend unlikely to be reversed.

A Note on the Little Blue Heron (*Egretta caerulea*)

Snooping in my brother's desk during a Christmas holiday many, many years ago, I discovered his present from our aunt: a gift certificate to an expensive Atlanta restaurant, on which she had written, "Favoritism is a secret thing." She had given me a carton of Winstons, which I thought was a pretty cool gift for a sixteen-year-old, but still . . .

I'm obviously not over the hurt but nevertheless heed the wisdom of the message, which is why I've appropriated this little aside to quietly divulge another personal secret: I have a special fondness for the little blue heron.

Why? I don't know. Maybe because I like all things blue, especially blue birds—like Eastern bluebirds, or indigo buntings, or blue grosbeaks, or even blue jays. And despite the typical photograph, in which it appears to be a dull slate-blue, this bird, caught in the sunlight, is really, beautifully, iridescently blue.

Maybe because I'm wowed by the fact that in its first-year plumage, before that blueness arrives, the bird is so purely white that it's often confused with the snowy egret. (Forbush wryly observes that this phenomenon must give pause to the proponents of the theory of protective coloration; by their logic, the young, still unaware of the world's myriad dangers, ought to be dark and easily camouflaged, and the parents should be white.)

Maybe because I see it so seldom. Though other writers deem it "common" and have hunted out its dense rookeries and roosting sites, they also describe the little blue as a "shy, retiring" species, one that has, in Bent's phrase, "retreated somewhat before the advance of civilization." Well, believe me, I have, too. Who wouldn't?

Maybe because it appears to be nobody else's favorite. Unlike its close relatives, the snowy egret and the tricolored heron, it has excited little rhapsody in the writings of our classic naturalists. "Lady of the Waters" indeed. The best Audubon can do for this bird is to report that the Creoles "not unfrequently eat the flesh of this species, and . . . some of them have assured me that it is not bad food."

The little blue heron has much in common with the tricolor, with which it often associates. The two species are the same size, with the same slender physique and graceful carriage, and the nesting behavior of the little blue is almost as highly ritualized as that of the tricolor. The two birds also inhabit much the same range, though the little blue is more likely than the tricolor to be found in inland, freshwater habitat.

Sadly, the little blue is also like the tricolor in that its population is declining, and for the same reasons.

It occurs to me that since the whole world seems to be going to hell in a handbasket, we may have more immediate problems than the declining population of a couple of bird species, however lovely. But, honestly, I don't believe we have a more ominous one.

Snowy Egret

Egretta thula

> It was as if three whirlwinds had drawn together at some center, to find there feeding in peace a snowy heron. Its own slow spiral of flight could take it away in its own time, but for a little it held them still, it laid quiet over them, and they stood for a moment unburdened.
> —Eudora Welty, "A Still Moment"

It's a special bird, no doubt about it. "This beautiful little heron," writes Bent, "one of nature's daintiest and most exquisite creatures, is the most charming of all our marsh birds." Thomas Burleigh agrees: "Its snow-white plumage and graceful movements give it the distinction of being the most attractive of all our marsh birds." Wilson writes about its "most distinguished ornament": the "long silky plumes proceeding from the shoulders, covering the whole back, and extending beyond the tail," which, when erected, give the bird its "very elegant appearance."

Many writers go on to note that the snowy egret's beautiful plumage, and especially those silky breeding plumes, came close to bringing about its destruction. Katharine Parsons and Terry Master, in BNA *Online*, offer a brief synopsis of the story: "This species was among the most sought-after of all herons and egrets for its delicate, recurved back plumes, used to adorn women's hats. In 1886, plumes were valued at an astounding $32 per ounce, twice the contemporary price of gold. Plundering for plumes began about 1880, peaked in 1903, and continued until 1910, when outraged citizens forced the passage of laws that reduced the slaughter." But this fascinating contest between wildlife preservation and the implacable engine of commerce is worth a closer look.

Bent writes that his trips to Florida in 1902 caught the snowy egret population at its "lowest ebb." There were none to be seen except for "a few left in the big rookeries on the upper St. Johns." He is keenly aware of the circumstances: "The little snowy egret was

slaughtered in much greater numbers than its larger relative, because it was originally much more numerous and more widely distributed, because it was much less shy and so more easily killed and because its short and delicate plumes were more in demand than the larger, stiffer plumes of the [great egret]. For these three reasons it suffered far more at the hands of the plume hunters and came much nearer being exterminated."

In fact, when Bent made those trips, the birding community at large was beginning to mobilize in protest against the "plume industry." He quotes an eyewitness to the slaughter, A. H. E. Mattingly, whose account was published in special leaflet number 21 of the newly formed National Association of Audubon Societies: "There, strewn on the floating water weed, and also on adjacent logs, were at least 50 carcasses of large white and smaller plumed egrets—nearly one-third of the rookery, perhaps more—the birds having been shot off their nests containing young. What a holocaust! Plundered for their plumes. . . . Fifty birds ruthlessly destroyed, besides their young (about 200) left to die of starvation! This last fact was betokened by at least 70 carcasses of the nestlings, which had become so weak that their legs had refused to support them and they had fallen from the nests into the water below, and had been miserably drowned."

As Scott Weidensaul wryly observes in *Of a Feather*, "Fashion in the 1880s had taken wing—and head, and tail, and plume, all stripped from wild birds and arrayed on increasingly flamboyant hats." The aigrettes*—those "long, airy, impossibly delicate breeding plumes grown each spring by herons and egrets"—excited an especially keen lust. Hat makers told their customers that the feathers were plucked harmlessly from live birds, or simply picked up off the ground, but, says Weidensaul, "this was feel-good hogwash; gunners shot the birds in their breeding colonies and stripped them of their skins, leaving their eggs and chicks to die and bringing many species to the brink of extinction."

---

*Yes, there's a connection: "egret" derives from the French *aigrette*, meaning "little heron." Today "aigrette" denotes only the plume, not the entire bird.

How many birds were slaughtered to satisfy this whim of fashion? Estimates vary. Diana Wells reports that in just one year, 1892, and in one city, New York, milliners were supplied with 130,000 egret "scalps." Theodore Cross puts the total annual take at 5 million birds. Weidensaul calculates the carnage to have been much greater still. He reports that a single London millinery firm went through a ton and a half of aigrettes in one year at the height of the craze, and, based on the weight of an individual plume, he figures that "almost two hundred thousand birds had been shot to supply them, never mind the multiplying loss in eggs and chicks." Overall, says Weidensaul, "the plume trade was chewing through an estimated 200 million birds a year."

The destruction became finally so alarming that the National Association of Audubon Societies began hiring wardens to police bird-nesting islands along the Atlantic coast, especially in the rich breeding colonies of south Florida, where legal protections for the birds were failing to put a dent in the illegal plume trade. This maneuver resulted in the slaying of three wardens—first Guy Bradley and later Columbus McLeod and L. P. Reeves—by poachers they were trying to arrest, incidents sufficiently shocking to spur a national outcry, and ultimately Congress, to bring an end to the feather industry. First written in 1913 and officially codified in 1918, the Migratory Bird Treaty Act at last gave native wild birds the protected status they still enjoy today.

Actually, if the sordid story can be said to have a happy conclusion, the landmark legislation is only part of it. As Sibley notes, the slaughter of the snowy and great egrets "spawned the conservation movement in the United States, including the establishment of the National Audubon Society."* With the cessation of the feather trade, the snowy enjoyed an especially remarkable resurgence, and its population today is generally stable.

---

*The complicated story of the founding, collapse, and resurrection of what we now know as the Audubon Society is deftly recounted by Weidensaul in *Of a Feather*.

. . . .

"Snowies, I guess," I replied to one of my birding companions who was asking about a couple of white herons feeding on a bank of the Altamaha away in the distance. I wasn't sure. They didn't look big enough to be greats, but they were too far away to tell whether their bills were yellow (great) or black (snowy), or to see if they wore the lovely "golden slippers" of the snowy.

"You're right," said our guide. "And one way you can tell, or at least make a good guess, from a distance is that they're feeding so actively. Greats do a whole lot of standing around. Snowies tend to stay busy."

Turns out that the snowy's resourcefulness at feeding itself is one of its most distinguishing characteristics. Audubon was sufficiently impressed to describe one of the bird's many eye-catching behaviors. When feeding in tidal creeks and marsh ponds, he writes, "their motions are generally quick and elegant, and, while pursuing small fishes, they run swiftly through the shallows, throwing up their wings. Twenty or 30 seen at once along the margins of a marsh or a river, while engaged in procuring their food, form a most agreeable sight." BNA *Online* confirms that the snowy has a more extensive repertoire of feeding techniques than any other heron, and the authors proceed to enumerate some twenty or more—including several that make use of those wonderful yellow feet: Foot-Stirring, Foot-Raking, Foot-Probing, and Foot-Paddling. "Foot-stirring," add Parsons and Master, "is particularly suited for small prey consumed by this heron."

Aerial foraging is another of its specialties. The tidal creek that feeds into Myrtle Pond on Little St. Simons Island was thick with greats and snowies, along with other waders, one early April morning during my visit there. Occasionally one of the snowies would take to the air, hover over the slow-moving water, then dip its bill down to snag its prey. "You'll never see a great do that," remarked our incomparable leader Stacia Hendricks.

The snowy's wide wandering after the breeding season, along with its varied diet and feeding behaviors, allowed the great naturalist Herbert Stoddard to watch this bird feed in the late-summer pastures of southwest Georgia. "A dozen or more may be seen associating with cattle or other grazing animals in closely cropped pastures either near or distant from water," he writes. "The birds dart about for insects, at times almost under the feet of the grazing herd. Sometimes one will pick at a fly or other insect on the tender belly of a cow, the reaction to the dagger-like beak being instantaneous and violent. . . . I have in one instance observed a Snowy Egret on the back of a cow; in another case standing sedately on the back of a hog."

Chances are if we've seen snowies at all, we've seen them feed. We're less likely to have seen them court. I haven't, so I'll turn to the experts: "In the full display," writes Bent, "the body is bent forward and downward, the neck is held in a graceful curve, the feathers of the head are raised in a vertical crest, the breast plumes are spread forward and downward, the wings are partially open and raised, and the plumes of the back are elevated and spread, with the curving tips waving in the air. Such a picture must be seen to be appreciated; no written words or printed photograph can do it justice."

Forbush reports that one day in 1877 he had the "good fortune" to watch the courtship rituals of a dozen of these birds from only thirty feet away. Against a dark background of mud and mangrove roots, "their immaculate forms stood out in such bold relief that every detail of movement, shape and plumage was plainly visible. They strutted about, raised, spread and lowered their lace-like plumes, pursued one another back and forth, bowed and turned about, . . . displaying all their airs and graces." He also remarks that if he had known what would happen to the species over the next couple of decades, he would have taken better notes.

Audubon witnessed this bird's most spectacular courtship behavior, though he mistook it for alarm caused by his own intrusion. When the pair are disturbed during their mating ritual, he writes, "they rise high in the air, sail about and over the spot in perfect silence, awaiting the departure of the intruder, then sweep along, exhibiting the most singular movements, now and then tumbling over and over like the Tumbler Pigeon, and at length alight on a tree." In fact, Parsons and Master describe what Audubon saw as "Tumbling Flight," a special aerial display that "consists of male, and perhaps his mate, flying upward and dropping earthward, tumbling over and over until individual rights itself just before landing."

I'm happy to report that I have seen snowy egrets on their nests. On coastal Georgia's St. Catherines Island, in sweltering mid-June, island manager Royce Hayes took us to Greenseed Pond, in the middle of which were two small tree- and shrub-covered islands. Here, relatively safe from the sorts of mammalian predators who prefer not to swim, the wood storks, herons, and egrets had established a dense rookery. At this midpoint in the season, with downy white chicks in many of the nests, we were treated to a graphic view of regurgitative feeding: the parent snowy's bill deep down the throat of its chick and the seemingly violent pumping-up of the food. We could also see several of the birds panting—or "gular fluttering"—to beat the heat, and it looked like their main brooding concern on this particular day was to keep their babies shielded from the sun.

Our proximity didn't seem to bother the birds, so I wasn't surprised to read later that egrets won't leave their young even when in danger themselves. Of course, this devotion made them easy to prey on, not only by humankind. Describing a rookery he visited on the coast of Cape May, Wilson writes, "Great quantities of egg shells lay scattered under the trees, occasioned by the depredations of the Crows, who were continually hovering about the place. On one of the nests I found the dead body of the bird itself, half devoured by the Hawks, Crows, or Gulls. She had probably perished in defence of her eggs."

In fact, snowies are remarkably dedicated parents. Nest construction and incubation are shared occupations, and both parents brood and feed the young. Bent writes that "either the father or mother bird watches the youngsters constantly, and when the absent mate returns they caress and coo, being a most loving pair, as if they had not seen each other for a week." More scientifically, Parsons and

Master talk about the "nest-relief ceremony," in which the returning parent often offers a twig to its partner, which is sometimes then incorporated into the nest.

These beautiful birds make good neighbors, too. They feed peaceably among a variety of other species, including gulls, terns, and ibises, as well as other herons. Their rookeries, like the one on St. Catherines, are sufficiently diverse to meet the most exacting contemporary standards. As Audubon observes, "So very social are they, that they do not appear even to attempt to disturb such other birds as are wont to breed among them, the Night Herons, for instance, the Green Herons, or the Boat-tailed Grackles."

Not that any more could be asked of a bird, but Audubon goes on to add that they even make "excellent eating," particularly after they've plumped up in the autumn. Happily for the lovely egret, we'll have to take his word for it.

. . . .

The "three whirlwinds" in the Welty story are the evangelist Lorenzo Dow, the outlaw James Murrell, and the naturalist John James Audubon. As a rationalist, law-abiding indoorsman, I can't claim kinship with any of the three, but . . .

For my last evening on North Carolina's Outer Banks I decided to return to the Bodie Island Lighthouse Pond. I had given up on the avocets and stilts, but I thought I might catch another glimpse of the bittern I had seen the day before, winging briefly across a neck of the pond then disappearing, utterly, into the marsh grass. Or the northern harrier I had watched as it cruised low, at its leisure, back and forth over the grass and water. Not that it mattered what I saw. John Fussell had steered me to this place—"a great place to be at sunset, especially when it is nearly calm"—and I already knew how right he was.

The October light had been beautiful all day, and the pond seemed absolutely still. I sat alone on the observation deck at the edge of the water, with the lighthouse behind me and, behind it, the setting sun. The marsh grasses began to turn golden, and one by one the great egrets arose from the water and made their graceful way into the lowering sun, toward their nighttime roost. Soon it was just me—and one snowy egret that seemed as reluctant to leave as I was. The bird was in the middle of the shallow water, continuing to feed, and its reflection was so mirror-clear that I wondered why it wasn't confused as to what it was stabbing at. Must not have been, though, because eventually I saw it come up with a little silver minnow, both ends wriggling as the bird held it sideways in its bill. How in the world could it turn the fish without dropping it? But this is what egrets do, and in an invisibly quick motion, the bird swallowed the fish.

Then the gold light faded to shadow, and the snowy at last spread its white wings, lifted itself, and flew slowly past the lighthouse and into the darkening trees.

winter

Sanderling
Calidris alba

My maternal grandfather had seven children. Those seven produced twenty-two, giving me a total of twenty-one siblings and first cousins just on that side of the family. If we drop down another generation — to nephews, nieces, and cousins-at-some-remove — we get a glimpse of overpopulation in action. But my family ain't got nothing on the sandpiper clan.

The family Scolopacidae includes forty-three species in North America alone, including several birds covered elsewhere in these pages: the willet, the ruddy turnstone, the red knot, the dowitcher, the Wilson's snipe, the whimbrel, and the yellowlegs. Knowing your armchair birder as you do, you can believe he is tempted to say, "Enough already." But he must resist. In the first place, casual beachgoing birders (himself included) don't think of any of those birds when they hear the name "sandpiper." And second, any book that purports to take as its subject familiar coastal birds probably ought to have something to say about the birds that people really do see every time they walk on the beach. That is, the peeps.

"Peep" is the general term applied to a few of the small, common sandpipers actually called "sandpiper" — the semipalmated sandpiper, the western sandpiper, and the least sandpiper — and to their close cousin the sanderling. Choate tells us that the name derives from their call notes, so we might say that these are the little shorebirds that, in fact, pipe, or "peep," on the sand. Of the four, the sanderling is the one that I would have the best chance of picking out from the others, so, since I'm the boss here, that's the one we'll focus on.

Not that identifying the little sanderling is at all times easy. In fact, quite unlike the black-bellied plover, for example, or the red knot, or the dunlin, all of which become distinctive during their summer breeding season, the sanderling then becomes more like the other peeps. As Peter Matthiessen writes, "The problem of identifying peeps is compounded in the summer and fall by molts and transitional plumages, which may assert themselves in such disorder that no two birds in ten of the same species look alike. Sanderlings and semipalmated sandpipers are the worst culprits in this respect and may range in August from spring red to winter gray, with myriad scraggy intermediates."

I had noticed this problem in May, in Sanibel, Florida, when I was no longer sure that the sanderlings I had been seeing during the winter and early spring were in fact sanderlings. Their faces, chests, and backs were turning darker, in some cases a rich, reddish brown, and when I looked in my book, I saw that the western and semipalmated sandpipers didn't look a whole lot different. I suppose that if I had been able to coax one into my hand, I could have looked for a hind toe (sanderlings don't have one; other peeps do), but I doubted that they would cooperate.

Now it's January, though, and the sanderlings I'm looking at along central Florida's eastern coast have once again become the conspicuously pale members of the tribe—white face, white underside, and pale gray topside. It's helpful, too, that this will be their look for just about the whole time we're able to see them. As with so many other Scolopacids, the arrival of the breeding plumage signals the departure of the birds.

And once again, it's likely to be a very long journey. As Bent writes, "To the ends of the earth and back again extend the migrations of the sanderling, the cosmopolitan globe trotter; few species, if any, equal it in world-wide wanderings. Nesting in the Arctic regions of both hemispheres, it migrates through all of the continents, and many of the islands, to the southernmost limits of South America and Africa, and even to Australia." The sanderling, however, won't necessarily have to endure the mind-boggling journey of a bird like the red knot because it won't necessarily have wintered at the very southern tip of South America. Its winter range is vast. As Bruce Macwhirter, and others, point out in BNA *Online*, the sanderling is probably the most widespread maritime shorebird wintering in North America, found from southern British Columbia and Massachusetts all the way down to southern Chile and southern Argentina. "Its wintering range thus spans some 100° latitude, encompassing most temperate and tropical beaches in the Americas."

So while you're sure to see sanderlings joining the red knots for the May to June horseshoe crab egg feast on Delaware Bay, they might not have traveled as far to get there. They might have flown up from the eastern coast of Florida, where I had just seen them, or from pretty much anywhere else along our southeastern or Gulf coasts.

Not that I'm any the less impressed — astounded really — by the sanderlings' choice of breeding destination. I understand, in the abstract, that for this brief period of time, conditions — weather, food, habitat — are conducive to reproductive success, but that doesn't stop me from whining, as I did recently to Theresa Hartz, one of our Atlanta Audubon experts: "I'm sorry, I just don't get it." "Well," Theresa replied, "that's because you've never seen the size of the mosquitoes in Alaska."

Still, it seems an arduous quest, and other writers acknowledge as much. Bent correspondent A. L. V. Manniche writes from northeastern Greenland as the sanderlings first arrive: "Here they led a miserable existence. Heavy snow storms and low temperature in connection with want of open water made the support of life difficult for the birds." Likewise Rachel Carson: "There was little food for the migrant birds — lovers of warm sun and green, tossing surf. The sanderlings gathered miserably under a few dwarf willows that were sheltered from the northwest winds by a glacial moraine. There they lived on the first green buds of the saxifrage and awaited the coming of thaws to release the rich animal food of the Arctic spring."

Why not Costa Rica? Why not Tahiti? I know, I know. We're all anthropomorphizing here. Who's to say the birds are miserable, or would be "happier" elsewhere? The system works, has worked forever, and will keep working forever — in the absence of human tinkering. The thaw will come, food will be plentiful, and the birds will go about their business.

Warming temperatures will induce the male sanderling to rise up into his hovering, erratic display flight—unusual in that he neither rises high (just a few feet) nor flies very far. Shortly he returns to his mate, who, says Manniche, awaits him in mute expectation. "He then tries by slow, affected, almost creeping movements to induce her to pairing, until at last the act of pairing takes place; when effected, both birds rush away in rapid flight to return soon after to the nesting place."

Macwhirter and his colleagues see the thing differently, beginning with the alleged silence of the female. "Female initiates copulation," they write, "by displaying in a precopulatory scrape . . . with head low and tail almost vertical, and gives rapid 'low buzzing notes' . . . not unlike the sound of a typewriter carriage in motion." While the simile will be lost on anyone under the age of forty-five, the vocalizations succeed in attracting the male, "who nudges female from scrape. Birds run side by side, rubbing bodies together vigorously" until "male stops female by pressing his lowered bill against her breast. Female stands still and male mounts her back. Male flutters for balance, jabbing at female's head and pulling feathers of her nape and crown. Female eventually dislodges male, usually by running in small circles."

I have to say I much prefer this action-packed account, which also improves on Peter Matthiessen's dismissive observation that the sanderling's lovemaking "has no finesse at all. In this species, tender behavior and an attractive voice are replaced by marked pugnacity and a kind of 'snarling.'" To give Matthiessen his due, though, it must be conceded that the sanderling has never been credited with a melodious voice.

As is typical of tundra-nesting shorebirds, the sanderling doesn't need to be much of an architect. The nest is a shallow scrape lined with a few leaves. Small depressions in the ground may offer some concealment, but better concealment comes from the fact that the nest, as well as the bird in breeding plumage, blends perfectly into the surroundings. Lest the hatched eggshells give away the nest's location, the parents remove them from the vicinity.

Producing precocial chicks reduces to some extent the burden of parenthood—no regurgitative feeding, for example—and the young are out of the nest practically as soon as they hatch. In BNA *Online*'s depiction of that first expedition, however, parenting skill is certainly in evidence. At the time for departure, "parent calls loudly from nest, then leaves and exhibits deliberate feeding motions. Offspring bound out of nest and scramble behind the parent, probing the ground as they go." Also, while the young may forage for their very first meal, they need protection to do so, and the sanderling parents are adept at providing it—often by leading predators on an injured-bird chase. Rachel Carson describes the ingenuity of a mother bird who has spied an Arctic fox nosing around the discarded shells: "As he started up the slope of the ravine the sanderling fluttered toward him, tumbling to the ground as though hurt, flapping her wings, creeping over the gravel. All the while she uttered a high-pitched note like the cry of her own young. The fox rushed at her. [She] rose rapidly into the air and flew over the crest of the ridge, only to reappear from another quarter, tantalizing the fox into following her. So by degrees she led him over the ridge and southward into a marshy bottom fed by the overflow of upland streams."

In fact, one or the other of the parents remains with the young until they fledge, and occasionally this responsibility is complicated by the production of a second set of eggs. A small percentage of sanderlings apparently engage in either "double-clutching" (the same pair producing a second clutch) or polyandry (the female producing a second clutch with a different mate). In such cases, according to Macwhirter, "male incubates first clutch and female leaves shortly after incubation to initiate, incubate, and rear the second clutch." Of course, many northern-nesting birds will try to produce a second set of eggs if the first are lost, but in the case of the sanderling, says Macwhirter, the why and the wherefore are as yet little understood.

Perhaps the reproductive instinct simply surges against the quick dying of the northern summer. In any event, soon enough the sanderlings, old and young, are fleeing the Arctic winter and settling for the off-season on the beaches of the world, much to the delight of beach-strollers everywhere. And, really, this is how we know the sanderling; it's the bird dashing maniacally along the retreating water line to see what food might be uncovered by the backwash, then skedaddling just as madly from the next incoming wave. "They are particularly active and happy during stormy weather," writes Bent, "for then a bountiful supply of food is cast up by the heavy surf. But at all times the surf line attracts them, where they nimbly follow the receding waves to snatch their morsels of food or skillfully dodge the advancing line of foam as it rolls up the beach."

Or we might just see the holes that their probing bills leave behind, which, to the cognoscenti, are as diagnostic as the birds' fast-running feet. "While the semipalmated sandpiper runs about with his head down dabbing irregularly here and there," writes Bent correspondent Charles Townsend, "the sanderling vigorously probes the sand in a series of holes a quarter of an inch to an inch apart in straight or curving lines a foot to 2 feet long. Sometimes the probings are so near together that the line is almost a continuous one like the furrow of a miniature plough."

Or we might see a flock of these birds roosting on the sand, faces to the wind—until the shadow of a raptor sets off their alarm and launches them into the air. "Flying collectively and in prefect unison," writes Theodore Cross, "they loop, weave, and dive at tremendous speed. Now they turn again as a single body, exposing their brilliant white underwings. This pattern of flight, called 'selfish herding,' produces a blinding and flashing effect that makes it difficult for a raptor to track a single bird."

In any case, the small, unobtrusive sanderling is, as Bent says, "one of the characteristic features of the ocean beach." Maybe its very ordinariness, or its wide familiarity, or its colorless winter plumage—one or all of those things—led Wilson to conclude, "The history of this species has little in it to excite our interest or attention."

But Matthiessen, seeing the same bird on the same beach, won't let us ignore the extraordinary accomplishment that brought it there. "One has only to consider the life force packed tight into that puff of feathers to lay the mind wide open to the mysteries—the order of things, the why and the beginning. As we contemplate that sanderling, there by the shining sea, one question leads inevitably to another, and all questions come full circle to the questioner, paused momentarily in his own journey under the sun and sky."

Other Peeps, Briefly

Like the sanderling, the semipalmated, western, and least sandpipers are northern-breeding birds (though not so extremely northern) and therefore more or less long-distance migrants. Our chance to enjoy them, then, is when they're migrating or, more typically, on their wintering grounds. But how do we tell them apart?

First, let's see what's in a name. Are the semipalmated's feet more webbed than the others? No. The semipalmated and the western are both described as having "black legs with small webs between the toes." Not that you'd ever get close enough to tell anyway.

Is the western more closely identified with West Coast than East? Well, yes. The huge migratory flocks of these birds—hundreds of thousands—are more likely to be seen in the West, for instance in Alaska's Copper River delta. But that doesn't help us identify the considerable numbers of these birds that winter along the Gulf and Atlantic coasts.

Is the least noticeably less? Oh heck yes. At a length of six inches from bill tip to tail tip, it's a quarter of an inch shorter than the semipalmated and a half inch shorter than the western. Actually, though (withering sarcasm aside), the least can be distinguished from the other two by having yellow-green legs rather than black. But remember that this is a small bird, usually seen from a distance.

In fact, the experts agree that these peeps can be very hard to tell from one another. Sibley suggests that we consider habitat: "Peeps on small weedy mudflats or grassy edges of freshwater ponds are almost certainly Least Sandpipers, while flocks of hundreds of peeps on open coastal mudflats are sure to be mostly Semipalmated or Western." The western, moreover, is "slightly more likely" than the semipalmated to be found on sandy beaches.

Okay, say I'm on the Florida panhandle in January. There's a small crowd of peeps down the beach, but even with my binoculars they just look like little blobs of grayness. They're on the sand, though—not on a "weedy mudflat"—so maybe I can rule out the least. Western or semipalmated? Wait a minute: my range map tells me, unequivocally, that the semipalmated winters in South America, so am I looking at western sandpipers? Of course, the map also tells me the least winters on the same coasts as the western, and I know it's not true that least sandpipers are *never* seen on the beach. With a spotting scope I could probably make out the color of those legs.

Dang it—I'm going with western. But I ain't betting the condo.

Roseate Spoonbill

Platalea ajaja

"The feathers of the wings and tail of the Roseate Spoonbill are manufactured into fans by the Indians and Negroes of Florida," wrote Audubon in the 1830s; "and at St. Augustine these ornaments form in some degree a regular article of trade."

What for Audubon was an item of curiosity had become by the end of the century a far different matter. Here is an uncharacteristically outraged Arthur Cleveland Bent: "This unique and beautiful species is one of the many which have paid the supreme penalty for their beauty and been sacrificed by the avaricious hand of man, who can never resist the temptation to destroy and appropriate to his own selfish use nature's most charming creatures. . . . All his sordid mind can grasp is the thought of a pair of pretty wings and the money they will bring when made into ladies' fans! And so a splendid bird, once common in Florida and all along the Gulf coast to Texas, has been gradually driven from its former haunts and is making its last stand in a few remote and isolated localities."

Bent goes on to quote noted ornithologist Frank Chapman, writing in 1914: "Only a remnant [of the spoonbill population] was left when the National Association of Audubon Societies protested against the further wanton destruction of bird life, and through its wardens and by the establishment of reservations, attempted to do for Florida what the State had not enough foresight to do for itself." By 1934 Edward Howe Forbush was also sounding the alarm: "Today the Audubon Societies are waging a desperate fight to save the small remnant from any of the several menaces which in a single season might wipe out the few breeding Spoonbills of Florida and add this species to the list of vanished or extirpated birds." Writing for BNA *Online*, Jeannette Dumas sums up the near catastrophe: "Breeders persisted in only a few locations in Florida and Louisiana into the 1940s, and the species was virtually extirpated in Texas until the 1920s."

I almost didn't know what I almost missed.

. . . .

"What a great look at that reddish egret," I said to the woman who happened to be standing next to me at the first big tidal pool along Wildlife Drive in Sanibel, Florida's "Ding" Darling NWR.

"Yeah," she said, "but how 'bout those spoonbills in the trees on the far bank?"

Dang! I looked where she pointed and caught a faint glimpse of pink dropping out of sight into the mangrove thickets. It wasn't much of a sighting, but it was a first, so I figured I'd better count it.

Two weeks later, mid-May, I was on the observation platform behind the visitors center on the causeway to Jekyll Island. The platform overlooks a wide marsh, so everybody's eyes were sweeping the spartina, hoping for the elusive rail or sora, when a voice called out and we all looked up to see a solitary spoonbill cruising lazily low overhead.

In mid-June Dede and I were visiting St. Catherines Island, off the Georgia coast. While our hosts Royce and Christa were taking care of island business, we hopped in their truck to explore the south end of the island. Bumping down an increasingly narrow track, we made it as far as "Jungle Road," where, appropriately, we saw a half-dozen buzzards ascend from the carcass of an animal that looked to be about the size of a wooly mammoth, at which point Dede persuaded me to turn around. On the way back, though, we stopped to walk out on a dike alongside an inviting marsh pond that was sure to be crowded with exotic waders. We saw . . . zilch.

Suddenly Dede said, "What's that?" She pointed to a smudge of pink on the far side of the marsh, but the binoculars brought the lovely bird into clear focus. A first for her, and still by no means old hat for me, but not exactly an intimate encounter. I would spend the rest of the summer and fall without improving much on my distant acquaintance with this bird.

But maybe I was lucky to have seen one at all. Alexander Wilson never did, except for a specimen sent to him in Philadelphia, and he apologized for his "present inability to throw any further light on [its] history and manners."* And though the roseate spoonbill was not, after all, wiped out completely by the fan-making industry, Sibley still classifies it as "uncommon" in its preferred habitats of marsh pond, mangrove swamp, and mudflat.

Then winter came around, and an expedition to central Florida

---

*Audubon had better luck than Wilson, but still had to work hard to secure specimens of this bird. In *Ornithological Biography* he tells a hilarious story about dispatching his son from their boat to wade through the shallow water of an inlet on Galveston Island, in pursuit of the three spoonbills on the further shore. As soon as he got close enough to fire his gun, the party noticed the "back fins of a large fish, resembling those of a shark." Upon its destruction, rendered in rich Audubonesque detail, the fish is discovered to be a "sawfish," twelve feet long, with ten young still alive inside, five or six of which "were put into rum, and ultimately carried to England."

with a party of fellow enthusiasts from the Atlanta Audubon Society. Our primary destination was the justly renowned Merritt Island NWR, a vast preserve spreading out to the north of the Kennedy Space Center, but our veteran leaders, Lisa Hurt and Theresa Hartz, first guided us to the nearby Blue Heron Water Reclamation Facility. Some people like to look at ducks, and those people were made happy by waterfowl species too numerous to keep track of. But this place was also full of waders—wood storks, snowy and great egrets, white and glossy ibises, yellowlegs, tricolored and little blue herons (including immatures still in white plumage), and, yes, at least a dozen roseate spoonbills. These birds, often as close as twenty-five or thirty yards, preened with blithe lack of concern as we scrambled out of automobiles with spotting scopes and binoculars. In the bright morning light they glowed an incandescent pink.

In the afternoon we crossed the Indian River and landed on Merritt Island proper. Lisa, who had been reconnoitering for a week before the rest of us arrived, cautioned us that because of a lingering drought Black Point Trail, usually a highlight, might not live up to expectations. The waterfowlers among us were no doubt disappointed to find wide stretches of cracking mud where, ordinarily, water would have flowed and ducks would have dabbled. But waders don't mind a muddy basin, where they might take their ease in the sun, and as we rounded one bend in the trail, we found ourselves even closer to the birds than we had been that morning. Wood storks sat back on their haunches, or tarsi (a most peculiar sight), and spoonbills rested with their heads turned backward and their bills snuggled between their wing coverts. Some wandered so close that with their "spoons" pinched shut, I could see daylight between their mandibles.

Just off the roadway, where a small creek was pooling with the incoming tide, two spoonbills and two wood storks were doing some fishing, and a great egret was watching with interest. Honestly, these birds were no more than ten feet away, and I am able to report to you that the very crown of a spoonbill's head is (1) featherless and (2) pale green. Both species were foraging in their characteristic manner—sweeping their submerged bills back and forth as they turned slowly through the water. The wood storks appeared to have better luck. Twice I saw one of these birds come up with a fish large enough to require some serious juggling to gulp down. But it's quite possible that the spoonbills were doing fine also—just locating smaller prey (little fish or crustaceans)—and swallowing them without raising their bills out of the water. Besides, as one of my companions astutely noted, "If they were going hungry, they wouldn't be here."

So I've at last had an up-close look at these beautiful and strange birds—so stunningly plumaged and yet equipped, in Forbush's words, "with the absurd spoon-like bill that adds a touch of comedy to what otherwise would be an ideal of beauty." Jeannette Dumas tells us that of the six species of spoonbills found worldwide, the roseate is the only one found in the New World, as well as the only spoonbill with brilliantly colored plumage. She also reports that the "pale-green head" is a feature of the breeding season, which raises a further question.

Roseate spoonbills are what you might call reverse migrators: they tend to disperse northward after the breeding season. And the breeding season can come very early. It's likely that the green-crowned birds I saw in central Florida were just coming into their breeding plumage and were about to head down to the tip of the peninsula to raise their families. But these warmth-loving birds have been known to breed as early as December, so it's possible that the birds we saw had already finished with that chore and wandered northward.

In any case, we saw no mating activity, and, based on the literature available in the visitors center, Merritt Island NWR boasts no roseate spoonbill rookeries. To glimpse these birds on their nests, I might have to make the kind of journey Bent recorded in 1903, to the "far-famed Cuthbert rookery" in "the almost impenetrable mangrove swamps of extreme Southern Florida." After an arduous trek through the swamp, the party at last emerged on the open waters of Cuthbert Lake and in the distance saw a mangrove island covered with birds: "It was a beautiful sight as the afternoon sun shone full upon it; hundreds of white and blue herons, and a score or two of beautiful 'pink curlews' could be plainly seen against the dark green of the mangroves, like feathered gems on a cushion of green velvet."

The nests, wrote Bent, were in the thickest tangles of the red mangroves, near the edge of the water, twelve to fifteen feet above ground. Constructed on horizontal branches, they were larger than the nests of the ibises or the small herons, made of larger sticks, and deeply hollowed and lined with strips of inner bark and water moss. Collecting and delivering the building material is apparently the male's job; actual construction falls to the female.

Of course, all that comes after the male selects his mate, which he does by foreswearing his days of bachelorhood, isolating himself on a potential nest site, and advertising his availability. A head-bob or two might suffice, but if the female is looking the other way, the male can always shake the nearby foliage or wave some sticks around to get her attention. Once she consents, the lines between courtship, nest building, and copulation become blurred.

As Dumas reports, the delivery of nest-building material becomes a form of courtship, leading to the crossing and rubbing of bills as the twigs or sticks are presented and transferred to the female. The female may even crouch and "beg" for the item, clearly a next step in the mating ritual. If the moment is propitious, the male extends a stick across female's back, and both birds take hold and give it a shake. Now the male mounts, and, having let go of the stick, he takes his mate's bill and shakes it instead. The deed is soon done, and once the male hops off, "both shake feathers and preen." Dumas adds that "once begun, copulations appear to occur frequently." One pair copulated three times in under three hours, during which time the male also made eleven stick-collecting trips. Whew.

Bent saw some just-hatched young in the nests he visited, and he describes them as "curious looking birds, flabby and fat, with enormous abdomens and soft ducklike bills." Interestingly, roseate spoonbills are already rosy the moment they enter the world: "their color including bill, feet, legs, and entire skin, was a beautiful, deep, rich, salmon pink," writes Bent, such that their white down could not conceal the color beneath. What Bent doesn't mention, but Dumas does, is that those "ducklike" bills are actually tubular at first, and that the bill tip starts broadening and flattening in the chick's second week.

Climate, it's been said, explains everything, so maybe the torpid heat in which they are engendered explains the spoonbill's slow development. In any case, adult spoonbills shoulder the full load of parenthood, feeding their young by regurgitation — at first even placing the bills of the helpless hatchlings inside their own. Though the young begin to clamber about on the surrounding branches at about two weeks, they return to the nest to be fed until they fledge, at about six weeks. Even then, they remain in the colony for another few weeks, still on the family dole. Moreover, Dumas reports that while they are full-grown when they fledge, they probably won't begin breeding until they are three years old, suggesting a long, carefree adolescence.

Well, who can begrudge these lovely birds whatever ease they might enjoy, especially given the hardships they've endured? Audubon, by the way, considered the spoonbill a wary species, which explained its fondness for the company of herons, "whose keen sight and vigilance are useful to it in apprising it of danger, and allowing it to take flight in due time." If feeding alone, these birds could only be approached by those "expert at crawling over the mud on hands and knees, through the tall and keen-edged saw grass." He recounts an experience in which he did just this, when he took "something short of half an hour" to approach three birds who were less than a quarter mile away.

History tells us that they were not wary enough, and today, if my experience is any indication, they are not wary at all. No doubt they've become accustomed to being shot with cameras rather than guns, and that's a good thing. But I'm not sure we have a conservation success story to celebrate here. The Florida breeding population of roseate spoonbills is a scant 1,100 pairs, and it's listed as a species of special concern, a designation that recognizes its vulnerability to habitat alteration and human disturbance.

In other words, the bird has done all it can. Vigilance now falls to us.

....
Short-Billed Dowitcher
Limnodromus griseus

The first thing that must be said about the short-billed dowitcher is that it has a remarkably long bill. And thus is ushered in a world of confusion. Because the long bill of the short-billed dowitcher is, in many cases, every bit as long as the long bill of the long-billed dowitcher. That's right: after protracted debate, bird experts have arrived at their final decision: the dowitcher comes in two species— the short-billed and the long-billed. The journey to that conclusion was apparently circuitous.

Our early ornithologists, like Wilson and Audubon, had no dog in the fight; every dowitcher they came across they called the red-breasted snipe. Bent would have preferred to take that route also, but by his day the battle had been engaged, though not concluded: "The dowitcher," he wrote, "or, as I should prefer to see it called, the red-breasted snipe, occurs as a species entirely across the American continent. The long-billed dowitcher, the western form, was originally described as a distinct, full species; it has since been reduced to the rank of a subspecies, because of very evident intergradations; and now some very good ornithologists are in doubt as to the propriety of recognizing the two varieties in nomenclature at all."

As Bent saw it, they look alike and they act alike. "I have never been able to discover any differences in behavior between the two forms of the dowitcher," he continues; "their habits are doubtless similar." Forbush, too, would seem to be among the "very good ornithologists" who doubt the wisdom of separating the two species: "It is impossible to distinguish the two forms in the field and an expert can tell them apart only with difficulty even when in the hand. The measurements of bills of the two forms often overlap in length so that the length of the bill cannot be relied upon as a field mark."

Forbush's comment implies, however, that the two species *can* be told apart, albeit with difficulty, and the fact is that the experts have agreed on a couple of distinctions. For example, during the breeding season, the rufous-red color of the underparts is richer and more ex-

tensive on the longbill, covering belly and breast more or less completely, while the shortbill, as Sibley puts it, has "variable rufous
underparts, brightest on foreneck." Another difference is that during
migration or on their wintering grounds (the situations in which we
are likely to see them), the shortbill prefers coastal mudflats with
saline or brackish water, whereas the longbill is more likely to be
seen on shallow freshwater ponds. Finally, while feeding in its preferred habitat, the longbill is inclined to indulge in a "constant soft
chatter," while the shortbill remains silent.

I must say I find it interesting that bill length is *never* mentioned
as a means of distinguishing between the short-billed and the long-
billed dowitcher. While we're at it, let's observe a few other points of
similarity: Difference in size — 11.5 inches for the longbill v. 11 inches
for the shortbill — has to be dismissed as negligible. Outside of the
breeding season, plumages of the two are virtually indistinguishable.
Both employ the same characteristic dowitcher feeding technique
(which we'll return to), and both flash the same white rump in flight.
Sibley sums it all up by saying that the two species are "extremely
similar" and, in effect, dismisses all the other alleged differences by
saying that the birds are "best distinguished" by their flight call: the
longbill's "high sharp *keek* or *pweek*" as contrasted to the shortbill's
"rapid liquid *kewtutu*."

I was the fortunate beneficiary of a pithy lesson in distinguishing
dowitchers on my wintertime excursion to the renowned Merritt
Island NWR in Titusville, Florida. Our Atlanta Audubon group made
a side trip to the nearby Blue Heron Water Reclamation Facility,
where we saw waterfowl and wading birds aplenty, including a
couple of dowitchers. Art Hurt, husband of one of our group leaders
and a fine birder in his own right, realized that these freshwater
ponds might have lured in a longbill, as opposed the shortbills that
would have been much more likely on Merritt Island proper, so he
took the opportunity to launch into a disquisition on the difference
between the two species. He was nailing down an abstruse point
having to do with the angle between bill and eye-stripe when wife
Lisa finally cut him off: "Give it up, Hurt. You can't tell 'em apart."

And there I would be happy to leave it. But the experts would not, and your dutiful armchair birder shouldered the responsibility of getting the rest of the story from BNA *Online.* As Jehl, Klima, and Harris tell it, "The Short-billed Dowitcher was—and long remained—one of the least understood shorebirds, largely because western populations were continually confused with the Long-billed. The situation was rectified when Frank Pitelka (1950) confirmed and extended William Rowan's (1932) thesis that there were 2 species of New World dowitchers and that the Short-billed was polytypic." Once I refocused my glazing eyes on that last word, I had an inkling what it meant, and I was right. Not only is the short-billed dowitcher a species distinct from the long-billed, but it itself has been subdivided into three subspecies, or "races"—*Limnodromus griseus griseus, L. g. hendersoni,* and *L. g. caurinus*—each with distinct breeding areas and migration routes, and separable, if you're Jehl, Klima, or Harris, by plumage and size. Yikes.

. . . .

As you know by now, I admire expertise from afar but warily guard against its coming too close, so let's take a breath and consider for a few moments this bird that lay people like us will do well to recognize as a dowitcher—any dowitcher. If we're on the southeastern Atlantic or Gulf shores in winter, the bird we see will probably be a short-billed dowitcher, but we don't care about that.

What we care about is recognizing that the bird we're looking at is not, for instance, a willet, another shorebird of the sandpiper family with which it shares a generally drab, gray wintertime plumage. But the willet is a taller, leaner bird, and although it has no reason to be ashamed of the length of its bill, it's no dowitcher in that department.

Along these lines, Bent's correspondent Elliot Coues writes of dowitchers that "when feeding at their ease, in consciousness of peace and security, few birds are of more pleasing appearance. Their movements are graceful and their attitudes often beautifully statuesque." But I've seen no other writer dwell on the dowitcher's elegance, and to my mind these words come closer to describing yet another gray sandpiper we have to rule out, the lesser yellowlegs. It's roughly the same size as the dowitcher, too, but, helpfully, it does have those yellow legs, as opposed to the dowitcher's greenish-gray ones. Trying to identify the bird by itself, we can't do much better than Bent's pointed description: "The dowitcher when standing is a fat, chunky bird with . . . a very long bill."

Where the bird most clearly gives its identity away is in its feeding behavior. As it searches for marine worms or crustaceans, it drives its bill into the mudflat or muddy estuary again and again, with an up-and-down action of its head so mechanically repetitive that it is universally described as like a sewing machine.* The dowitchers also proceed methodically forward as they feed, rather than running here and there like so many sandpipers and peeps. As Jehl and his colleagues observe, the bird "most commonly probes around itself with pivoting movements of the body, then makes a step or 2 and repeats process." Audubon noted that in water up to their bellies, "they immersed the head and a portion of the neck, and remained thus sufficiently long to satisfy me that, while in this position, they probed several spots before raising their head to breathe"—an interesting quirk confirmed by later writers.

Foraging behavior might not be an absolute giveaway because the dowitchers could very well be feeding in the company of other birds—like the aforementioned willet, for example, or smaller sandpipers and plovers—who may also be feeding by jabbing their bills into the muck. But if you see, as I did, on Watchtower Pond in northwest Florida's St. Marks NWR, a formation of fifteen of these birds, lined up abreast of one another, sewing-machining their way across the shallow water, you're by golly looking at some dowitchers.

---

*John Murphy, who first pointed this behavior out to me on the Florida panhandle's Alligator Point, said he had heard it suggested that the sewing-machine motion was the source of the name "dowitcher," as a corruption of "dowager." Not so, says Choate: "Before crystallized into its present spelling, it was dowitchee, doewitch, and do-witch from Deutsher (German) or Duitsch (Dutch) snipe to distinguish it from the English (common) snipe."

The short-billed dowitcher nests across northern Canada, though it wasn't easy for ornithologists to pin this breeding territory down. Bent regularly watched the birds pass through Massachusetts in late May, but he hadn't yet learned just where they were headed: "The breeding range of the eastern dowitcher is imperfectly known or not known at all," he wrote in 1927. One of his correspondents located a couple of nests in the "tundralike muskeg" of Alberta, but William Rowan, the dowitcher specialist cited by Jehl, reported that "the nests . . . must be about the hardest of all shore-birds to find." Even today the bird on territory remains somewhat elusive, such that Jehl reports that actual nest-building has never been observed.

Still, nests have been found (simple bowls scraped out of the muskeg and lined with grass and leaves), and breeding behavior has been studied sufficiently to establish one particularly arresting fact: raising the precocial young is the male's responsibility. Both parents incubate the eggs, but as hatching time nears, the mother begins to absent herself, and in one study cited by Jehl, the male by himself oversaw hatching in 90 percent of the nests. If the female is still around when the hatchlings emerge, she's typically gone within a day or two, already migrating southward. It's up to the male to brood, protect, and lead the young to feeding areas during the two weeks before they're able to fly. Shortly thereafter, the season is over, and the males first, followed by the young, head for their wintering grounds.

Maybe the departure of the females has an effect on the male dowitcher's testosterone level. By all accounts, he is a gentle creature, with "aggression toward other species," in Jehl's words, "much less than expected for a bird of its size." Even the approach of a human intruder fails to arouse a defensive response: the birds "simply slink away, looking over shoulder, and disappear into marsh vegetation."

Bent observed that this laid-back personality almost brought about the bird's undoing. "Dowitchers are the gentlest and most unsuspicious of shore birds," he wrote, "which has made them easy prey for the avaricious gunner." Even when flying with other small waders, "the dowitchers generally bunched together in the flock; I once shot four dowitchers out of a mixed flock without hitting any of the smaller birds." Moreover, when the shooting begins, the uninjured birds refuse to flee. "If a flock is shot into, the sympathetic and confiding birds return again and again to their fallen companions until only a pitiful remnant is left to finally escape. Such slaughter of the innocents well-nigh exterminated this gentle species; but, now that it is protected, it is beginning to increase again."

At least there was some rationale for the "slaughter." Wilson, who reported that the dowitchers settle together in such numbers that "eighty-five have been shot at one discharge of a musket," went on to observe that "of all of our sea-side Snipes, it is the most numerous, and the most delicious for the table. From these circumstances . . . it is the most eagerly sought after by our gunners, who send them to market in great numbers." Audubon, likewise, notes that when the huge flocks alight together, "then is the time when the gunner may carry havoc amongst them. . . . It is not at all uncommon to shoot twenty or thirty of them at once. I have been present when 127 were killed by discharging three barrels, and have heard of many dozens having been procured at a shot." This last is undoubtedly a reference to the account from Wilson, whom he does not name, but whom he is, as always, happy to contradict: "When they are fat, they afford good eating, but their flesh is at no time so savoury as that of the common American snipe."

As Bent notes, the passage of the Migratory Bird Treaty Act brought an end to dowitcher hunting, and the bird's numbers began to rebound. Unfortunately, that trend has apparently been reversed in recent decades. Sibley tells us that a "significant" decline in the short-billed dowitcher's numbers over the past thirty years has landed it on the North American Watchlist. How significant? Jehl reports that shorebird surveys in the 1970s, 1980s, and 1990s found such a steady rate of decline that, at least along the East Coast, the short-billed dowitcher may now be "only about half as common as several decades ago."

Curiously, Jehl doesn't offer so much as a hypothesis to explain this decline, so, in the absence of actual information, I'll suggest a few of the usual suspects: changes in the ecology of their breeding grounds resulting from global warming; trashing of their migratory staging areas along the East Coast by human intrusion; and the generally deplorable condition to which Mother Earth's children have rendered her.

There. I've whined. I feel better.

Greater Yellowlegs

Tringa melanoleuca

Lesser Yellowlegs

Tringa flavipes

Carrabelle Beach, along the Florida panhandle, early March: "Yellowlegs, probably lesser. Feeding in shallow water frenziedly. Running and plunging head and chest into the water while legs still moving forward. Comical."

Little St. Simons Island, Georgia, April: "Greater yellowlegs (bill longer than head) running through the shallow surf, stabbing at little silver fish glinting in the sunlight. Also, as they land, spreading tail feathers into a pure-white fan."

Blue Heron Water Reclamation Facility, Titusville, Florida, January: "A close look at a pair of yellowlegs, bobbing their heads, and, taking off, treating us to a ringing alarm call."

I study these journal entries with some amusement. What in the world made me think that the yellowlegs I saw on Carrabelle beach was a lesser? As for the apparently slam-dunk ID on Little St. Simons Island, it's true that the greater does have a longer bill than the lesser, but how good a look could I have possibly have gotten? I know that I did get a good look in Titusville (the most recent of the sightings, and the only one of which I still have an actual memory), but you'll notice that in this case I make no attempt to specify which of the two I'm observing.

So, you see, I've learned something in my months of shorebirding: I've learned how little I know.

I will say this, though: Except for the very possible misidentification, what I had to say about these birds does hit on the peculiarities of their behavior. Here's Sibley's capsule description of the two sandpiper cousins: "Both yellowlegs are tall elegant shorebirds. Alert, noisy, and active, they walk briskly or even run in shallow water, and bob the head and body emphatically when alarmed. . . . Although difficult to tell apart, they are easily distinguished from all other sand-pipers by long yellow legs and long neck, usually graceful actions, and simple gray-brown plumage."

Actually, they're not hard to tell apart if they're standing next to one another; in body mass, the greater is about one-third greater than the lesser. Otherwise, they're quite alike, particularly with re-gard to that eponymous feature—the bright yellow legs—that im-mediately sets them apart from, say, the willet. Audubon, for ex-ample, never realized that there were two species. Though over the course of his wanderings he surely saw both, he described only one, which he called the yellowshank.

Moreover, we birders along the Atlantic and Gulf coasts are about as likely to see the one as the other. Like so many sandpipers, they're northern breeders, but after the season's work is done, both species head for a vast wintering range that includes U.S. coastal areas from California to the mid-Atlantic and on down to Mexico and South America. Forbush writes that the spring migration of the lesser "goes largely up the Mississippi Valley," rather than up the coast, so maybe that really was a greater I saw on Little St. Simons Island in April. But I'm still not looking to take credit.

Plus, if I'm right about the St. Simons sighting, I'm almost cer-tainly wrong about the one on the beach in Carrabelle. Michael O'Brien, in *The Shorebird Guide*, describes the greater yellowlegs as an active forager that "walks quickly with jerky motions and swiftly stabs at the water when prey is found. In deeper water, often runs frantically to chase small fish (a behavior seldom seen in lesser yel-lowlegs)." Likewise, Paul Bartsch, contributing to *Life Histories*, re-ports that he has many times watched the greater yellowlegs "wade out into the shallow water of the bars, moving slowly along with a tilting gait, suddenly lower that long head and neck and proceed to run through the water at a speed which would have done credit to a college sprinter, quickly striking to right and left with its bill."

Now, all observers agree that the lesser is also a "very active for-ager," typically seen moving rapidly through the shallow water and jabbing with its bill at whatever prey might be available. Also, both species occasionally "scythe" their bills back and forth under the water's surface, in the manner of the avocet and others. As one content to deal in broad generalities, I would be happy to conclude that in foraging style, as in so much else, the greater and the lesser are more alike than different. But Chris Elphick and Lee Tibbitts won't have it. Writing in BNA *Online*, they note that the greater "sometimes captures small fish by running toward surface ripples with bill open and lower jaw submerged; will plow surface in this way for some distance, sometimes simultaneously with 1–5 conspecifics, which turn in unison. In contrast, Lesser Yellowlegs rarely feeds on fish." As for the bird I saw in Carrabelle, clearly I was guessing.

If you make the trip to the subarctic regions of Canada or Alaska, you might notice some differences in the two species' breeding behavior also. Sure, both males engage in an "undulating display flight" and sing loudly while they're at it. But once the pair bond has been established, the species take different routes toward the moment of truth. As H. S. Swarth reports to Bent, the "courting antics" of greater males include "running in circles on the sand bars around the object of their attentions," or "posing with upraised, quivering wings," all the while "incessantly uttering the shrill whistle peculiar to the species."

The female of the lesser yellowlegs, however, does not submit to having circles run around her; instead, according to Lee Tibbits and William Moskoff, she leads the ardent male on a "Ground Chase"—sometimes brief, sometimes as long as a couple of minutes. He follows closely behind, uttering increasingly urgent "copulation chatter," until she at last relents and comes to a stop. Now come the "upraised, quivering wings," which these authors designate the "Wing-lifting Ceremony." By whatever name, it is a prelude to what the male must regard as "a consummation devoutly to be wished."

Both species are ground nesters whose habit is to scrape a cup out of the muskeg, and more than anything else they have in common, both defend their nests with noisy vehemence. Bent writes of the greater yellowlegs that the male bird "[flies] out to meet the intruder while he is a long way from the nest, alighting on any available spruce tree, stump, rock, or other eminence, pouring out a steady stream of invective cries and showing the greatest anxiety, but giving not the slightest clue as to the location of the nest. And the female sits so closely on the nest that it is only by the merest chance that she can be flushed."

Contributing to *Life Histories*, J. Fletcher Street describes the behavior of the lesser female: "Once her eggs are laid the female becomes frantic at any intrusion on the nesting grounds, flying from one stub to the next and crying incessantly." But if the intruder conceals himself, she will "at length become silent, look about inquiringly and take a short flight to the ground and run to the nest [where] she sits low and close." So low and close, in fact, that I've seen reports of lesser females allowing researchers to lift them off their nests.

Moreover, Elphick and Tibbits note that, in both species, defense of the nest often goes far beyond perching and scolding. The treetop vantage allows for long-range vigilance, and when a potential predator approaches, scolding gives way to chasing, circling, and mobbing. "Alarming birds will persist for considerable time, often following intruder until it has retreated some distance." The two species might even team up: "During late brood-rearing period, parents of neighboring Greater and Lesser Yellowlegs broods jointly mob predators." Of which there are plenty, by the way: In addition to the intrusive human type, yellowlegs must fend off airborne predators like bald eagles, northern harriers, merlins, peregrine falcons, herring gulls, and American crows, to name a few of the most familiar.

The birds seem to have both courage and resiliency. Theodore Cross has a vivid memory of a day in Manitoba when a lesser yellowlegs, "intent on protecting her nearby nest, perched on [his] head." Peter Matthiessen writes that the only time he ever saw a peregrine falcon actually succeed in overtaking a fleeing shorebird, "the victim was a lone yellowlegs, caught low over the Sagaponack flats." The bird "was knocked spinning to the ground like an old feathered pin-wheel," he recounts. "But the falcon, out of apathy or inexperience, did not turn fast enough to pin it down, nor did it pursue the wind bird very far when the latter pulled itself together and took off again with an impressive turn of speed."

Indeed, whether breeding during the summer or foraging during the winter, it is their remarkable wariness — and readiness to cry out at the first hint of danger — that finally renders the two species indistinguishable. As Bent puts it, both birds have justly earned the sobriquets "telltale" and "tattler," "for their noisy talkative habits are their best known traits. They are always on the alert and ever vigilant to warn their less observant or more trusting companions by their loud, insistent cries of alarm that some danger is approaching." Many sportsmen have been vexed when the shriek of the yellowlegs has frightened away more desirable game, he continues, "and many a yellow-legs has been shot by an angry gunner as a reward for his exasperating loquacity."

Cross goes so far as to credit these birds with altruism: "When the yellowlegs gives the screaming warning call, she is directing the predator's attention to herself, thus giving other birds a better chance of survival." Well, maybe. But I believe I prefer Forbush's assessment: "This shy, wild bird seems always on the lookout for danger and its cries of alarm are well understood by every wild denizen of marsh and shore."

Another feature of the alarm system exhibited by both species is the characteristic head-bobbing. Audubon wrote that, when alarmed, the birds "generally run to some distance before they take wing, stop as if to discover your intention, vibrate their body backwards and forwards, . . . and, as if convinced that you are bent on mischief, spring up." Similarly, William Brewster reports to Bent that the lesser seems the "exact counterpart" of the greater with respect to general appearance and behavior — including "the same habit of tilting its body and alternately lengthening and shortening its neck with a bobbing motion, when suspicious of danger and about to take wing."

And so it goes, with one writer after another—including yours truly, above—taking note of this curious tic. As far as I can tell, though, only Peter Matthiessen offers a physiological explanation: The head-bobbing, he writes is "executed while the bird is standing still, in open surroundings; the birds are thus enabled to judge the distance of the approaching threat by obtaining a fix at different angles to the horizon."

Finally, the two species have in common a history of being hunted quite mercilessly. Presumably, the larger bird would make the likelier target, but perhaps because of its overall greater population and stronger tendency to flock together, the lesser yellowlegs has been slaughtered in more remarkable numbers. According to Bent, a gunner from the mid-1800s reported that he killed 106 of the birds "by discharging both barrels of his gun into a flock while they were sitting along the beach." Forbush adds that the lesser yellowlegs is more easily hunted because it is less shy than its larger cousin, but he adds that both birds are "persistently sought by the gunner" and that the numbers of the greater yellowlegs, in particular, "have been greatly reduced in the last twenty years."

Bent never liked hunting any bird that, like the yellowlegs, "decoys very easily [and] returns again and again to the slaughter," and he hoped to see the species removed from the list of game birds. In fact, that's what happened, with the passage of the Migratory Bird Treaty Act of 1918. And if, before that time, hunting had indeed diminished the numbers of these birds, they have since rebounded. Populations of both species are deemed stable, and neither is considered threatened or endangered.

. . . .

I'm so glad of that, so glad that I've seen these wonderful birds and can hope to see them again. I'm editing my journal, though. I'm saying that both on the beach in Carrabelle and on Little St. Simons Island in April, it was the greater yellowlegs I saw. As for the two birds at that water treatment facility in January, I'm still holding fire.

And I'll add this: sometimes it just ain't easy. I saw a pair of yellowlegs another time—on the little preserve that surrounds the

Georgia DNR station in Brunswick. A bunch of birders were on a walkway over a stretch of marsh pond, and way off—I mean *way* off—across the water the birds flew in and landed in the shallows. With my binoculars I could just make out the yellow legs when I heard an authoritative voice behind me: "Greater yellowlegs."

Unh unh. No way he coulda known that.

Wilson's Snipe

Gallinago delicata

> For here thy bill
> Suited by wisdom good
> Of rude unseemly length doth delve and drill
> The gelid mass for food.
> —John Clare

Todd Engstrom and I were heading back toward Highway 98, the quiet stretch of the old two-lane blacktop that runs along Florida's "forgotten coast." We had been birding on Bald Point, which juts out into Ochlockonee Bay so you can look back across the water toward Panacea. It was a chilly but beautiful February morning, not a breath of wind rippling the bay water, and we had seen some fine birds, including a bald eagle with a couple of young out on a distant oyster bar.

I probably ought to mention that Todd didn't know me from Adam, and while I'm at it I'll throw in that this was Valentine's Day. Point being: he probably had better things to do than serve as birding guide to some stranger who, at the suggestion of a mutual friend, had e-mailed him from out of the blue a couple of days earlier. But what I was discovering in these months of actual birding, as opposed to the armchair variety, was that a lot of birders are like that. It's an enthusiasm they seem to enjoy sharing, and, mercifully, they're not real picky about whom they share it with.

Still, it was getting on past noon and Todd had obligations, so we were making time back down Bald Point Road when he suddenly slammed on his brakes and threw his Toyota truck in reverse. He backed up fifty yards or so and rolled to a stop.

He leaned over to look out my window. "Snipe."

"What? Where?"

"Right there on the side of the road."

I saw nothing except the mottled browns, grays, and yellows of a boggy coastal roadside in winter.

"Straight out your window, twelve feet away, on the ground."

"Well, I'll be doggone." There they were, two of them, emerging from invisibility, absolutely motionless. We watched for a full minute — with binoculars, a great look. "Are they, like, holding still waiting for prey?" I asked, dimly.

"They're hiding from us," replied Todd, kindly. Another car was coming down the road behind us, so we pulled away at last.

With his Ph.D. from Florida State and long experience as a wildlife biologist (including a stint as the associate director of FSU's Coastal and Marine Laboratory in nearby St. Teresa), Todd had plenty of street cred. But somehow spotting those snipe as we sped by at fifty miles an hour — that's *road* cred.

. . . .

"Note the *extremely long bill*," says Peterson. It's hard not to. The thing seems as long as the bird's entire body. And with such an apparatus, of course, a snipe doesn't *wait* for prey; it probes for prey, often plunging that three-inch dagger into the soft ground all the way to the hilt. What then, though? If it discovers a little morsel in the muck, can it use its bill as a straw and just suck it up? This was "a question still undetermined in my mind," Benjamin T. Gault reported in *Life Histories*. "The glasses however brought out the important information that the probing or feeling movements of the bill were accompanied every now and then with a guttural or swallowing motion of the throat, which at times developed into a decided gulp, as though large morsels of some kind were being taken down, and this *without the removal of the bill from the muck*."

Writing for BNA *Online*, Helmut Mueller confirms that snipe sometimes do "swallow small prey without withdrawing bill from soil," but he cites current opinion that, rather than being vacuumed, food is "moved up the backward-projecting serrations inside the bill by movements of the tongue." If the item is too big — an earthworm, for example — the snipe will "extract and beat into several pieces before swallowing." Or, if the muck isn't mucky enough, the snipe might feed "by stamping feet or bouncing up and down, apparently to startle prey into moving. Can thus find prey near surface or in soils too hard for probing."

Now, as to just what these prey items are, I prefer Audubon's account: "The food of our Common Snipe* consists principally of ground worms, insects, and the juicy slender roots of different vegetables, all of which tend to give its flesh that richness of flavor and juicy tenderness, for which it is so deservedly renowned." He goes on to note that many "epicures" prefer their snipe with viscera included, "the intestines in fact being considered the most savoury parts." But he's had a close look and isn't buying. "On opening some newly killed Snipes, I have more than once found fine large and well-fed ground worms, and at times a leech, which I must acknowledge I never conceived suitable articles of food for man."

As I can testify, along with its fabulous bill, the snipe is most notably equipped with an incredible talent for camouflage. Its characteristic behavior is to move around on the ground, bill pointed downward, looking for likely probing spots. But at the first sign of disturbance, says Bent, "it squats for concealment . . . ; the longitudinal stripes on its back and head so closely resemble prostrate stems of dead grass that the bird is difficult to distinguish." You have to just about step on one to get it to move, and if you do, you're treated to another bit of characteristic snipe behavior — the familiar *scaipe* note sounded as the bird suddenly flushes and flies off in its zigzag pattern. "This note has been variously expressed in writing," says Bent, "perhaps best by the word 'escape,' which the snipe often does, unless the sportsman is smart enough to say 'no you don't,' and prove it."

The snipe makes another, more musical sound, which has caught the admiring attention of writers throughout the ages. Bent, as well as anybody, captures its haunting quality: "All through the spring migration and all through the nesting season we may hear the weird

---

*Learned ornithological disputations notwithstanding, for the purposes of this essay the Wilson's snipe and the common snipe are interchangeable. Period.

winnowing sound of the snipe's courtship flight, a tremulous humming sound, loud and penetrating, audible at a long distance. One is both thrilled and puzzled when he hears it for the first time, for it seems like a disembodied sound, the sighing of some wandering spirit, until the author is discovered, a mere speck sweeping across the sky."

Audubon, too, was enchanted by the snipes' "rolling notes mingling together . . . falling faintly on the ear," and, predictably, he had his opinion as to how the sound is produced, already a subject of debate way back in his day. It cannot result, he writes, "simply by the beatings of the wings, as at this time the wings are not flapped, but are used in sailing swiftly in a circle not many feet in diameter." He was right, in so far as he went. The eerie "winnowing" is not produced "simply" by the wings, but neither is it a vocalization. "It is produced," says Mueller, "by airflow over outstretched outer rectrices of spread tail, modulated by beating of wing." Mueller compares the sound to a screech owl's call, and based on the recordings I've heard, that's close enough to be helpful.

Back on terra firma after the aerial maneuvers, two males might have to square off. At the pitch of the battle, they leap up, beat on each other with their wings, and duel with those awesome bills. The winner gets to strut before his chosen spouse, tail erect and fanned wide, like so many of our gallinaceous birds. When the eggs come along, though, you'll need a DNA test to determine the father. Both male and female are promiscuous. Leslie Tuck (Mueller's primary source) reported an incident in which two males copulated with the same female and then tried to copulate with each other. "Although occasional sparring occurred, episode lasted 42 min."

If you live up north, and get lucky, you might come upon a snipe nest. Just be careful. You won't see the sitting mother, and she's so protective she won't leave unless she *really* has to. W. J. Brown reported to Bent that in one instance he was able to stroke the bird on the back and then had to lift her off the nest to photograph the eggs. If she does flush, however, she'll do her damnedest to get you to come after her and leave the nest alone. After accidentally frightening a mother from her nest, wrote another of Bent's correspondents, "looking ahead I saw the creature, who with outspread tail and wings, was fluttering on the damp earth, and with her long bill down in the mud, was giving vent to a series of squeaking sounds. I knew at once that . . . the object of her actions was to draw my attention from something that she was very desirous to conceal."

If the mother's vigilance is rewarded, the precocial hatchlings start to get restless as soon as they are out of the shell. On long legs and big feet, they scramble up onto their mother's back or over the edge of the nest and out into the wide world—until the mother is able to brood them back home again. Mueller adds this interesting note: "Male usually leaves nest with first 2 of hatched chicks; female takes last 2. Apparently no contact between mates afterward."

. . . .

Given that the snipe is one of the world's most popular game birds, it's odd to me that "snipe hunt," used figuratively, has come to denote the sort of prank wherein the credulous city slicker is left "holding the bag," alone, in the middle of the woods—to the great amusement of the local folk. The fact is that some snipe hunters have been so spectacularly successful that Bent, writing in the first half of the twentieth century, became alarmed about the bird's population. In particular, he had in mind "the oft-quoted achievements" of one James J. Pringle, who "was not a market hunter but a gentleman (?) sportsman" [question mark Bent's].

"The birds being such great migrants," Pringle had written, "and only in the country for a short time, I had no mercy on them and killed all I could, for a snipe once missed might never be seen again. I shot with only one gun at a time; had no loader, but loaded my gun myself; had I shot with two guns and had a loader I would, of course, have killed a great many more birds, but in those days and in those parts it was impossible to get a man that could be trusted to load."

How did Pringle fare under these harsh constraints? "His best day, undoubtedly a world record," writes Bent, "was December 11, 1877, when he shot in six hours 366 snipe and 25 other birds." During the winter of 1874–75 he killed 6,615 snipe. The grand total for the 20 years 1867 to 1887: 69,087 snipe (along with three thousand other game birds).

Given such a record of mayhem, it was easy for Bent to conclude that this bird "was formerly exceedingly abundant, but its numbers have been sadly depleted during the past 50 years by excessive shooting." Actually, his fears may have been misplaced. Though snipe hunters are still having plenty of luck (with an estimated annual take of 500,000 to 900,000 birds), there's no agreement that this prodigious haul has any impact on the bird's population, which apparently remains stable.

But now I'm rethinking: If "snipe hunt," in that other sense, means "making a fool out of yourself looking for something you'll never see," maybe I do get it. They say that the winter snipe population in Florida pushes 11 million, but based on my experience with Todd, if I set out by myself to try to find one, the locals would be smirking.

· ·

American White Pelican
Pelecanus erythrorhynchos

"Have you seen the white pelicans yet?" asked Dale Henderson, whom I had called as soon as I arrived on Cedar Key. John Murphy, my old friend on the Florida panhandle, had put me in touch with Dale. He told me she was the best bird person he knew on the island.

"Where are they?" I asked. "I'm dying to see the white pelicans."

"Just head back out the causeway in the morning. The tide will still be low. You'll see 'em."

Cedar Key, on Florida's Gulf coast due west from Gainesville, is a quiet little island town favored by birds, artists, and clammers. I knew of the place only because my cousin Elsa, who lives in Atlanta, had recently inherited a small cottage there, hidden away behind an overgrown privet hedge on Sixth Street. About all that needs to be said about the condition of the house is conveyed by the signs posted in the kitchen. On the oven door: "No oven." On the wall above the microwave, toaster, and coffeemaker: "Caution! Use only one appliance at a time." Above the toaster: "Toast does not pop up on its own."

But I can't resist saying a little more. Because the artist aunt from whom Elsa had inherited the house had made the long trip from her home in the North Carolina mountains only rarely in recent years, the place had fallen into disrepair. After the change in ownership, Gerald, the artist from across the street, had moved several tons of his equipment, supplies, and works in progress into the formerly spacious front room, with the understanding that in exchange for this usurpation he would undertake the house's gradual renovation. Cousin Elsa is also a painter, but she had found the old house more a tax liability than an artistic asset and finally put it on the market, bringing the restoration project to an untidy halt.

I wasn't complaining. The plumbing worked, two of the eyes on the gas range worked, and, propped up on a makeshift table, the half-sized refrigerator hummed away. Stepping through the wall (a frame of studs from which ruined plaster had been stripped away)

183

and into what was apparently the one bedroom, I found two couches facing each other, and I was welcome to sleep on whichever I chose.

Some neighborhood bird's loud trill woke me up at seven. I didn't know how long that tide would still be low, so I put the water on for coffee and was out of the house by eight, walking east toward the mainland. A mile or so later, at the bridge over the Number Three Channel, I saw something soaring over the mudflats way off to the south.

There they were, sure enough. A dozen in the air, those beautiful black-and-white wings stretched out in a graceful glide. As they dropped down to land, I saw more, dozens more, maybe hundreds, taking it easy on the flats, probably waiting for what the tide would bring in.

In fact, this wasn't my first look at these majestic birds, but the white pelican is not a bird you see every day, nor one you quickly tire of looking at. But there was a cold February wind blowing hard across that bridge, and I was still tired from the long drive the day before, so I said "mission accomplished" and turned back toward town to find some breakfast.

About the time I lowered my nocs, though, a pickup truck rolled to a stop beside me, and a curly haired brunette woman leaned out the window.

"You birding?" she asked.

"Yeah. I'm getting a look at all the white pelicans out there on the flats." I probably said that like I knew something, but she wasn't impressed.

"You need to go another half mile out of town," she said. "On your left. There's an old clamming operation. They're all there."

Birders. Sheesh. I started walking, but without much enthusiasm. Hadn't I already seen the white pelicans? I walked on for a few minutes, wondering if this woman had any concept of "half mile." I checked the time on my cell phone and told myself that I would walk another ten minutes. In about five I got to the place, a wide tidal basin surrounded by marshland.

Hundreds more white pelicans, but now the feeding frenzy had begun. They flattened themselves in the shallow (but obviously food-filled) tide pools, then scooted forward with those enormous bills wide open, stood up to swallow, then did it again. It was quite a thing to see.

Of course, the woman hadn't meant that all the white pelicans were there; she meant all the wading birds. And she was right. Great blue, little blue, and tricolored herons. Great and snowy egrets. Dowitchers. Willets. Black-necked stilts, for God's sake. Dozens of white ibises. And that brown bird feeding among the ibises, with a decurved bill like theirs—was that a whimbrel? (No, Dale would tell me later on the phone. It was probably an immature ibis.)

Watching birds like this is like eating great food. After a while, you can't take any more in. Like the woman had said, they were all there. I watched as long as I could stand it.

. . . .

Where I had already seen white pelicans, most spectacularly, was on Cat Island, a tiny but incredibly bird-dense rookery out in the middle of the Mississippi Sound. Sto Stowers had showed me this amazing place, a thirty-minute boat ride from his house on Dauphin Island, just off of Mobile. The great birds rose from the beach at our approach, circled and settled out on the water, where they would patiently await our departure. Up close like that I could appreciate their size, but I was still surprised to read that they weigh twice as much as brown pelicans and that their wingspan is thirty—that's right, thirty—inches greater.

Sto pointed out that they had already developed the knobby protrusion on top of their bill that indicated the onset of breeding season, which meant that we had caught them just in time. In another week—maybe in another day—the white pelicans would be gone from the Gulf coast and from the Atlantic beaches of Florida and Georgia. They would be headed north to the upper Midwest and Canada, where (oddly to me) they nest on islands in freshwater lakes and change their diet to perch, trout, and carp.

Roger Evans and Fritz Knopf, writing for BNA *Online*, offer a detailed account of how these birds go about their business on their breeding grounds. To summarize briefly, the thing often gets under way with a "strutting walk," the two birds parading single file with heads erect, the male following the female and (presumably to keep her on task) jabbing at her all the while. When the female bows at the nest site, the time has come: "Male mounts and grasps back of female's head or neck, waves wings, grunts."

They don't build much of a nest. Bent describes it as a "mere depression in the bare earth, with usually a more or less complete rim of dirt and rubbish raised around the edges." Neither parent leaves the site to fetch nesting material; the sitting bird simply scrapes up whatever is at hand. Evans and Knopf note that the end result is "often trampled and poorly defined, providing only limited protection against eggs rolling out or movements of chicks."

The mama bird typically lays two eggs, and the hatchlings are altricial—"naked, blind, and helpless," writes Bent, "of a livid flesh color, and most unattractive in appearance." One of his correspondents, William Finley, vividly describes the process by which the young are fed: "The parent regurgitated a fishy soup into the front end of its pouch and the baby pelican pitched right in and helped himself out of this family dish. As the young bird grew older and larger, at each meal time he kept reaching farther into the big pouch of his parent until finally, when he was half grown, it was a remarkable sight. The mother opened her mouth and the whole head and neck of her nestling disappeared down her capacious maw while he hunted for his dinner in the internal regions."

That part of the survival game sounds simple enough, but the life of the young pelican has its hazards. Bent writes that "as is generally the case with the larger birds, pelicans are not at all solicitous for the welfare of their eggs or young." At the approach of intruders, they think of their own safety first. Conveniently for bird collectors and hungry gulls, he notes, "the white pelicans promptly depart and leave their nests to be despoiled." If that danger is escaped, a greater one awaits—for the smaller of the two nestlings. The first-hatched and therefore larger chick will make every effort not only to hog all the food, but also to abuse its poor sibling, constantly biting or pecking it on its head or back. The result is usually siblicide, the smaller chick dying either from starvation or from being driven from the nest and devoured by those rapacious gulls.

Does this Cain-like malevolence bring retribution from an angry God? Actually, if I may mix my Biblical references, when white pelican parents and their new-fledged children arrive on their mild wintering grounds—stretching from southern California and across Mexico to the southeastern coasts—they find a land of milk and honey.

Their food arrives dependably on the incoming tide, and white pelicans are adept at securing it. Every observer has noted that, unlike the brown pelican, which dives headfirst into the water to catch fish, the white pelican uses a coordinated flanking maneuver to drive its prey shoreward for easy pickings. In a single extended line, writes Audubon, the pelicans "at once spread out their broad wings, press closely forward with powerful strokes of their feet, drive the little fishes toward the shallow shore, and then, with their enormous pouches spread like so many bag-nets, scoop them out and devour them in thousands."

There didn't seem to be a lot of teamwork involved in the scoot-

and-gobble method I witnessed on Cedar Key, but apparently the birds' cooperation can be pretty remarkable. Sibley writes that the pelicans sometimes divide into two lines, "'mirroring' each other and driving the fish into the narrowing space between them." Or the birds might deploy a semicircular formation, which Evans and Knopf describe as "highly coordinated, with almost perfectly synchronized bill dipping."

So is that about it, then, in terms of having to get out there and earn a living? Audubon seems to think so: White pelicans "appear almost inactive during the greater part of the day, fishing only soon after sunrise, and again about an hour before sunset." But take a closer look at that inactivity. Those bills are pretty doggone critical, and they need to be kept in serviceable condition. So what these pelicans are really doing, says Sibley, is maintaining their elasticity by "performing pouch exercises, throwing the head back with the bill open, or even tucking the head down and turning the pouch inside-out over the breast."

With the exercise out of the way, all that's left is soaring, another occupation for which these birds show great aptitude, and at which they seem to expend very little effort. "I know of no more magnificent sight in American bird life," writes Bent, "than a flock of white pelicans in flight. . . . At intervals it sails for long distances on motionless, decurrent wings, a perfect picture of aerial grace and dignity." The majesty of the performance survives even the telegraphic syntax of BNA *Online*: "Much thermal soaring on sunny days. . . . Soaring birds attract others into flock. Soar upward, often beyond view of unaided eye or binoculars (10X). At destination, set wings, circle downward without flapping, often from great heights."

Eating, sunning, and soaring. Forbush admirably sums up this diurnal cycle: "On the coast they sat on the sands at low water, and as the tide flowed in, they sailed calmly and majestically out over the shallows, formed long lines at a distance from the shore and parallel to it, and then beating the water with their great wings, closed in toward the beach, driving before them the little fish, which they scooped up in their capacious pouches. Then after sitting sluggishly for a time the great white birds, with heads drawn backward on their shoulders, rose into the air in flocks and sailed grandly, sweeping in wide circles up into the blue dome, rising to enormous heights and floating there for long periods apparently to enjoy the cooling breezes of those high altitudes."

An enviable life, but this great bird inspires no resentment. A "truly beautiful bird," writes Audubon, with "the natural cleanness of its plumage" and "the brightness of its eyes [that] seemed to me to rival that of the purest diamond." Bent calls it "really a glorious bird, the spotless purity of its snow-white plumage offset by its glossy black wing feathers and enriched by its deep orange bill and feet."* He adds to the encomium by describing the white pelican as "a gentle bird of mild disposition" that "never makes any trouble for its neighbors on its breeding grounds" and, except for the occasional predatory gull, "seems to have no enemies."

Bent correspondent (and noted turn-of-the-century ornithologist) Frank Chapman lists one more virtue: the bird's ancient pedigree: "We must also accord to pelicans that respectful attention which is the due of extreme age," he writes. "Pelicans became pelicans long before man became man, a study of the distribution of the eleven existing species leading to the conclusion that at least as late as the latter part of the Tertiary period our white pelican, and doubtless also other species, presented much the same appearance as it does today."

Audubon worried that "the constantly increasing numbers of our hostile species" were forcing the white pelican to migrate ever further northward, seeking "security from molestation" in "wild and uninhabited parts of the world." *BNA Online* confirms that until the 1960s the continental population of white pelicans was considered threatened by a variety of circumstances, including human distur-

---

Erythrorhyncos combines the Greek words *erythro* ("red") and *rhyncos* ("beak"). Ernest Choate glosses this etymology by noting, "At least it is of an orange color."

bance. The good news is that improved protective legislation and greater public awareness have helped not just to arrest but to reverse the bird's decline, and that its population has been gradually increasing in recent years.

So, yes, I've seen the white pelicans. They're fine, thanks.

Black Skimmer
Rynchops niger

The more I watch all these shorebirds, the more tempted I become
to generalize that songbirds have it easy. A good many of them, of
course, have figured out that if they just make an appearance in a
suburban yard, the homeowner will come running out with a bushel
of sunflower seeds. Those that don't like seeds can find a thousand
insects per square inch of plant material, it seems, and for the fruit-
and berry-pickers, well, the food's just sitting there, right?

These fish-eaters, though. . . . Heck, I can't catch a fish with a
hook, worm, and bobber unless the farm pond's been overstocked.
But we have dozens of species of birds who make their living catching fish—without the first tool to abet the enterprise. Some, like
brown pelicans and terns, dive from on high, head-first, to catch fish
in their bills; ospreys do likewise, but somehow pull out at the last
instant and sink their talons into the fish's back. Great blue herons
stand motionless, then stab like lightning when prey comes near.
Cormorants and anhingas just dive under and swim after the fish, for
goodness' sake. And then we have the black skimmer.

The first time you saw this bird feeding, (1) did you know what
it was doing? And (2) if you did, could you believe it? Of course,
the facts are familiar to even casual bird-watchers. The black skimmer skims along just above the surface, slicing the water with his
longer lower mandible, then, when it touches something, the bill
snaps shut to trap the prey. But the wonder remains: how could such
a thing be? Theodore Cross observes that "the skimmer is the only
bird that has been clever enough to develop a lower jaw that is not
only springloaded but longer than its upper beak." But what I want
to know is when the bird got so clever. Did the skimmer start skimming and then gradually develop the special adaptation to make
the technique productive? Or did the bird find itself with this oddly
adapted bill and then decide it ought to start skimming to put it to
use? (As Bent points out, young skimmers, before they learn to fly,

have to feed on what they can pick up along the water's edge. "At this time," he writes, "the mandibles are of equal length. The long lower mandible of the adult would be a serious handicap in feeding, and therefore it is not developed until the bird has learned to skim the surface of the water for its food.")

In any case, no writer can fail to comment on this wonderfully bizarre feeding technique. Audubon's account is notable for what he apparently got wrong. With the lower mandible slicing the water, he writes, and "with wings raised and extended, [the skimmer] ploughed as it were, the element in which its quarry lay to the extent of several yards at a time, rising and falling alternately, and that as frequently as it thought it necessary for securing its food when in sight of it; for I am certain that these birds never immerse their lower mandible until they have observed the object of their pursuit, for which reason their eyes are constantly directed downwards like those of Terns and Gannets."

On the contrary, experts today agree that the skimmer is purely a tactile, not visual, feeder. "Skimmers feed by touch," writes David Allen Sibley, "which allows them to feed at dawn, dusk, and even at night, when prey may be closer to the water's surface than during the day." He goes on to explain that "when the lower jaw contacts prey, the head snaps downward and the prey is gripped by the bill, tossed up, and swallowed. This method, which relies entirely on chance contact with fish, requires a high density of prey at the water's surface. Skimmers forage mainly at night when small fish rise to the surface of sheltered waters."

I confess that I had never thought about when skimmers skim. I know I've seen them during the day; otherwise I wouldn't have seen them. But it could have been late afternoon or early evening. Audubon, along with other writers, agrees with Sibley that skimmers are for the most part nocturnal feeders. "They spend the whole night on wing," he writes, "searching diligently for food." Bent, however, having often seen this bird feeding in broad daylight, suggests that "it is more influenced by the tides than by anything else, for these at certain stages make its food more accessible."

Right, says Rachel Carson; the skimmers like to feed on the rising tide, which is why they are called "flood gulls." The black skimmer is one of the species Carson focuses on in her lovely book *Under the Sea-Wind*, and in this passage she credits the bird with ingenuity as well as technique: "Sometimes the vibrations [of the bill slicing the water] tell of food animals like small shrimps or oar-footed crustaceans moving in swarms overhead. And so at the passing of the skimmer the small fishes came nosing at the surface, curious and hungry. Rynchops, wheeling about, returned along the way he had come and snapped up three of the fishes by the rapid opening and closing of his short upper bill."

Whenever it happens, it's a hell of a thing to watch. Bent writes of the sheer pleasure he feels as the skimmers "quarter back and forth over the same ground again and again, cutting the smooth surface of the water with their razor-like bills, scaling, wheeling, and turning like giant swallows, silently engrossed in their occupation for which they are so highly specialized."

. . . .

"That's my favorite bird!" hollered my sister Susan when we saw a skimmer skimming at Fripp Island, South Carolina, on a recent family vacation. Why not? It's a looker on the ground—sharp black-and-white plumage and fabulous two-toned bill—beautiful in flight, and amazing when it drops that mandible into the surface and glides along like sharp scissors through gift wrap. As Peter Cashwell puts it, "Cool just drips from these birds." We sat on the patio of our rented beachfront house, sipped our beverages, and took in the performance.

That was typical of my experience with this bird—seeing an individual skimmer, maybe two, cutting the surf on a given day at the beach. Then I made my memorable trip to Cedar Key, on Florida's west coast, where I had found the tidal creeks and estuaries brimming with white pelicans, waders, and shorebirds. As I was leaving the island, I decided to have another go at the renowned Shell Mound, situated a few miles out of town in the middle of Cedar Key National Wildlife Refuge. Dale Henderson, my contact in Cedar Key, had agreed to meet me there the day before, but we arrived at high tide and in a steady rain, and the mudflats that would otherwise have been covered with feeding birds were covered with water, so we sat in her car and marveled at the variety of marsh grasses surrounding the flats.

This time the day was beautiful—sunny, cool, and breezy—and I could walk out on the little fishing pier and enjoy the vista. Not surprisingly, since I was there at about the same hour as the day before, the tide was again in, and I saw a lot of water, broken by a couple of the refuge's coastal islands off in the distance. I was standing in the middle of the 50,000-or-so acres where the Lower Sewanee River breaks apart to feed into the Gulf, one of those beautiful places of shifting boundaries between land and water and, except for that dock, nary a trace of human habitation as far as the eye can see.

But how about birds? Yes, it was high tide, but just a hundred yards or so off the pier was an exposed oyster bar, covered in black. I took a look through my binoculars and saw a blanket of black skimmers, maybe two hundred, maybe more. Just beyond was another exposed bar, equally covered. I had never seen anything like it.

While I watched, I was joined on the pier by two middle-aged couples, who, with one pair of binoculars among them, also began looking at the skimmers. "What kind of bird is that?" they asked me. "Black skimmers," I announced. "Fabulous birds." I could have stopped there, but I had these people pretty much at my mercy. "Really unusual to see a whole bunch of them like that. You usually just see one or two."

Oops. "No bird is more gregarious by nature," writes Thomas Burleigh; "during the fall and winter months large flocks can be seen resting much of the day on a sand bar or stretch of open beach. Such flocks are not scattered out, but invariably occupy the smallest possible area, the birds being so close together that at a distance a large flock suggests a black patch on the sand." Skimmers are even more gregarious than usual "in the fall and winter," agrees Bent, "when they gather in large flocks, flying in close formation, or roosting in dense masses on sand bars or beaches."

They're plenty gregarious during the summer breeding season, too, it turns out, and establish their big nesting colonies up and down the eastern seaboard and along the Gulf of Mexico. Those that nest north of the Carolinas might come south for the winter, but many of the southerly nesters can just stay put year-round.

Black skimmers often choose to nest among their cousins in the Laridae family, the gulls and terns — especially terns, whose early warning systems and greater aggressiveness enhance the skimmers' defense against predators. By all accounts, though, the skimmers are pretty aggressive on their own. "They have a great enmity towards Crows and Turkey Buzzards when at their breeding ground," observes Audubon, "and on the first appearance of these marauders, some dozens of Skimmers at once give chase to them, rarely desisting until quite out of sight." His friend Dr. Bachman, of South Carolina, described a rookery of some 20,000 nests on the islands of Bull's Bay: "The sailors collected an enormous number of their eggs. The birds screamed all the while, and whenever a Pelican or Turkey

Buzzard passed near, they assailed it by hundreds, pouncing on the back of the latter, that came to rob them of their eggs, and pursued them fairly out of sight."

Burleigh, checking out a nesting colony on Oysterbed Island near the mouth of the Savannah River, writes that as soon as he got out of his boat, "the birds left their nests and literally charged at me with quite an uproar, turning aside when possibly a hundred feet away and then circling overhead." When charging and screaming don't work, skimmers, unlike their cousins, revert to distraction displays. Michael Gochfield and Joanna Burger, writing for BNA *Online*, note that at their "highest intensity" displays "include belly-flopping in front of intruder, culminating in apparent collapse on the ground with struggling hops and apparently vain, symmetrical, flapping of wings."

It makes sense that breeding skimmers need all the ingenuity they can muster, along with defensive help from other species. Their nests are fully exposed, nothing more than a shallow scrape in the sand. The mated pair take turns at the excavation, turning around and around as they kick the sand backward, eventually creating a "saucer-shaped depression." The scrape takes only a few minutes, write Gochfield and Burger, "but the process of nesting may involve several scrapes and nest-showing behavior," requiring as much as a week between the first scrape and the first egg.

In a gesture of decency uncharacteristic of avian species generally, skimmers usually copulate at night. "Typically," according to BNA *Online*, "the male turns and presents fish to female (in absence of fish, a leaf, stick, or nest marker may be offered). . . . Female takes offering and immediately turns and crouches. Male mounts and raises wing." There's no postcopulatory display as such, write Gochfield and Burger, but the "Wing-flagging Display" during copulation "acts as stimulus for neighboring pairs, and several pairs may copulate simultaneously."

White sand might offer the skimmer's white eggs some concealment from predators, but there's no escape from the sun. Prolonged exposure can be lethal, write Gochfeld and Burger, "and parents incubate tenaciously on hot afternoons." If eggs and hatchlings survive, the young skimmers start to jump and flap their wings in their fourth week, and their maiden voyage is likely to take place during the fifth. Before that time, they might have run long distances to avoid danger, but having once taken wing, the skimmer will never run again.

And having once taken wing, the young bird is presumably ready to put its lower mandible to the test—along with a couple of other distinctive skimmer features. Cross writes that while the purpose of the bill is obvious, "there continues to be a mystery about why the skimmer barks like a dog and has the elliptical, vertical eyes of a cat." As for the first of these, to my way of thinking the cry of the skimmer is no more mysterious than, say, the hooting of an owl, but it is kind of yippy. Audubon is not the only writer to compare the "notes" of the skimmer, giving chase to a predator, to "the barkings of a very small dog." A fuller description of the skimmers' music comes from Carson: "As they flew they raised their voices in the weird night chorus of the skimmers, a strange medley of notes high-pitched and low, now soft as the cooing of a mourning dove, and again harsh as the cawing of a crow; the whole chorus rising and falling, swelling and throbbing, dying away in the still air like the far-off baying of a pack of hounds."

As for the second mystery, the eyes of the black skimmer are indeed an avian anomaly. In the first place, they're relatively small, but have unusually large pupils when fully dilated, an advantage for nighttime foraging. But much more remarkable, as Sibley explains, is the fact that skimmers are the only birds in the world "known to close their pupils vertically, with a slit very much like that of a cat's eye. This structure, found mostly in aquatic and nocturnal vertebrates, allows a skimmer to close its pupils tightly, which protects the retina in bright sunlight."

So not only the bill but also the eyes make this bird a phenomenon of evolutionary biology.

. . . .

Having read the journals of Samuel de Champlain, Forbush concluded that the skimmer was "undoubtedly one of the summer birds of Massachusetts when the Pilgrim Fathers settled in Plymouth." What happened? "While its plumage was of no great value in the millinery market and its flesh was not valued as food, its eggs were prized on account of their large size. As Skimmers deposit their eggs without concealment on the open sands, the same fate overtook them along the northern coast of the Middle States, where they have been extirpated in recent times."

It's true that the black skimmer population declined during the late 1800s (Forbush was writing in 1925), but it rebounded with the passage of the Migratory Bird Treaty Act of 1918, and the skimmer once again nests as far north as the coast of Massachusetts. More recently, coastal development has threatened this bird's nesting grounds, but according to *The Breeding Bird Atlas of Georgia*, the skimmer population today is generally stable.

Along those lines, I'm also able to report that the flock of skimmers I saw on Cedar Key paled in size compared to the one Dede and I saw on Jekyll Island during an end-of-winter getaway a couple of weeks later. In the company of equal numbers of royal terns and laughing gulls (in a congregation totaling some thousands), we marveled at untold hundreds of skimmers—all of them, like their cousins, turned headfirst into a northerly breeze. As we were watching, a man and woman headed down the beach in our direction, in the company of a dog the size of a small horse. Dogs are forbidden on the south end of Jekyll beach, and we were properly indignant. But then, as the intruders drew closer, we saw a glory of skimmers rise into the air, wheeling and crying, and who could really mind such a sight?

(return to)
spring

Red Knot
Calidris canutus

Except during the relatively brief breeding season, you can forget the "red" in red knot. To identify the bird in flight, Sibley says to "note plain gray rump and tail." Brian Harrington, writing for BNA *Online*, attributes to this bird the "characteristic calidridine profile," meaning that it looks a whole lot like a bunch of other sandpipers. And Bent, to sum it up, points out "the absence of any conspicuous field mark" on this "plain gray bird. . . . Its larger size will hardly distinguish it from the smaller sandpipers except by direct comparison."

For most of the year, then, the red knot* is a bird unlikely to grab our attention—which, now that I think about it, doesn't matter anyway because even if we know what to look for, the bird ain't here. It breeds on top of the world and winters on the bottom. Unless you've caught it passing through, there's every chance you've never seen this bird.

But if you've been on the Atlantic coast in April or May, and been with people who could tell you what you were looking at, you just might have caught the red knots passing through. On Little St. Simons Island's Sancho Panza Beach in late-April, we saw huge flocks of these plump sandpipers, their undersides beginning to take on a russet tinge. By mid-May, when I returned to the Georgia coast with a group from Atlanta Audubon Society, the knots were in full breeding plumage, bright salmon from cheek and chin to bottom of belly. Suddenly they were unmistakable, whether sitting quietly massed, heads to the wind, waiting for the tide to recede or feeding ravenously in order to continue their northward migration.

They were even more striking when they burst into flight—a thousand birds wheeling and turning in symphonic harmony, silent

---

*"Knot" is an odd name for a bird, isn't it? A popular theory is that the name derives from King Canute (Cnut, Knut) of Denmark (1018–35), based at least in part on the belief that the bird was the king's favorite food. Seems far-fetched, but a better explanation hasn't arisen.

music of some unseen conductor. "Their aerial evolutions are very beautiful," writes Audubon, "for . . . they follow each other in their course, with a celerity that seems almost incomprehensible, when the individuals are so near each other that one might suppose it impossible for them to turn and wheel without interfering with each other. At such times, their lower and upper parts are alternately seen, the flock exhibiting now a dusky appearance, and again gleaming like a meteor." Peter Matthiessen, waxing metaphysical, observes that the birds' evolutions "are so unified and intricate and marvelous that one can scarcely believe that they fly by sight or signal. The flock seems to travel as a single bird, a single soul—as if, in the intensity of flight, it had pierced some dimension of knowing in which all signals were superfluous."

On Jekyll Island's south beach, your own armchair birder spotted an orange band around the leg of one of the knots, a sight that aroused much excitement on the part of guide Lydia Thompson and the other knowledgeable knot-watchers in the group. A band of that color signified that that particular bird's migratory journey had indeed originated in Tierra del Fuego.

Where, I might have asked, is Tierra del Fuego? But I kept my mouth shut, content to assume that it was way the heck down there somewhere. I have since found out—have found out, in fact, that the life of the red knot is a testament to the irrepressible power of the reproductive urge.

. . . .

I've just read in my Atlanta Audubon Society newsletter that thanks to a new gizmo—the sunrise- and sunset-sensitive geolocator—a revised nonstop red knot distance record has just been officially established. A bird outfitted with one of these devices flew for six straight days and nights, covering 5,000 miles from southern Brazil to the coast of North Carolina. That was just the longest single leg in a much longer journey. The bird was equipped with the geolocator in May 2009 during its stopover on Delaware Bay; by the time it returned a year later, it had covered an astonishing 16,600 miles.

The southernmost point of the round trip may very well have

been Tierra del Fuego (at the very tip of South America, it turns out). But how about the northernmost, the breeding home to which the bird's hormones ultimately push it? That was a question even the intrepid Audubon couldn't answer. "As to its habits . . . during the breeding season," he writes, "I am sorry to inform you that I know nothing at all, for in Labrador, whither I went to examine them, I did not find a single individual." Nor did he find red knots breeding in Nova Scotia or Newfoundland, from which he inferred, correctly, "that those which betake themselves to the fur countries, turn off from our Atlantic shores when they have reached the entrance of the Bay of Fundy."

So they continue their journey north and west, but where to? "The nesting habits of the knot long remained unknown," reports Bent. "Arctic explorers were baffled in their attempts to find the nest; and the eggs were among the greatest desiderata of collectors." The story goes that it was Admiral Robert Peary, returning through Ellesmere Island after his discovery of the North Pole in 1909, who came upon the first knot nests ever seen by man. As Matthiessen observes, "In ornithological circles this discovery was scarcely less momentous than the one he had made en route, for the nest of the knot had been hunted assiduously for half a century."

You know how when you think about the universe you feel like your head will explode? That's how I feel when I think about why this six-ounce bird must push itself into the remotest land masses of northern Earth in order to breed. The rationalist in me has to declare it a mystery and let it go.

How the bird manages this trip is more comprehensible — is, in fact, well documented. The red knots have several established stopovers along the Argentine coast and up to the southern coast of Brazil. At these places they gorge themselves on clams, snails, and other invertebrates, adding on enough body fat to make it to their next destination. Wilson describes one of their favorite foods: "a small, thin, oval, bivalve shellfish, of a white pearl color, and not larger than the seed of an apple," which they swallow whole. "If we may judge from their effects," he adds, "they must be extremely nutritious, for almost all those tribes that feed on them are at this season mere lumps of fat."

Now comes the long flight, around the eastward bulge of South America up to the East Coast of the United States. The birds may stop in Florida, or Georgia (where I've seen them), or the Carolinas. But there is one destination for which virtually all of them are headed: Delaware Bay. Here, in May, another migration is in progress — that of millions of horseshoe crabs who are laboring up out of the muck and onto the beach to breed and lay their eggs — and one of nature's greatest spectacles is about to unfold. As though in anticipation of the birds' arrival, the female crabs are digging holes in the sand and laying their eggs — "billions of greenish globes the size of tapioca beads," as Scott Weidensaul puts it. "Latecomers plow up the nests of those that have finished spawning, until in places the beach has an olive tinge, more eggs than sand."

Into this cornucopia come the voracious knots, along with huge numbers of semipalmated sandpipers, ruddy turnstones, and sanderlings, among others. Maybe a million birds in all, writes Weidensaul, all in search of, and finding, the nourishment they must have at this juncture. "Within two weeks, they must be airborne again, making another 2,400-mile leap to the Arctic breeding grounds. The fat they accumulate here must be enough not only for the flight but also to carry them through the beginning of the breeding season, when they have more on their minds than food."

The fact that so many red knots (maybe 80 percent of our hemisphere's population) partake of this feast is all the more remarkable because horseshoe crab eggs are utterly atypical of the birds' normally crustacean-based diet. It's unclear what causes this sudden change in preference, writes Harrington, but one theory is that "the species' ability to digest hard-shelled prey may atrophy following sustained fasting, which presumably occurs during flight from South America to North America."

In any case, the eggs apparently do the job, and the knots continue on to their breeding grounds in northernmost Alaska, Canada, and Russia. It's so cold when they first arrive — snow and ice still on the ground—that they're obliged to change diet again, subsisting on seeds and plant shoots until the insects begin to hatch. But the thaw is coming, and the males, who shoulder most of the load of propagating the species, get busy brightening up the landscape.

They begin their courtship with an aerial song-and-dance routine. Bent correspondent W. E. Ekblaw vividly describes the bird's mating-season ecstasy: "He rises high above the hills, sweeping the sky in great graceful circles not unlike the stately flight of the sparrow hawk, so smooth and calm it seems. . . . Then suddenly he drops wildly, tumbling and tossing like a night jar at sunset, as suddenly to break his fall and soar for miles on still outstretched wings, not a movement noticeable." Another contributor to *Life Histories* documents the male's "beautiful flutelike notes . . . heard far and wide over the country, bringing joy to other birds of his own kin. . . . This fine pairing song may be heard for more than a month everywhere at the breeding places, and it wonderfully enlivens this generally so desolate and silent nature."

The hopeful bridegroom is plenty busy on the ground as well. He's got to mark off and defend his territory and make a number of nest-scrapes in order to attract his mate. Harrington, in BNA *Online*, describes the process: "Removes vegetation by pulling with bill, and by sitting in nest depression and pivoting on breast while kicking backward with feet." As soon as an interested female settles into one of his scrapes, and makes her own modifications, the pair bond is established.

Both parents incubate the eggs, sharing the work equally, and their defense of the nest is interesting. During the early stages, says Harrington, they simply fly away in response to any human intrusion, sometimes taking several hours to return. Later on, though, perhaps calculating their greater investment, they sit so tight that they'll sometimes allow themselves to be touched or even lifted off their eggs. Ekblaw reports that a sitting bird remained on the nest even when he placed his camera only a foot away.

It seems counterintuitive to imagine that the bird sitting so determinedly might be the father, or that it might be the father clucking the alarm signal ("Be still!") to the tiny precocial chicks. But, apparently, when the red knot daddy commits, he means it. Ekblaw reports that "all the birds caring for the young that I collected were males, beyond doubt." And Harrington's research confirms the finding: "All adults seen with chicks, including small chicks . . . were males. Adults collected while with well-grown broods . . . were males; females evidently leave broods and breeding haunts at about the time of hatching."

. . . .

I'm not criticizing the distaff side. You can't call any of these birds a slacker. Its own DNA sets the red knot on a rigorous course through life, and, sad to say, humankind has done little to ease its passage. Fattening itself on its way up the Atlantic coast, the knot became a favorite game bird (and "good table bird" in Bent's phrase) during the second half of the nineteenth century. When the knots weren't being shot, they were being taken by the "vicious practice of fire-lighting," of which Bent offers the 1893 account of George Mackay: "The mode of procedure was for two men to start out after dark at half tide, one of them to carry a lighted lantern [by which the birds were effectively blinded], the other to reach and seize the birds, bite their necks, and put them in a bag slung over the shoulder." Mackay had it on "excellent authority" that six barrels of these birds were taken on a single night and put on a Cape Cod packet bound for Boston. If each barrel held the estimated sixty dozen knots, for a total of 4,320 birds, we can understand Bent's assertion that shooting and market hunting eventually reduced the species to "a pitiful remnant of its former numbers."

Fire-lighting, thankfully, had been banned by the turn of the century, and the knot also was removed from the list of game birds. As a result, in 1929, wrote Bent, its population was increasing slowly, "but it is far from abundant now, and makes only a short stay on Cape Cod."

Unfortunately, the red knot population is no longer increasing but rapidly decreasing. The number of birds wintering in South America dropped more than 50 percent from the mid-1980s to 2003.

The knot is now listed by the Fish and Wildlife Service as a bird of conservation concern and is considered a continentally threatened species. Most recently, it has been listed as a candidate for the Endangered Species List.

What's happening is that their chief survival strategy—their ability to find and fatten up at those key staging areas along their northward migration—is turning into a liability. If one of these places fails to provide the necessary nourishment, the knots don't have a readily available Plan B. Delaware Bay again offers the most dramatic example. During the 1990s, the commercial demand for horseshoe crabs began to surge. The crabs don't make good food, it seems, but they make good bait—especially for eel. As the Asian market for American eel started to boom, so did the horseshoe crab harvest. According to Weidensaul's figures, fishermen took about 100,000 crabs out of the bay in 1990. By 1996 the haul was something like 900,000—possibly a third of the total population. Sure enough, the number of shorebirds showing up for the 1997 feast was far below average, leading New Jersey governor Christine Todd Whitman to impose an immediate moratorium on horseshoe crab fishing. Since that time, both New Jersey and Delaware have prohibited the harvesting of horseshoe crabs.

From a broader perspective, though, commercial fishermen comprise but one threat to the bay's ecological balance. Constant oil tanker traffic, pollution from heavy industry and agricultural runoff, and human encroachment are among the others. Widening the lens further, Delaware Bay is but one of many critically important staging areas for red knots and other migrating shorebirds. Identifying and protecting these areas has come under the purview of the Western Hemisphere Shorebird Reserve Network (WHSRN), originally established in 1986 and now including eighty-three sites in thirteen countries. As Weidensaul points out (and as is often the case with conservation initiatives), "WHSRN's weight is moral and scientific, rather than legal, but that can be potent."

Let's hope so. The migration of the red knot is miraculous enough already.

Whimbrel

Numenius phaeopus

From old favorites Wilson and Audubon, we don't get much help with the life history of the whimbrel, our familiar member of the curlew family. Mostly we get nomenclatural confusion. Wilson is probably talking about the whimbrel when he describes the "Esquimaux Curlew" or "Short-billed Curlew" arriving "in large flocks on the sea-coast of New Jersey early in May, from the south, frequent[ing] the salt marshes, muddy shores and inlets, feeding on small worms and minute shellfish."

But maybe not, because in his day there did exist a distinct species known as the Eskimo curlew. However, that close relative of our whimbrel would probably have been migrating up the Mississippi River valley in the spring, rather than up the East Coast. I say "there did exist," and since we're in no hurry, let's take a moment to lament the passing into extinction of this fine bird. Here is Forbush's succinct obituary:

> The destruction of the Eskimo Curlew followed that of the Passenger Pigeon, whose place it took in the markets of the country. In the spring migration in the West it was slaughtered at times by wagonloads. Market hunters made it their business to follow the birds from state to state during the migration. On the Atlantic coast in autumn the curlews met with a similar reception, while the South Americans hunted them in winter. From 1870 to 1880 they began to decrease. Between 1886 and 1892 they diminished very rapidly and after that were never seen in numbers on the Labrador coast. Since that time the records show comparatively few birds killed in any part of their range. The last specimen known in New England was a lone bird shot September 5, 1913, at East Orleans, Massachusetts.

Requiescat in pace.

Additional evidence that Wilson was describing our whimbrel comes from Audubon, in his account of what he called the "Hudsonian" or "Short-billed" curlew. He was so certain that he and Wilson were talking about the same bird that he, having little knowledge of the species, deferred to Wilson's account, with due credit to his sometime rival. From that point, it's not hard to trace the evolution of the "Hudsonian Curlew" into our whimbrel. Forbush called *Phaeopus hudsonicus* the Hudsonian curlew; Burleigh jumped from that familiar name to "Hudsonian Whimbrel"; and BNA *Online* declares our eastern race of the whimbrel to be *Numenius phaeopus hudsonicus*.* There. I believe that should settle the nomenclature issue to everyone's satisfaction.

I might add that what Wilson has to say about the "Esquimaux Curlew" seems applicable enough to the whimbrel: that during their spring migration they are commonly seen on mudflats at low water, feeding in the company of other waders. On their preparing to head north, he writes, "they collect together from the marshes, as if by premeditated design, rise to a great height in the air . . . and, forming in one vast line, keep up a constant whistling on their way to the north, as if conversing with one another to render the journey more agreeable." To be perfectly honest, I've seen no other reference to this companionable whistling en route, but there's no question that these birds do fly north. That fabulous bill notwithstanding, the whimbrel's long-distance migration might very well be the most remarkable aspect of its life.

. . . .

I count myself fortunate to have seen the whimbrel, a bird Sibley describes as "uncommon in grassy marshes and tidal flats." But Brad Winn and Tim Keyes of the Georgia DNR certainly weren't surprised to see them along the Georgia coast during spring migration. Leading our small party out into St. Catherines Sound on his nice little DNR boat, Brad assured us we would see the birds fattening up on

---

*Since it's lovely, I'll pass along from Choate that *numenius* is Greek for new moon, a reference to the bird's long, decurved bill. While I'm at it, Choate translates *phaeopus* as "dusky foot," referring to the grayish legs and feet. And finally, to complete the record, *BNA Online* disagrees, translating *phaeopus* as "dark countenance."

fiddler crabs, and that they would double their body weight before they left Georgia at the end of May.

As it happened, the first shorebird we saw was a whimbrel, standing alone in lordly fashion—with striped crown and scythe-like bill—at the top of the bank on a skinny sand and grass island. The bird had apparently been diligent at its feed, because when it flew off at our approach, Tim pointed out that it looked like a flying football. (Reading Peter Matthiessen, I would later learn that the curlew takes on so much weight in preparation for its long-distance migrations that, "in the days when it was shot by thousands from the sky, the fat would sometimes burst out of its breast when it struck the ground.")

Later that day we would see a small group of maybe half a dozen whimbrels feeding on a tidal pool on St. Simons Island, and at sunset, on the beach at Gould's Inlet, we saw a larger crowd gathering on a distant sandbar. Not surprising: Brad had mentioned that they roost offshore to avoid being preyed on by great horned owls.

It had turned out to be a fine day for whimbrel spotting, thanks to our Georgia DNR experts. But what Brad and Tim hadn't told us was that, in partnership with the Center for Conservation Biology at the College of William and Mary, they were hip-deep in a study of whimbrel migration patterns. As I discovered in a subsequent issue of my DNR online newsletter, about the time we were there, Brad and Tim were helping equip a couple of whimbrels with radio transmitters in order to be able to determine exactly where they headed after leaving Georgia. By the time the story appeared, one of the birds, named Chinquapin, had taken care of business up north and returned south for the winter. The transmitter filled in the details.

After leaving the Georgia coast, the bird headed north toward Hudson Bay in Canada and ultimately settled down to nest about 350 miles west of the bay, below the Arctic Circle in the Northwest Territories. He left his breeding grounds in mid-July and made his way to Coats Island in Hudson Bay, where he spent a couple of weeks fattening up for the marathon migration to come. According to the transmitter, Chinquapin departed Coats Island on August 5, flew

600 miles south over Hudson Bay, then continued east over Quebec, over Maine, and finally out over the Atlantic, where he pursued a southerly route. The approach of Tropical Storm Colin on August 8 apparently necessitated a detour that took him 300 miles east of Bermuda. On August 10 the transmitter beeped from the beaches of northwest Puerto Rico, indicating that Chinquapin had at last made landfall after a nonstop journey of 3,470 miles—the equivalent, according to the newsletter account, of flying "about five days around-the-clock from Boston to Anchorage, Alaska."

Puerto Rico, though, wasn't the bird's ultimate destination. After two weeks of rest and refueling, Chinquapin finished his journey with a quick 1,300-mile dash to his winter home in Suriname, along the northeastern coast of South America.

If Chinquapin had been equipped with a tiny camera along with that radio transmitter, we might have evidence of just what went on during those six weeks in the Northwest Territories. He didn't, but with the help of Margaret Skeel and Elizabeth Mallory, writing for BNA *Online*, we can play voyeur. Shortly after his arrival on the breeding grounds, Chinquapin would have laid claim to a bit of territory by flying up and over it, gliding down and rising again. No doubt he sang a pretty song—a low, lonesome whistle—to the female below, and once he had her attention, he would've set his wings and circled down to the ground. He might well have discovered, though, that the hard work of courtship was just beginning. Let's imagine that she ran from his approach, that he gave chase. As he closed in, his instinct reminded him to gently pluck a few feathers from her tail. This endearment had done the trick in years past, but this time, instead of stopping to crouch, she ran on ahead, wings flapping. When at last she submitted, Chinquapin sensed that he had found what every whimbrel looks for—a mate he might pair with again next year, a mate he might even look up on their wintering grounds.

By all accounts, a whimbrel pair are fierce guardians of nest and young. Any potential predator, whether from the air or on the ground, is aggressively driven away. While one bird incubates, the other keeps watch, and if that bird's efforts are not enough to repulse the intruder, the other leaves the nest to join in. Human interlopers, equally intolerable, will be met with a swift, low attack flight and a raucous scolding until they are put to rout. The precocial chicks are foraging for their own food from Day One, so this kind of protective aggression is pretty much the only parenting skill required. If the skuas, jaegers, and arctic foxes can be kept at bay, the young will fledge in a month or so, and the long southbound migration will commence—females first, males next, young last.

Among its many points of interest, I notice that the migration route, as a whole, is somewhat elliptical: up the East Coast of the United States, back down over the Atlantic, from Bermuda to Puerto Rico and on down to South America. Assuming, as Brad Winn does, that this route is typical of the species, one of the things it tells us is that we Georgia birders don't need to look for whimbrels in the fall. Which makes me wonder what the heck Forbush was talking about when he wrote that the Hudsonian curlew "is considered rare in spring, when a few may be seen, but many small companies pass along the coast from the latter part of July until well into September."

To suggest that he might have been writing of a different curlew would be to revive disputes safely laid to rest, and we won't do that. Instead, we'll agree that either Forbush was wrong or that the whimbrel has changed its migration route—which is not unthinkable. Writing of the black-bellied plover along the coast of Massachusetts, Bent noted that "formerly they were much more abundant in the fall than in the spring, but the reverse is now the case. He believed that they had changed their migratory pattern to avoid the autumn hunt in that area, which he saw as "a striking example of the bird's sagacity."

The whimbrel, similarly, is said to be a wary bird, and some writers speculate that its cautious nature helped it avoid the fate of the Eskimo curlew. In *The Shorebirds of North America*, Ralph Palmer suggests that the whimbrel "escaped the thorough slaughter" because "it was not as available (due to its migration routes) or as unwary as the Eskimo Curlew." Skeel and Mallory add that prior to the Migratory Bird Treaty Act, hunters did in fact pose a serious threat to the whimbrel, especially hunters who "sought the challenge of so vigilant a bird." The authors go on to note that "owing to its wary nature and habit of migrating in smaller flocks, the Whimbrel was not slaughtered in the same excessive numbers as some large shore-birds."

To be fair, Skeel and Mallory also write that while many whim-brels in their southbound migration fly directly over the Atlantic to the Caribbean and South America, "some" do move south along the East Coast and can be seen along the mid-Atlantic and southeastern shores from mid-July to mid-October. Still, these findings are quite the reverse of Forbush's observation that the birds are rare along our coast in spring and numerous in the fall, so I am quite willing to conjecture that, between his time and ours, the birds indeed have gradually altered their southbound route. Having watched their close cousins blasted from the sky as they migrated down the East Coast in the fall (as Forbush vividly documents, above), the wary whimbrels decided that a flight over the Atlantic, while maybe more exhausting in the short run, would ultimately prove more salutary.

What matters, of course, is that although we do not have Eskimo curlews, we do have whimbrels, in healthy numbers, using the bounty of our seacoasts to make the crucial trek to their breeding grounds. That's certainly how Brad Winn sees it, noting that the fiddler crabs they pluck from our marshes make possible the next 2,000- to 3,000-mile leg of their northward migration. These things matter. "If our marshes are destroyed or become polluted," Brad points out, "the crabs will be gone and this vital link in the migra-tory chain will be lost." That hasn't happened yet. Maybe it won't.

Contemplating the whimbrel's northward migration, Peter Mat-thiessen writes that "in the sense that they are birds of passage, . . . in the wild melodies of their calls, in the breath of vast distance and bare regions that attends them, we sense intimations of our own mortality." It's not death they represent, however, "but only the memory of a life, of a high beauty passing swiftly, as the curlew passes, leaving us in solitude on an empty beach, with summer gone, and a wind blowing."

Whoa. Talk about your *lachrymae rerum*, your "sadness at the heart of things." But I can deal. As long as spring comes round again, and the whimbrels with it.

American Avocet
Recurvirostra americana

A return visit confirmed it: Cedar Key is my kind of town. No hassle. No hustle. No nothing, mostly. I came in on a Wednesday evening, late April, and cruised Dock Street looking for an adult beverage. I found one at the Black Dog, same place I found one last time was here, back in the winter. It looked like pretty much every other place along the strip was closed.

"Well," the bartender explained, "after the weekend, most everybody takes Monday and Tuesday off."

"But this is Wednesday."

"Well, you know. It takes a while to gear back up."

The power went off while I was sipping my cab. It was about 6:30. I settled up (in cash) and walked over to the Island Hotel to get some supper. Power off there, too, and with the beer getting hot, they decided to go ahead and close down for the evening. At the restaurant of the hotel where I was staying, the Cedar Cove Beach and Yacht Club, a "limited menu" was available. I got a shrimp cocktail and a tossed salad and headed back to my room.

I was sitting on my little patio, looking at the stars, when the lights came twinkling back on along the dock. It was after ten. The power had been off over the whole island for close to four hours. Nobody gave a rat's butt.

On my earlier trip to Cedar Key, I had found the majestic white pelicans. This time I hoped to catch sight of the American avocet. It had been a long search. They breed along lake shores in the West and upper Midwest, but some migrate back southward along the Atlantic coast, and some stay for the winter along Florida's eastern coast or along the Gulf. I thought I might see some of those migrating birds on North Carolina's Outer Banks in the fall, but they failed to show. My Atlanta Audubon friends told me we would have a great chance of seeing avocets wintering in Merritt Island NWR, midway down Florida's Atlantic coast, on our trip there in January.

Nope, didn't happen. Still, both those trips had yielded their own pleasures, and I wasn't obsessing.

But then spring rolled back around. Soon the avocets would head up to their breeding grounds again, and, doggone it, I wanted to see 'em before they took off. I called St. Marks NWR, on Florida's Big Bend, where I had seen the lovely black-necked stilts more than a year earlier. Avocets and stilts are related and sometimes hang out together, so I thought maybe a colony of the birds had wintered there. The wildlife folks there said they hadn't seen any. It was a long shot, but I e-mailed my acquaintance at the Georgia DNR, Brad Winn, to ask if any were being spotted headed north along the Georgia coast. Brad e-mailed me back: "Sorry."

Hmm. I started looking a little further afield. I found mention in BNA *Online* of a couple of counties along Texas's Gulf coast where avocets were reported to breed. Well, shoot—that wasn't too far. And if they were going to be nesting there, I would be sure to get as long a look as I wanted. I was all set to jump on a plane when I called Aransas NWR, which looked like the major refuge in that area, to make sure the reports were accurate. The expert from the Texas Fish and Wildlife Department told me that if there were any avocets nesting along the Texas Gulf coast, he didn't know anything about it.

About that time I got an e-mail response from Captain Doug Maple, proprietor of Tidewater Tours on Cedar Key. On my first visit to the island I had signed up for one of Captain Doug's excursions, but the wind came up that morning and he had to cancel. At this point he was just another of my last-ditch attempts—until I got his answer: "We've had about 100 avocets down here over the winter. They've started to leave, so I can't guarantee anything, but I've got two seats left on a special bird outing Thursday at 1:30." That was Tuesday. I left the next morning.

By the time I checked in to the hotel and opened my laptop e-mail, his wife had booked the final two seats, but Captain Doug told me to come on; they might get a cancellation, and he would manage to squeeze me on even if they didn't. They didn't but he did. While twelve passengers luxuriated on comfortably upholstered

seats (with backs) underneath the flat-bottomed boat's blue canopy, I perched underneath the captain's elbow on top of his stern-end storage bin.

Captain Doug is a big man and might have been imposing in his Teddy Roosevelt hat and Hemingway beard, but his demeanor was well suited to a Cedar Key kind of life. He moved about his tasks (lowering the canopy to squeeze under the canal bridges, for example) with slow deliberation and spoke in a soft, high, nasal whine. Unfortunately, about the first thing he said was, "Tide's coming in fast. I didn't want it to be this high. I'm afraid those avocets might have already moved on from where I usually see 'em."

We were headed southeast to a place he called Coogan's Reef, and we were seeing a lot of fine shorebirds—willets, dowitchers, black-bellied plovers starting to turn, lots of oystercatchers and turnstones, hundreds of black skimmers, even whimbrels and marbled godwits—but there were no avocets, and I began contemplating an essay on failing to find my own grail bird.

Why the avocet? "Well, if nothing else," writes Peter Cashwell, who documented a quest somewhat like mine in his book *The Verb "To Bird,"* "the Avocet is striking, a slender wader, standing almost two feet high, with its back and wings boldly pied black and white; in breeding plumage, its gray head turns a rich, warm, almost rosy shade of tan." He doesn't mention that those long thin legs are blue, but he does highlight the bird's most remarkable feature: "its long, black, slender bill, which curves gracefully and noticeably upwards, something like Nixon's nose in the political cartoons of my youth."

It doesn't look much like any other kind of bird, Cashwell concludes, and nobody disagrees. "[It] could not be mistaken for anything else," writes Bent matter-of-factly. "A white tail, a black V on a white back, black wings with white secondaries and blue legs are all distinctive marks." More poetically, Scott Weidensaul describes these birds as "so delicate that they seem more like paintings than living birds. . . . A single avocet is breathtaking, a flock of them beautiful beyond belief."

When their head and neck turn from pale gray-white to that remarkable rusty buff, the avocets are ready to head north and west to
breed in their favored habitat of salt ponds, shallow alkaline lakes,
and salt- or freshwater marshes. What they do when they get there
has been the subject of varied commentary. Bent quotes Julian Huxley as writing that the avocet "has no courtship[;] . . . no songs or
aerial displays; no posturing by the male; no mutual ceremonies;
no special courtship notes." Bent then immediately contradicts
Huxley based on his own observation of a breeding colony in southwestern Saskatchewan. With nests and eggs not yet in evidence, he
writes, the birds "were still apparently conducting their courtships,
wading about gracefully in the shallow water, frequently bowing or
crouching down close to the water; sometimes they danced about
with wings widespread, tipping from side to side like a balancing
tight-rope walker; occasionally one, perhaps a female in an attitude of invitation, would lie prostrate on the ground or water for
a minute or more, with the head and neck extended and the wings
outstretched."

Julie Robinson, and others, writing for BNA *Online*, confirm that
it is indeed the female, in "Solicitation Posture," who prostrates herself, and the writers add that she sometimes extends her neck so far
that her bill is submerged in the water. Meanwhile, the male en-
gages in precopulatory preening, with an interesting twist. He begins calmly enough, dipping his bill in the water and working on his
breast feathers, but as his excitement builds, the dipping becomes
splashing, and soon enough the preening is an afterthought: "Intensity increases during the course of display, culminating in vigorous
splashing immediately prior to mounting the female." In the postcoital glow, the pair "stands side to side with necks entwined."

The authors are at pains, however, to assert that the famous "circling display" is *not* a courtship ritual, though it is "sometimes mis-
interpreted" as such. The clarification comes as a relief, since our
already overheated imaginations don't need the stimulation that this
kind of "group interaction," were it sexual in nature, might supply.
What happens is that two pairs of birds form a circle, with heads

facing inward and downward toward the water. All four birds make a high trumpeting sound, then the circle rotates slightly in one direction or the other.* Robinson and her team note that the display is often instigated by the arrival of a new pair innocently looking to move into the neighborhood, and we're invited to see it as more polka than tango.

Accounts generally agree that the mated avocet pair scrape out a simple nest in the soft ground close to the water's edge, with little vegetation to obscure the view. Audubon's experience differed on this point—and was all the more memorable as a result. The nests he discovered on an island pond in Indiana "were placed among the tallest grasses," difficult to locate, and not easy to approach. Ever undaunted, and determined to see the sitting female, Audubon set out across fifty yards of sucking mud. "Softly and on all fours I crawled toward the spot, panting with heat and anxiety," finally arriving "within three feet of the unheeding creature, peeping at her through the tall grasses. Lovely bird! . . . There she sits on her eggs, her head almost mournfully sunk among the plumage, and her eyes, unanimated by the sight of her mate, half closed, as if she dreamed of future scenes."

When the female finally sees Audubon and scrambles off the nest in alarm, he learns something about the behavior of these birds that later writers confirm: "Until that day I was not aware that gregarious birds, on emitting cries of alarm, after having been scared from their nest, could induce other incubating individuals to leave their eggs also, and join in attempting to save the colony. But so it was with the Avosets, and the other two sitters immediately rose on wing and flew directly at me."

---

*BNA Online includes a fine illustration of the Circling Display by an artist identified simply as B. Keimel. A bit of Internet sleuthing on the part of yours truly turned up a biologist, naturalist, and artist of that name based in California, home to a large population of avocets. Against my better judgment, I attempted to "friend" Ms. Keimel on Facebook to ask if she had actually witnessed this remarkable display. I received no reply, which is as it should be.

Though tame and unsuspicious most of the time, writes Bent, avocets are "very solicitous and aggressive on their breeding grounds," where "their demonstrations of anxiety . . . are amusing and ludicrous. Utterly regardless of their own safety, they meet the intruder more than half way and stay with him till he leaves." This behavior is all the more noticeable when the nests are in the open and "can be seen from afar." In this kind of circumstance, he writes, "long before we reach their haunts, the avocets are flying out to meet us, advertising the fact that we are approaching their home, making the air ring with their loud yelping notes of protest, circling about us and darting down at us in threatening plunges."

Robinson agrees that, when threatened by predators on the ground (including, presumably, human beings), pretty much every adult avocet in the breeding colony comes to its defense. Those that attacked Bent from the air were most likely nonincubating birds, Robinson implies, but even the sitting birds rise from their nests and engage in a variety of distraction displays—including a particularly clever one it shares with its close cousin the black-necked stilt. In "false incubation," the bird crouches on the ground as if incubating eggs, then gets up, moves to another spot, and sits again. If I were a gopher snake I believe I'd fall for that.

In fact, the avocets' parenting instinct produces a number of interesting behaviors. In hot weather, when the eggs need to be cooled rather than warmed, the parent will soak its belly feathers before settling down on the eggs. Also, the bird arriving to take its turn at incubation will generally turn the eggs with feet or bill. Most ingeniously, once the chicks are hatched, the telltale shells are sunk below the surface of the water—unless they've been crushed in the nest such that the white insides are not visible, in which case they are not removed. The young are precocial, so their survival is largely dependent on their own instinct. Fortunately, they are innately capable of hiding, swimming, and even diving under water to avoid capture.

Apparently, we southeastern birders will have to venture somewhere beyond Texas to see any avocet breeding behavior. The best we can hope for is to watch them feed, which, as you might guess given those long, fine, upturned bills, is pretty interesting. "They search for food precisely in the manner of the Roseate Spoonbill," writes Audubon, "moving their heads to and fro sideways, while their bill is passing through the soft mud." Frank Chapman reported to Bent that the birds drop their bills below the surface "until the convexity of the maxilla probably touches the bottom," then move forward sweeping their bill "through an arc of about 50 degrees in search of shells and other small aquatic animals. . . . It is evident that birds with a straight or downward curved bill could not adopt this method of feeding."

It is also evident, as another of Bent's correspondents points out, that this method of feeding makes the avocet essentially a scavenger, with sometimes unpleasant results. Noting that the birds have no choice but to take recently dead prey along with living, Alexander Wetmore adds, "The large tapeworms found almost without fail in the duodenum of the avocet are transmitted from one bird to another in this manner. The cast-off terminal segments of the worms (bearing the eggs) are picked up and swallowed by other avocets, a proceeding which the author has personally observed." (Robinson adds that the avocet's bill "is so sensitive that a bird in the hand will recoil at the gentlest touch"—information that would make a finer impression if we hadn't already learned about the tapeworms.)

Back quickly to the big picture: we should know that this beautiful bird used to breed along the East Coast but that by the end of the nineteenth century shooting and trapping had driven it from this portion of its range. Bent, for one, could not understand why. "There is no excuse for treating it as a game bird. It is so tame and so foolishly inquisitive that it would offer poor sport and . . . its flesh is said to be worthless for the table." Moreover, he was uncharacteristically pessimistic about the chances of its survival: "The destruction of its breeding grounds will exterminate it soon enough."

That hasn't happened yet, and to its benefit, the avocet is adaptable and willing to look around for suitable habitat. Suitable habitat is a finite resource, however, and one that's under ever increasing pressure from agricultural and other interests. Robinson points out that many breeding areas that depend on spring flooding don't get flooded anymore; the water is diverted for other uses. In other cases, traditional avocet habitat has simply become degraded. As Robinson writes, "Major breeding, staging, and wintering areas in Pacific Flyway, such as San Francisco estuary, San Joaquin Valley, and Salton Sea, are already seriously polluted."

Grim as that sounds, I'm happy to report that the avocet population appears to be stable, and that we are not currently in danger of losing this spectacular representative of the avian world.

. . . .

We were headed toward the No. 3 bridge, which we would be going under to get to the islands, marshes, oyster bars, and sand spits of the vast Lower Sewanee NWR. There was a sandbar full of birds just ahead of us—willets, dunlin, dowitchers, a whimbrel or two—when Captain Doug nodded my way: "There they are. We'll head straight for them before they take a notion."

They were on beyond the group I had been looking at, a dozen of them, by themselves, standing in shallow water just off the end of a little spit of grass, in the middle of nowhere. At ease in the warm sun, most had their heads turned back, nestled between their scapulars. But a few were standing up so we could marvel at that bill. Coming into their breeding plumage, too, necks and heads bright orange-rust. Fabulous birds. Incredible that we had come upon them.

I probably whooped or something.

"Those aren't your first, are they?" asked Captain Doug.

"They are," I said.

"Big day for a birder."

"It is," I said.

BIBLIOGRAPHY

Audubon, John James. *Ornithological Biography, or, an Account of the Habits of the Birds of the United States of America*. Philadelphia: E. I. Carey and A. Hart, 1832. This invaluable resource is now available, in its entirety, at the University of Pittsburgh's Darlington Digital Library (http://digital.library.pitt.edu).

Bent, Arthur Cleveland. *Life Histories of North American Birds*. New York: Dover, 1962–65. The first of Bent's volumes, *Life Histories of North American Diving Birds*, appeared in 1919, and the series continued for forty years, producing twenty-one volumes in all. The work was undertaken by the Smithsonian Institution, and the volumes appeared as *Bulletins* of the U.S. National Museum. Dover set about reprinting all the volumes in the series in the early 1960s.

The Birds of North America Online. The print version of this comprehensive resource (eighteen volumes covering 716 species and consisting of individual accounts by many of North America's leading ornithologists) was edited by Alan Poole and Frank Gill and appeared in 2002. Published by Birds of North America Inc. in Philadelphia, it represents the culmination of at ten-year effort on the part of the American Ornithologists' Union, the Cornell Lab of Ornithology, and the Academy of Natural Sciences. Now, thanks to the Cornell Lab, the complete work, with audio, video, and recurrent updating, is available online—for a small subscription fee.

Burleigh, Thomas D. *Georgia Birds*. Norman: University of Oklahoma Press, 1958. This is the classic "Georgia bird book," with beautiful illustrations by George Miksch Sutton.

Carson, Rachel. *Under the Sea-Wind*. New York: Simon and Schuster, 1941. New York: Penguin, 1996.

Cashwell, Peter. *The Verb "To Bird."* Philadelphia: Paul Dry, 2003.

Choate, Ernest A. *The Dictionary of American Bird Names*. Rev. ed. Boston: Harvard Common, 1985.

Cross, Theodore. *Waterbirds*. New York: Norton, 2009.

Elphick, Chris, John B. Dunning Jr., and David Allen Sibley, eds. *The Sibley Guide to Bird Life and Behavior*. New York: Knopf, 2001; Flexibind edition, 2009.

Forbush, Edward Howe, and John Bichard May. *A Natural History of*

American Birds of Eastern and Central North America. New York: Bramhall House, 1939. This is the abridgment of Forbush's three-volume work, *Birds of Massachusetts and Other New England States*, with material on 100 additional species supplied by J. B. May. It retains the illustrations of Louis Agassiz Fuertes and Allan Brooks, with four new plates by Roger Tory Peterson.

Fussell, John O., III. *A Birder's Guide to Coastal North Carolina*. Chapel Hill: University of North Carolina Press, 1994.

Lembke, Janet. *Dangerous Birds: A Naturalist's Aviary*. New York: Lyons and Burford, 1992.

Martin, Laura C. *The Folklore of Birds*. Old Saybrook, Conn.: Globe Pequot, 1993.

O'Brien, Michael, Richard Crossley, and Kevin Karlson. *The Shorebird Guide*. Boston: Houghton Mifflin, 2006.

Peterson, Roger Tory. *Eastern Birds*. 4th ed. Boston: Houghton Mifflin, 1980.

Schneider, Todd M., Giff Beaton, Timothy S. Keyes, and Nathan A. Klaus. *The Breeding Bird Atlas of Georgia*. Athens: University of Georgia Press, 2010.

Sibley, David Allen. *The Sibley Field Guide to Birds of Eastern North America*. New York: Knopf, 2003.

Spohrer, John B., Jr. *Florida's Forgotten Coast*. Eastpoint, Fla.: Two Dogs, 2004.

Stoddard, Herbert L., Sr. *Birds of Grady County, Georgia*. This bulletin of the Tall Timbers Research Station in Tallahassee, Florida, brings into book form the unpublished manuscript of noted ornithologist Herbert Stoddard Sr., who moved to Grady County in southwest Georgia after many years of work with the Milwaukee Public Museum and the Field Museum of Natural History in Chicago. He came south to lead the Cooperative Quail Investigation, and the result—*The Bobwhite Quail: Its Habits, Preservation and Increase* (1931)—earned Stoddard the coveted Brewster Award of the American Ornithologists' Union.

Stout, Gardner D., ed. *The Shorebirds of North America*. New York: Viking, 1968. This big, beautiful book features a long essay by naturalist and novelist Peter Matthiessen, lovely full-color illustrations by Robert Verity Clem, and species accounts by noted zoologist Ralph S. Palmer. The editor, Gardner Stout, was for ten years chairman of the Executive Committee of the National Audubon Society.

Voight, Ellen Bryant. *Claiming Kin*. Middletown, Conn.: Wesleyan University Press, 1976.

Weidensaul, Scott. *Living on the Wind: Across the Continent with Migratory Birds*. New York: North Point, 1999.

————. *Of a Feather: A Brief History of American Birding*. New York: Harcourt (Harvest edition), 2008.

Wells, Diana. *100 Birds and How They Got Their Names*. Chapel Hill, N.C.: Algonquin, 2002.

Wilson's American Ornithology, with Notes by Jardine—To Which Is Added a Synopsis of American Birds, Including Those Described by Bonaparte, Audubon, Nuttal, and Richardson; by T. M. Brewer. New York: Magagnos, 1854. I would love to lay eyes on an original copy. The book I have is a product of Cornell University Library's Digital Collections, the original having been digitized and scanned "cover to cover."

INDEX

Note: Page numbers in *italics* refer to illustrations.

Alligator Point, Fla., xiii, 4–5, 59, 166n

Anastasia State Park (St. Augustine, Fla.), 99–100

Anhinga (*Anhinga anhinga*), 51–58, *52, 75, 191*

Anhingidae family, 51

Ardeidae family, 42–43

Audubon, John James, xvii; on American avocet, 220, 222; on American oystercatcher, 13, 14–15, 16; on American white pelican, 187, 188, 189; on anhinga, 51, 53, 55, 56, 57, 58; on black-bellied plover, 26–27; on black-necked stilt, 8; on black skimmer, 192, 193, 195, 197; on brown pelican, 90–91, 92, 93, 94; on clapper rail, 113–14, 115, 116–17; on double-crested cormorant, 108, 111; on laughing gull, 81–82, 83, 84, 86–87; on least tern, 104; on reddish egret, 40–42, 45; on red knot, 202, 203; on roseate spoonbill, 155, 157n, 161, 222; on royal tern, 67–68, 69; on ruddy turnstone, 32–33, 36; on short-billed dowitcher, 166, 168; on snowy egret, 139, 140–41, 142; on tricolored heron, 129, 131, 132, 134; on whimbrel, 208–9; on white ibis, 20, 21, 24; on willet, 123–24, 126; on Wilson's plover, 62; on Wilson's snipe, 179, 180; on wood stork, 76–77, 79; on yellowlegs, 171, 174

Avocet, American (*Recurvirostra americana*), 5–6, 9, 172, 215–23, *217*

Bent, Arthur Cleveland, *Life Histories of North American Birds*: on American avocet, 218, 219, 221, 222; on American oystercatcher, 13, 14–15, 16; on American white pelican, 186–87, 188, 189; on anhinga, 51–52, 56, 57, 58; on black-bellied plover, 26, 27, 30, 31; on black-necked stilt, 6–7, 8; on black skimmer, 191–92, 193, 195; on brown pelican, 90, 91, 92, 93; on Caspian tern, 71; on clapper rail, 114, 115, 118; on double-crested cormorant, 108–9, 111; on Forster's tern, 100, 102, 103; on glossy ibis, 25; on laughing gull, 81, 82, 84, 85, 86; on reddish egret, 44, 45, 46–47; on red knot, 201, 203, 205, 206; on roseate spoonbill, 155, 159, 160–61; on royal tern, 68, 70; on ruddy turnstone, 35, 38; on sanderling, 148, 149, 152; on short-billed dowitcher, 163, 165, 166, 167, 168; on snowy egret, 135–36, 140, 141; on tricolored heron, 129, 130, 131–32, 134; on whimbrel, 212; on white ibis, 21–22, 23; on willet, 121, 123, 124–25, 126; on Wilson's plover, 61, 62, 64; on Wilson's snipe, 179–80, 181–82; on wood stork, 75, 76, 77, 78, 79; on yellowlegs, 172–73, 174, 175

Birds of North America Online, The (BNA Online): on American avocet, 216, 220n; on American oystercatcher, 14, 17; on American white pelican, 186, 188, 189–90; on anhinga, 54, 55, 56–57; on black-bellied plover, 27, 28, 29; on black-necked stilt, 6, 8; on black skimmer, 196–97; on brown pelican, 90, 92–93, 94, 95, 96; on clapper rail, 117; on common tern, 100; on double-crested cormorant, 106–7, 108, 109; on Forster's tern, 101, 102–3; on herring gull, 86–87; on laughing gull, 81, 82, 83, 86; on least tern, 105; on reddish egret, 43, 44–45; on red knot, 201, 205, 206; on roseate spoonbill, 155, 159, 160, 161; on royal tern, 69, 70; on ruddy turnstone, 37, 38; on sanderling, 148–49, 150, 151; on short-billed dowitcher, 165, 167; on snowy egret, 135, 142–43; on tricolored heron, 129, 131; on whimbrel, 209, 211, 213; on white ibis, 21, 22–23; on willet, 119n, 122, 123, 124, 125; on Wilson's plover, 61–62, 65; on Wilson's snipe, 178–79, 180, 181; on wood stork, 77–78; on yellowlegs, 172, 173

Blue Heron Water Reclamation Facility (Titusville, Fla.), 158, 164, 170

Bunting, indigo, 18

Burleigh, Thomas D., *Georgia Birds*: on black skimmer, 195, 196; on brown pelican, 95; on Forster's tern, 100; on laughing gull, 81; on ruddy turnstone, 32; on sanderling, 149, 151; on snowy egret, 135; on whimbrel, 209

Carrabelle Beach, Fla., xii, xiii, 3–4, 170, 171, 175

Carson, Rachel, *Under the Sea-Wind*: on black skimmer, 193, 197; on laughing gull, 82–83, 87; on royal tern, 69

Cashwell, Peter, *The Verb "To Bird"*: on American avocet, 218; on black skimmer, 194

Cat Island, Miss., xiv, 18–19, 185–86

Cedar Key, Fla., 183–85, 194–95, 215–18, 223

Charadrius family, 59n

Choate, Ernest A., *The Dictionary of American Bird Names*: on American white pelican, 189n; on anhinga, 51–52; on double-crested cormorant, 107n; on dowitcher, 166n; on gull, 86n; on plover, 59n; on reddish egret, 42n; on royal tern, 67; on sanderling,

147; on Sandwich tern, 72; on whimbrel, 209n; on white ibis, 19n

Cormorant, 4, 53, 54, 56; double-crested (*Phalacrocorax auritus*), 106–11

Cross, Theodore, *Waterbirds*: on anhinga, 53; on black skimmer, 191, 197; on brown pelican, 88, 94–95; on Caspian tern, 71; on common tern, 100; on ruddy turnstone, 35; on sanderling, 152; on snowy egret, 138; on wood stork, 76; on yellowlegs, 173, 174

Dauphin Island, Ala., 18, 40, 43, 71
"Ding" Darling National Wildlife Refuge (Sanibel Island, Fla.), 24, 30, 55–56, 58, 83–84, 156
Dowitcher (aka red-breasted snipe), 6, 33, 35, 147, 185, 218, 223; short-billed (*Limnodromus griseus*), 163–69

Egret, 6, 19, 25, 73, 75, 77, 121; American, 132; cattle, 104–5; compared to heron, 40–43, 44–45, 46–47; great, 6, 19, 25, 75, 129, 137, 138, 142, 158, 185; reddish (*Egretta rufescens*), 40–47, 41, 129; snowy (*Egretta thula*), 6, 25, 133, 134, 135–43, 136, 185

Elphick, Chris, John B. Dunnings Jr., and David Allen Sibley, eds., *The Sibley Guide to Bird Life and Behavior*: on American oyster-catcher, 14, 16; on American white pelican, 188; on anhinga, 51, 54, 56; on black-bellied plover, 30; on black-necked stilt, 5; on black skimmer, 193, 197; on clapper rail, 113, 117–18; on double-crested cormorant, 110–11; on gull family, 81, 86; on peeps, 153; on reddish egret, 43; on short-billed dowitcher, 168; on snowy egret, 138; on tricol-ored heron, 129; on wood stork, 77, 78, 79; on yellowlegs, 170–71

Forbush, Edward Howe, and John Bichard May, *A Natural History of American Birds of Eastern and Central North America*: on American white pelican, 188–89; on anhinga, 51; on black-bellied plover, 28, 31; on black-necked stilt, 8, 9; on black skimmer, 197–98; on brown pelican, 90; on double-crested cormorant, 109, 110; on dowitcher, 163; on Eskimo curlew, 208; on Forster's tern, 100–101; on least tern, 104; on little blue heron, 133–34; on roseate spoonbill, 155, 159; on snowy egret, 140; on whimbrel, 209, 212, 213; on wood stork, 75; on yellowlegs, 171, 174, 175
Fripp Island, S.C., xii, 194
Fussell, John O., III, *A Birder's Guide to Coastal North Carolina*: on Bodie Island Lighthouse Pond, 142; on North Pond, 127

Gull, 4, 9, 15, 23, 29, 91, 102, 103, 121, 142, 173, 187, 195; herring, 86–87; laughing (*Larus atricilla*), 68–69, 70, 81–87, 99, 115–16, 119, 198

Harris Neck National Wildlife Refuge (McIntosh County, Ga.), 73–75, 78, 79
Heron, 19, 21, 23, 56, 73, 75, 141, 142, 161, 185; blue, 159–60; compared to egret, 40–43, 44–45, 46–47; great blue, 18, 99, 129, 185, 191; green, 142; little blue (*Egretta caerulea*), 6, 25, 43, 132, 133–34, 158, 185; night, 19, 23, 112, 142; tricolored (*Egretta tricolor*), 6, 25, 127–34, *128*, 185

Ibis, 142, 160; glossy (*Plegadis falcinellus*), 25, 40, 158; white (*Eudocimus albus*), 18–25, 20, 40, 128–29, 158, 185; wood (*see* Stork, wood)

Jekyll Island, Ga., 39, 60, 68–69, 73, 76, 78, 122, 156–57, 198, 202

Knot, red (*Calidris canutus*), 35, 147, 148–49, 201–7

Laridae family, 195
Lembke, Janet, *Dangerous Birds*: on brown pelican, 88, 94; on double-crested cormorant, 110
Little St. Simon's Island, Ga., 7, 11–12, 17, 25, 66, 139, 170, 201

Merritt Island National Wildlife Refuge (Titusville, Fla.), 158, 159–60

Nag's Head, N.C., 119–21, 122–23

O'Brien, Michael, Richard Crossley, and Kevin Karlson, *The Shorebird Guide*: on black-bellied plover, 30; on yellowlegs, 171
Ochlockonee Bay, Fla., xiii, 3, 177
Oriole, orchard, 18
Outer Banks, N.C., 107–8, 110, 119–21, 122–23, 127–29, 142–43
Oystercatcher, American (*Haematopus palliatus*), 11–17, *12*

Pea Island National Wildlife Refuge (Hatteras Island, N.C.), 107–8, 127–29
Pelican: American white (*Pelecanus erythrorhynchos*), 18–19, 40, 183–90, *184*, 194, 215; brown (*Pelecanus occidentalis*), 82, 88–96, *89*, 99
Plover, 39; black-bellied (*Pluvialis squatarola*), 26–31, 212, 218; distinguishing between different species of, 63–65; golden, 4; piping, 64; semipalmated, 64; snowy, 64; Wilson's (*Charadrius wilsonia*), 59–65, 73

Rail, clapper (*Rallus longirostris*), 112–18
Rallidae family, 113
Recurvirostridae family, 6

St. Catherines Island, Ga., 141, 157

St. Catherines Sound (Ga.), 33, 209–10

St. Marks National Wildlife Refuge (St. Marks, Fla.), 3, 5–6

St. Simons Island, Ga., 73, 210

Sanderling (*Calidris alba*), 30, 35, 87, 120, 147–54, 204

Schneider, Todd M., Giff Beaton, Timothy S. Keyes, and Nathan A. Klaus, *The Breeding Bird Atlas of Georgia*: on anhinga, 54; on black skimmer, 198; on brown pelican, 95–96; on glossy ibis, 25; on tricolored heron, 133

Scolopacidae family, 33, 147

Sibley, David Allen, *The Sibley Field Guide to Birds of Eastern North America*: on red knot, 201; on roseate spoonbill, 157; on short-billed dowitcher, 164; on whimbrel, 209; on willet, 120–21

Skimmer, black (*Rynchops niger*), 60, 68–69, 70, 191–98, *192*, 218

Snipe, 35n, 166n; red-breasted (*see* Dowitcher); Wilson's (*Gallinago delicata*), 177–82

Spohrer, John B., Jr., *Florida's Forgotten Coast*: on brown pelican, 91, 92; on least tern, 104–5

Spoonbill, roseate (*Platalea ajaja*), 73, 112, 132, 155–62, *156*

Stilt, black-necked (*Himantopus mexicanus*), 3–10, *4*, 25, 185, 221

Stoddard, Herbert L., Sr., *Birds of Grady County, Georgia*: on snowy egret, 139–40

Stork, wood (*Mycteria americana*), 73–80, *74*, 141, 158, 159

Stout, Gardner D., ed., *The Shorebirds of North America*: on American oystercatcher, 14n; on whimbrel, 212–13

Tanager, scarlet, 18

Tern, 9, 81–82, 91, 121, 142, 195; Cabot's, 70, 82; Caspian, 67; common, 82, 100–101, 102–3; distinguishing between crested terns, 70–72; Forster's (*Sterna forsteri*), 99–105; gray-backed, 35–36; least (*Sterna antillarum*), 104–5; roseate, 82; royal (*Sterna maxima*), 60, 66–72, *68*, 82, 101, 198; Sandwich, 71; sooty, 81

Threskiornithidae family, 19n

Turnstone, ruddy (*Arenaria interpres*), 31, 32–39, *34*, 204, 218

Voight, Ellen Bryant, *Claiming Kin*: on stork, 80

Warbler, prothonotary, 18

Weidensaul, Scott

—*Living on the Wind*: on American avocet, 218; on Forster's tern, 101; on red knot, 204; on shorebird consumption of crabs, 34, 207

—*Of a Feather*: on snowy egret, 137, 138

Wells, Diana, *Birds and How They Got Their Names*: on anhinga, 51; on brown pelican, 95; on ibis, 19n; on snowy egret, 138

Whimbrel (*Numenius phaeopus*), 99–100, 185, 208–14, 218, 223

Willet (*Catoptrophorus semipalmatus*), 6, 33, 99, 119–26, *120*, 165, 166, 185, 218, 223

Wilson, Alexander, *Wilson's American Ornithology, with Notes by Jardine*: on American oystercatcher, 19; on anhinga, 51; on black-bellied plover, 26–27; on clapper rail, 114, 115, 116, 117; on dowitcher, 163, 168; on laughing gull, 81; on least tern, 104; on red knot, 203–4; on roseate spoonbill, 157; on sanderling, 152; on shorebird consumption of crabs, 34–35n; on snowy egret, 135, 141; on tern, 101; on whimbrel, 208–9; on white ibis, 24; on willet, 123, 125; on wood stork, 76

Yellowlegs, greater (*Tringa melanoleuca*) and lesser (*Tringa flavipes*), 158, 170–76

26.00   5/24/12.

LONGWOOD PUBLIC LIBRARY
800 Middle Country Road
Middle Island, NY 11953
(631) 924-6400
mylpl.net

LIBRARY HOURS

Monday-Friday	9:30 a.m. - 9:00 p.m.
Saturday	9:30 a.m. - 5:00 p.m.
Sunday (Sept-June)	1:00 p.m. - 5:00 p.m.